A Compendium of
KNITTED STITCH PATTERNS

A Compendium of
KNITTED STITCH PATTERNS

Shelagh Hollingworth

Schocken Books · New York

ACKNOWLEDGEMENTS

The author would like to acknowledge with thanks the following who, with their patience and help assisted with the preparation of this book: Jasmin Suter of Wendy Wools for arranging supply of the yarn with which to work the samples; Denise Wykes of Wycraft for supplying beads and sequins; Joan Edwardes for knitting all the squares; Eleanor Chester for her eleventh-hour co-operation, and especially Simon Tuite of Batsford Ltd for his encouragement in this and past works.

**Photographs by Keith Hills
and Brian Hollingworth**

First American edition published by Schocken Books 1985
10 9 8 7 6 5 4 3 2 1   85 86 87 88
Copyright © Shelagh Hollingworth 1985
Published by agreement with B. T. Batsford Ltd., London

Library of Congress Cataloging in Publication Data
Hollingworth, Shelagh.
    A compendium of knitted stitch patterns.
    Bibliography: p.
    Includes index.
    1. Knitting—Patterns.   I. Title.
TT820.H773   1985   746.43'2041   85–1998

Manufactured in Great Britain
ISBN 0–8052–3992–8

CONTENTS

INTRODUCTION

There can be little doubt that the craft of knitting is amongst the most popular of leisuretime pursuits. Although knitters from earlier centuries – many of them men – might be surprised at the tools we use now, they would still recognize that the basic principles have not changed and that this relaxing pastime can produce an abundance of articles, from the most utilitarian to the very glamorous.

Those knitters from the past belonged to two groups: those who diligently learned their patterns by heart and repeated them so often that they gradually passed on from generation to generation, and those who occasionally had a small lapse in their patterns and, either by accident or design, invented a whole new pattern stitch. However the invention of pattern ingenuity came about, the popularity of knitting today owes much to the persistence and artistry of our predecessors.

In this book you will find stitches with which you are already familiar and be introduced to some new ones. It is assumed that the initial knitting skills have been acquired and that this technique, applied to the infinite variety of patterns available today, can be used to enhance every aspect of the craft.

ABBREVIATIONS

The abbreviations listed below are considered to be in common usage; special abbreviations, where they occur, are given above individual patterns.

k.	knit
p.	purl
st.(s.)	stitch(es)
cm	centimetre(s)
in	inch(es)
alt.	alternate
beg.	beginning
foll.	following
p.s.s.o.	pass slipped stitch over
rep.	repeat
sl.	slip
tog.	together
t.b.l.	through back of loop(s)

ONE

THE USE OF KNITTING PATTERNS

During the past 50 years or so, the expression *pattern*, when applied to knitting, has come to mean two things. One is the set of directions, a commercial leaflet or magazine feature, outlining the method for making garments, household articles etc., and the other is the very fabric stitch from which the items are evolved. It is with the latter that this book is concerned.

Stitch patterns, no matter how intricate, are all initially derived from plain knitting (garter stitch) or purl knitting. These two stitches, if worked in separate squares, will each produce garter stitch, since purl stitch is simply the reverse of plain, or knit, stitch. With the knitwise stitch, the loop is directed away from the knitter; with the purlwise stitch, the loop is directed towards the knitter. However, once one works a knit row followed by a purl row, the first real pattern emerges – stocking stitch (stockinette). After this it is just a case of applying variations in graduating stages of difficulty. Even the most complicated patterns will soon become manageable to the inexperienced knitter after a little practice. It is not unusual for a novice to progress fairly rapidly from early pattern stitches to highly complicated cabled patterns, if making an Aran sweater is her goal.

Between stocking stitch and the intricacies of Aran knitting, there is an abundance of patterns. Stitches can be joined together in varying numbers and there are divers methods for doing this. They can be joined by knitting two loops together as one stitch, through either the front or the back of the loops; by slipping a stitch without knitting it, knitting the following stitch and passing the slipped stitch over the knit stitch; by purling two stitches together, and many other methods. Bringing stitches together has to be balanced by adding stitches, or the work would simply decrease out of all proportion. There are many methods for adding stitches, too: winding yarn forward or completely round the needle; working twice (or more) into a stitch; picking up the loop lying between the stitches and knitting or purling it, etc. The manner in which stitches are joined together or created is seldom chance. Experience will show that the surface of the knitted fabric is altered according to the type of stitch join or increase; each method shows differently on the work and frequently provides an influence on the finished pattern. One of the most obvious examples is in lace patterned diamond shapes. The directions for working may seem rather elaborate but these will, however, give the intrinsic shape to the motifs without which the quality of the pattern would be lost.

Apart from making intentional eyelet holes in the fabric, the other popular textures are made by ribbing variations, raising and crossing stitches by twisting or cabling, loops and bobbles. Each of these skills is fun to work at alone and will produce attractive fabric but, by learning them all and having so many methods to hand, the permutations are endless. With so many pattern stitches already available, it may be difficult to invent a completely new one, but by combining two or three and, maybe, adding some colour, a truly original design will result.

To the keen knitter, the very challenge of trying a new pattern is enough. One sign of a dedicated knitter is that she is no longer intent on an end product, but may well indulge her love of the craft by simply producing sample squares of beautiful patterns, in the same way that ladies of bygone ages worked sewing or knitted lace samplers. The squares can, of course, be useful too: joined together to make a bedspread or cushion covers, they can be left on show for all to enjoy.

Possibly the most popular reason for using knitting patterns is to create a new design from another pattern. This is not how a knitting designer works: she finds it easier to begin every new design from scratch, since each article brings its own problems. By using a commercial pattern, however, most of the design problems will have been removed, and substituting personal ideas for colour and pattern stitch is the easiest way to individuality.

Altering a pattern in this way is not difficult once the basic principle is understood. The designer calculates the number of stitches required for each size, according to the tension she has obtained when working a sample square of the pattern stitch in the yarn to be used. A straight substitution may only take place when using similar yarn and a pattern stitch with the same number of stitches in each repeat: follow the method below for comparing the number of stitches in a pattern repeat. On the commercial pattern the pattern stitch is set out row following row. The main part of each row (the repeat) will usually be either preceded by an asterisk * and concluded by a semi-colon, or will be outlined by brackets (parentheses). Count the number of stitches that need to be repeated across the row – this is called a stitch multiple – plus the end stitches. Above each pattern in this book a number of stitches is given: this is the number of stitches required plus the end stitches. A relatively inexperienced worker will need to find a pattern that has a corresponding number above the pattern so that a direct substitution may take place. Those with greater understanding of the complexities involved will soon be able to use patterns of different multiples. Notice that patterns are almost always arranged to have the end stitches equally balanced at each end. Try to follow this idea when altering a pattern.

To create a new design using a chosen pattern is considerably more complicated. It is necessary not only to grasp the fundamental principle of pattern repeats but also to understand the shape of the pattern pieces. A knowledge of dressmaking is beneficial but not necessary if the knitter has a great many years of experience and can recognize the basic shapes of various knitted articles. The design begins with a tension sample in the chosen pattern. Having decided on the finished shape, the knitter should use the working sketch provided to indicate the basic finished measurements, remembering to allow at least 5 cm (2 in) extra all round for movement. The measurement across each piece must be multiplied by the number of stitches to the cm (in) to obtain the number of stitches to cast on. Bear also in mind the number of stitches in the pattern repeat, plus the end stitches. Combining the two may give a few more or less stitches than the original calculation. This will not matter in a fine yarn but could make a big difference when very thick yarn is being used, where the difference of 1 stitch in each pattern repeat could alter the size by a matter of several centimetres (inches).

The real key to success in using new patterns is to knit with understanding. Try to follow the instructions when you knit, not just accepting what is written but realising the cause and effect of each step. It is by this method that you are most likely to achieve originality; by learning how others arrange their patterns and, with this knowledge, gradually realising that you can do it too. One or two basic designs will make many garments with the addition of different stitches, different colours and different yarns. A little experimenting will show which patterns suit which yarns and colours, and the picture on page 189 demonstrates just how different the same pattern stitch will look when worked in a variety of yarns ranging from wool and cotton to luxury yarns like mohair and lurex. Each new yarn and pattern produces a novel and attractive effect.

A significant reason for turning to a fund of knitting patterns for new ideas is that the average commercial pattern does not have the space to reproduce many of the lovely stitches available. The more elaborate the finished fabric, the more written directions required, and the condensed wording of commercial patterns cannot always cope with this.

Without doubt the most obvious problem when compiling a selection of knitting patterns is deciding which to include and which to leave out. Pattern devotees may well thumb through the pages and wonder how their favourite has been excluded, but hopefully the inclusion of others previously unknown to them will compensate for the omission. There are many hundreds of patterns and many of these have variations of their own: far too great a number to be contained in one book. The fairest decision seemed, therefore, to provide as wide a selection as possible.

Since the craft of knitting and the resultant stitches have such ancient beginnings, it is not feasible that all patterns should have recognized titles. The names given above each pattern in the book are either the common name most frequently used, or the name that the writer has come to associate with it. In no way is it intended that these are authoritative names but more a means of identification.

Often the origins of these patterns are, like the very beginning of the craft itself, obscure. What makes this

simple, gentle craft so rewarding, is perhaps the sense
that, in working, for example, feather and fan, old shale
or even the humble garter stitch, one is continuing a
timeless tradition.

TWO

PLAIN AND PURL TEXTURES

All the stitch patterns in this book are based on knit plain and purl. All are within the scope of the experienced knitter, but the novice is advised to practise these simpler examples before progressing to the more elaborate patterns.

The samples in this chapter are variations of textured all-over patterns suitable for all types of garments and generally readily interchangeable. Despite their simplicity, care should be taken to work the stitches evenly, since an irregular stitch will mar these patterns more obviously than, say, a loose stitch in a lacy pattern.

Interesting effects may be obtained by substituting fancy yarns: the very first stitch we learn – plain knit (garter stitch) – takes on a totally different look when worked in bulky yarn, fluffy yarns or yarn mixed with lurex thread. These early patterns open a whole new knitting fabric world with experimentation.

No. 1   Garter Stitch Any number of sts.
1st row: K. to end.
2nd row: Sl. 1 knitwise, k. to end.
Repeat 2nd row for garter stitch.

No. 2   Stocking Stitch (Stockinette) Any number of sts.
1st row: K. to end.
2nd row: P. to end.
These 2 rows form the pattern.

No. 3   Moss Stitch (Seed Stitch) Uneven number of sts.
1st row: K.1, *p.1, k.1; rep. from * to end.
Repeat this row for pattern.

1 Garter Stitch

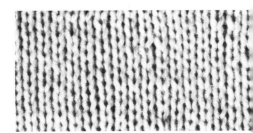
2 Stocking Stitch (Stockinette)

3 Moss Stitch (Seed Stitch)

13

4 Irish Moss Stitch

No. 4 Irish Moss Stitch 2 sts. plus 1
1st row: K.1, *p.1, k.1; rep. from * to end.
2nd row: P.1, *k.1, p.1; rep. from * to end.
3rd row: As 2nd row.
4th row: As 1st row.
These 4 rows form the pattern.

5 Simple Basket Pattern

No. 5 Simple Basket Pattern 4 sts. plus 2
1st row: K.2, *p.2, k.2; rep. from * to end.
2nd row: P.2, *k.2, p.2; rep. from * to end.
3rd row: As 2nd row.
4th row: As 1st row.
These 4 rows form the pattern.

6 Broken Stocking Stitch (1)

No. 6 Broken Stocking Stitch (1) 4 sts. plus 5
A useful background pattern where plain stocking stitch may be considered too dull. Although this pattern is unlikely to alter the stitch tension, notice that a set number of stitches is required, unlike stocking stitch for which any number of stitches is suitable.
1st row: (right side) K.4, *p.1, k.3; rep. from * to last st., k.1.
2nd row: K.1, p. to last st., k.1.
3rd row: K. to end.
4th row: As 2nd row.
5th row: K.2, *p.1, k.3; rep. from * to last 3 sts., p.1, k.2.
6th row: As 2nd row.
7th row: As 3rd row.
8th row: As 2nd row.
These 8 rows form the pattern.

7 Broken Stocking Stitch (2)

No. 7 Broken Stocking Stitch (2) 2 sts. plus 1
The note for No. 6 applies to this pattern also.
1st row: *P.1, k.1; rep. from * to last st., p.1.
2nd row: P. to end.
3rd row: K. to end.
4th row: As 1st row.
5th row: As 3rd row.
6th row: As 2nd row.
These 6 rows form the pattern.

No. 8 Simple Ringwood Pattern 2 sts. plus 1

A very popular pattern much used for sweaters and gloves.

1st row: K. to end.
2nd row: K.1, *p.1, k.1; rep. from * to end.
These 2 rows form the pattern.

8 *Simple Ringwood Pattern*

No. 9 Ringwood Pattern reversed 2 sts. plus 1

Worked in reverse to pattern No. 8, this texture is equally useful and makes an excellent pattern in its own right.

1st row: P. to end.
2nd row: K.1, *p.1, k.1; rep. from * to end.
These 2 rows form the pattern.

9 *Ringwood Pattern reversed*

No. 10 Spanish Basket Pattern 3 sts.

1st row: K.1, *p.1, k.2; rep. from * to last 2 sts., p.1, k.1.
2nd row: K.2, *p. to end.
3rd and 4th rows: Rep. last 2 rows.
5th row: P.1, *k.1, p.2; rep. from * to last 2 sts., k.1, p.1.
6th row: As 2nd row.
7th and 8th rows: Rep. last 2 rows.
These 8 rows form the pattern.

10 *Spanish Basket Pattern*

No. 11 Broken Garter Stitch (1) 6 sts. plus 5

1st row: (right side) K. to end.
2nd row: K.5, *p.1, k.5; rep. from * to end.
These 2 rows form the pattern.

11 *Broken Garter Stitch (1)*

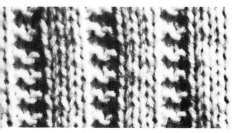

12 Broken Garter Stitch (2)

No. 12 Broken Garter Stitch (2) 5 sts. plus 3
1st row: (right side) K.3, *p.2, k.3; rep. from * to end.
2nd row: P. to end.
These 2 rows form the pattern.

13 Purl and Garter Stitch Pattern

No. 13 Purl and Garter Stitch Pattern 6 sts. plus 3
1st row: *P.3, k.3; rep. from * to last 3 sts., p.3.
2nd row: K. to end.
These 2 rows form the pattern.

14 Reversible Garter Pattern

No. 14 Reversible Garter Pattern 4 sts.
1st row: *K.3, p.2; rep. from * to end.
2nd row: *P.2, k.2; rep. from * to end.
These 2 rows form the pattern.

15 Broken Rib Pattern

No. 15 Broken Rib Pattern 2 sts.
1st row: (right side) *K.1, p.1; rep. from * to end.
2nd row: P. to end.
3rd row: *P.1, k.1; rep. from * to end.
4th row: P. to end.
These 4 rows form the pattern.

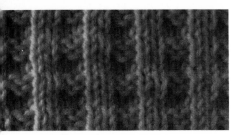

16 Betty Martin Pattern

No. 16 Betty Martin Pattern 4 sts. plus 2
Various traditional patterns are given this name. While this may not be its true name, it is frequently used in Guernsey patterns.
1st row: (right side) *K.2, p.2; rep. from * to last 2 sts., k.2.
2nd row: *P.2, k.2; rep. from * to last 2 sts., p.2.
3rd row: K. to end.

4th row: P. to end.
These 4 rows form the pattern.

No. 17   Basket Stitch Blocks 6 sts. plus 4
1st row: (wrong side) K.4, *p.2, k.4; rep. from * to end.
2nd row: P.4, *k.2, p.4; rep. from * to end.
3rd and 4th rows: As 1st and 2nd rows.
5th row: K.1, p.2, *k.4, p.2; rep. from * to last st., k.1.
6th row: P.1, k.2, *p.4, k.2; rep. from * to last st., p.1.
7th and 8th rows: As 5th and 6th rows.
These 8 rows form the pattern.

17 *Basket Stitch Blocks*

No. 18   Irish Moss Blocks 6 sts. plus 3
This attractive reversible pattern is simply formed by
moss stitch variations.
1st row: P.1, *k.1, p.1; rep. from * to end.
2nd row: K.1, *p.1, k.1; rep. from * to end.
3rd row: As 2nd row.
4th row: As 1st row.
5th row: P.3, *k.3, p.3; rep. from * to end.
6th row: K.3, *p.3, k.3; rep. from * to end.
7th and 8th rows: As 5th and 6th rows.
9th and 10th rows: As 3rd and 4th rows.
11th and 12th rows: As 1st and 2nd rows.
13th to 16th rows: [Rep. 6th row, then 5th row] twice.
These 16 rows form the pattern.

18 *Irish Moss Blocks*

No. 19   Beechers Rib 2 sts.
Despite its name this is not a true rib pattern, since it
forms a flat fabric.
1st and 2nd rows: *K.1, p.1; rep. from * to end.
3rd row: P. to end.
4th row: K. to end.
These 4 rows form the pattern.

19 *Beechers Rib*

No. 20   Ladder and Moss Pattern 11 sts. plus 2
This pattern is reversible.
1st row: K.2, *p.2, k.5, p.2, k.2; rep. from * to end.
2nd row: P.2, k.2, p.5, *k.2, p.2, k.2, p.5; rep. from * to
last 4 sts., k.2, p.2.
3rd row: As 2nd row.
4th row: As 1st row.
These 4 rows form the pattern.

20 *Ladder and Moss Pattern*

21 Classic Triangle Pattern

No. 21 Classic Triangle Pattern 5 sts.

1st row: *K.4, p.1; rep. from * to end.

2nd row: K.1, *p.3, k.2; rep. from * to last 4 sts., p.3, k.1.

3rd row: P.2, *k.2, p.3; rep. from * to last 3 sts., k.2, p.1.

4th row: K.1, *p.1, k.4; rep. from * to last 4 sts., p.1, k.3.

5th row: K.3, *p.1, k.4; rep. from * to last 2 sts., p.1, k.1.

6th row: P.1, *k.2, p.3; rep. from * to last 4 sts., k.2, p.2.

7th row: K.1, *p.3, k.2; rep. from * to last 4 sts., p.3, k.1.

8th row: *P.1, k.4; rep. from * to end.

These 8 rows form the pattern.

22 Flag Pattern

No. 22 Flag Pattern 8 sts.

The slightly pleated look of this pattern makes it very suitable for skirts, but its most common use is in tradition Guernsey sweaters.

1st row: (right side) *K.1, p.7; rep. from * to end.

2nd row: *K.6, p.2; rep. from * to end.

3rd row: *K.3, p.5; rep. from * to end.

4th row: *K.4, p.4; rep. from * to end.

5th row: *K.5, p.3; rep. from * to end.

6th row: *K.2, p.6; rep. from * to end.

7th row: *K.7, p.1; rep. from * to end.

8th row: P. to end.

These 8 rows form the pattern.

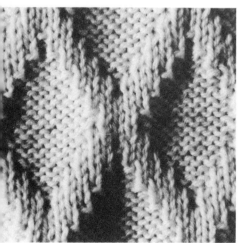

23 Shadow Diamond Pattern

No. 23 Shadow Diamond Pattern 12 sts. plus 13

1st row: (right side) P.4, *k.5, p.7; rep. from * to last 9 sts., k.5, p.4.

2nd row and foll. alt. rows: K. all k. sts. and p. all p. sts. as they present themselves.

3rd row: P.3, *k.3, p.1, k.3, p.5; rep. from * to last 10 sts., k.3, p.1, k.3, p.3.

5th row: P.2, *k.3, p.3; rep. from * to last 5 sts., k.3, p.2.

7th row: P.1, *k.3, p.5, k.3, p.1; rep. from * to end.

9th row: K.3, *p.7, k.5; rep. from * to last 10 sts., p.7, k.3.

11th row: K.2, *p.9, k.3; rep. from * to last 11 sts., p.9, k.2.

13th row: As 9th row.

15th row: As 7th row.

17th row: As 5th row.
19th row: As 3rd row.
21st row: As 1st row.
23rd row: P.5, *k.3, p.9; rep. from * to last 8 sts., k.3, p.5.
24th row: As 2nd row.
These 24 rows form the pattern.

No. 24   Moss Diamond Outline 6 sts. plus 7

1st row: K.3, *p.1, k.5; rep. from * to last 4 sts., p.1, k.3.
2nd row: P.2, *k.1, p.1, k.1, p.3; rep. from * to last 5 sts., k.1, p.1, k.1, p.2.
3rd row: K.1, *p.1, k.3, p.1, k.1; rep. from * to last 6 sts., p.1, k.3, p.1, k.1.
4th row: K.1, *p.5, k.1; rep. from * to end.
5th row: As 3rd row.
6th row: As 2nd row.
These 6 rows form the pattern.

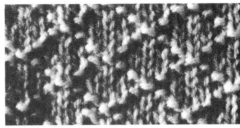

24 *Moss Diamond Outline*

No. 25   Moss Diamond on Stocking Stitch 15 sts.

1st row: (right side) K. to end.
2nd row: P.7, k.1, p.7.
3rd row: K.6, (p.1, k.1) twice, k.5.
4th row: P.5, (k.1, p.1) 3 times, p.4.
5th row: K.4, (p.1, k.1) 4 times, k.3.
6th row: P.3, (k.1, p.1) 5 times, p.2.
7th row: K.2, (p.1, k.1) 6 times, k.1.
8th row: P.1, (k.1, p.1) 7 times.
9th row: P.1, (k.1, p.1) 7 times.
10th row: As 8th row.
11th to 16th rows: As 7th to 2nd rows in backward rotation.
These 16 rows form the pattern.

25 *Moss Diamond on Stocking Stitch*

No. 26   Vandyke Moss Pattern 8 sts.

1st row: (right side) *P.1, k.3; rep. from * to end.
2nd row: *K.1, p.5, k.1, p.1; rep. from * to end.
3rd row: *K.2, p.1, k.3, p.1, k.1; rep. from * to end.
4th row: *P.2, k.1, p.1, k.1, p.3; rep. from * to end.
These 4 rows form the pattern.

26 *Vandyke Moss Pattern*

27 Marriage Lines

No. 27 Marriage Lines 11 sts.

The name is given to many variations of this pattern. It is frequently found in Aran and other traditionally patterned garments.

1st row: (right side) ★K.5, p.1, k.2, p.1, k.2; rep. from ★ to end.

2nd row: ★P.1, k.1, p.2, k.1, p.6; rep. from ★ to end.

3rd row: As 1st row.

4th row: ★P.3, k.1, p.2, k.1, p.4; rep. from ★ to end.

5th row: ★K.3, p.1, k.2, p.1, k.4; rep. from ★ to end.

6th row: ★P.5, k.1, p.2, k.1, p.2; rep. from ★ to end.

7th row: ★K.1, p.1, k.2, p.1, k.6; rep. from ★ to end.

8th row: ★P.5, k.1, p.2, k.1, p.2; rep. from ★ to end.

9th row: ★K.3, p.1, k.2, p.1, k.4; rep. from ★ to end.

10th row: ★P.3, k.1, p.2, k.1, p.4; rep. from ★ to end.

These 10 rows form the pattern.

No. 28 Broad Marriage Lines 15 sts.

1st row: P.1, k.1, p.1, k.12.

2nd row: P.11, (k.1, p.1) twice.

3rd row: K.2, p.1, k.1, p.1, k.10.

4th row: P.9, k.1, p.1, k.1, p.3.

5th row: K.4, p.1, k.1, p.1, k.8.

6th row: P.7, k.1, p.1, k.1, p.5.

7th row: K.6, p.1, k.1, p.1, k.6.

8th row: P.5, k.1, p.1, k.1, p.7.

9th row: K.8, p.1, k.1, p.1, k.4.

10th row: P.3, k.1, p.1, k.1, p.9.

11th row: K.10, p.1, k.1, p.1, k.2.

12th row: (P.1, k.1) twice, p.11.

13th row: K.12, p.1, k.1, p.1.

14th row: (P.1, k.1) twice, p.11.

15th row: K.10, p.1, k.1, p.1, k.2.

16th row: P.3, k.1, p.1, k.1, p.9.

17th row: K.8, p.1, k.1, p.1, k.4.

18th row: P.5, k.1, p.1, k.1, p.7.

19th row: K.6, p.1, k.1, p.1, k.6.

20th row: P.7, k.1, p.1, k.1, p.5.

21st row: K.4, p.1, k.1, p.1, k.8.

22nd row: P.9, k.1, p.1, k.1, p.3.

23rd row: K.2, p.1, k.1, p.1, k.10.

24th row: P.11, (k.1, p.1) twice.

These 24 rows form the pattern.

28 Broad Marriage Lines

No. 29 Tile Pattern 8 sts.

1st row: K.6, *p.3, k.5; rep. from * to last 2 sts., p.2.
2nd row: *K.1, p.1, k.1, p.3, k.1, p.1; rep. from * to end.
3rd row: K.4, *p.1, k.2, p.1, k.2, p.1, k.1; rep. from * to last 4 sts., p.1, k.2, p.1.
4th row: *K.1, p.3; rep. from * to end.
5th row: *K.7, p.1; rep. from * to end.
6th row: *K.1, p.7; rep. from * to end.
These 6 rows form the pattern.

29 *Tile Pattern*

No. 30 Serried Pattern 2 sts. plus 1

1st row: K. to end.
2nd row: P. to end.
3rd row: K. to end.
4th row: P.1, *k.1, p.1; rep. from * to end.
5th row: K. to end.
6th row: As 4th row.
These 6 rows form the pattern.

30 *Serried Pattern*

No. 31 Wide Serried Pattern 6 sts. plus 3

1st row: (right side) P.1, *k.1, p.2; rep. from * to last 2 sts., k.1, p.1.
2nd row: K.1, *p.1, k.2; rep. from * to last 2 sts., p.1, k.1.
3rd row: As 1st row.
4th row: As 2nd row.
5th row: *P.1, k.1, p.1, k.3; rep. from * to last 3 sts., p.1, k.1, p.1.
6th row: *K.1, p.1, k.1, p.3; rep. from * to last 3 sts., k.1, p.1, k.1.
7th row: As 5th row.
8th row: As 6th row.
9th to 12th rows: As 1st to 4th rows.
13th row: P.1, *k.1, p.5; rep. from * to last 2 sts., k.1, p.1.
14th row: K.1, *p.1, k.5; rep. from * to last 2 sts., p.1, k.2.
15th to 18th rows: Rep. 13th and 14th rows twice.
These 18 rows form the pattern.

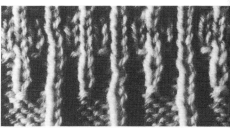

31 *Wide Serried Pattern*

32 Clare's Pattern

No. 32   Clare's Pattern 6 sts.
1st row: K.1, *k.4, p.2; rep. from * to last 5 sts., k.5.
2nd row: P. to end.
3rd row: K.2, *p.2, k.4; rep. from * to last 4 sts., p.2, k.2.
4th row: P. to end.
These 4 rows form the pattern.

33 Prince William Pattern

No. 33   Prince William Pattern 4 sts. plus 2
1st row: K. to end.
2nd row: P. to end.
3rd row: K.2, *p.2, k.2; rep. from * to end.
4th row: P.2, *k.2, p.2; rep. from * to end.
5th and 6th rows: As 1st and 2nd rows.
7th row: As 4th row.
8th row: K.2, *p.2, k.2; rep. from * to end.
These 8 rows form the pattern.

34 Serried Checks

No. 34   Serried Checks 5 sts. plus 4
1st row: K. to end.
2nd row: P.4, *k.1, p.4; rep. from * to end.
3rd to 6th rows: Rep. 1st and 2nd rows twice more.
7th and 8th rows: K. to end.
These 8 rows form the pattern.

35 Serried Blocks

No. 35   Serried Blocks 5 sts.
1st row: (right side) K. to end.
2nd row: P. to end.
3rd, 5th and 7th rows: P.2, *k.1, p.4; rep. from * to last 3 sts., k.1, p.2.
4th, 6th and 8th rows: K.2, *p.1, k.4; rep. from * to last 3 sts., p.1, k.2.
These 8 rows form the pattern.

36 Tulip Pattern

No. 36   Tulip Pattern 5 sts. plus 2
1st row: *P.3, k.1, p.1; rep. from * to last 2 sts., p.2.
2nd row: *K.3, p.1, k.1; rep. from * to last 2 sts., k.2.
3rd row: As 1st row.
4th row: As 2nd row.
5th row: *P.2, k.1, p.1, k.1; rep. from * to last 2 sts., p.2.
6th row: *K.2, p.1, k.1, p.1; rep. from * to last 2 sts., k.2.

7th row: As 5th row.
8th row: As 6th row.
These 8 rows form the pattern.

SLIP STITCH VARIATIONS

The following patterns produce all-over textured fabric but incorporate the use of slipped stitches. None of the samples is difficult to work but care should be taken to slip the stitches either knitwise or purlwise, as given.

No. 37   Garter Slip Stitch 3 sts. plus 2
1st row: *K.2, sl. 1 purlwise; rep. from * to last 2 sts., k.2.
2nd row: K. to end.
These 2 rows form the pattern.

37 Garter Slip Stitch

No. 38   Gosling Pattern 2 sts. plus 1
1st row: (wrong side) K. to end.
2nd row: K.1, *keeping yarn back, sl. 1 purlwise, k.1; rep. from * to end.
3rd row: K.1, *yarn forward, sl. 1 purlwise, yarn back, k.1; rep. from * to end.
4th and 5th rows: K. to end.
6th row: K.2, *keeping yarn back, sl. 1 purlwise, k.1; rep. from * to last st., k.1.
7th row: K.2, *yarn forward, sl. 1 purlwise, yarn back, k.1; rep. from * to last st., k.1.
8th row: K. to end.
These 8 rows form the pattern.

38 Gosling Pattern

No. 39   Slip Stitch and Garter Fabric 4 sts. plus 1
To avoid working too densely, try using knitting needles one size thicker than usual for this pattern and keep the yarn loose behind the slipped stitches.
1st row: (right side) K. to end.
2nd row: K. to end.
3rd row: K.1, *keeping yarn back, sl. 1 purlwise, k.1; rep. from * to end.
4th row: K.1, *yarn forward, sl. 1 purlwise, yarn back, k.1; rep. from * to end.
These 4 rows form the pattern.

39 Slip Stitch and Garter Fabric

40 Fabric Weave Pattern

No. 40 Fabric Weave Pattern 4 sts. plus 3
See note below No. 39. All stitches to be slipped purlwise for this pattern.
1st row: K.3, *yarn forward, sl.1, yarn back, k.3; rep. from * to end.
2nd row: P. to end.
3rd row: K.1, *yarn forward, sl.1, yarn back, k.3; rep. from * to last 2 sts., yarn forward, k.1, yarn back, k.1.
4th row: P. to end.
These 4 rows form the pattern.

41 Miniature Honeycomb

No. 41 Miniature Honeycomb 2 sts. plus 1
All stitches to be slipped purlwise for this pattern.
1st row: (right side) P.
2nd row: P.1, *keeping yarn forward, sl.1, p.1; rep. from * to end.
3rd row: P.1, *yarn back, sl.1, yarn forward, p.1; rep. from * to end.
4th row: P.
These 4 rows form the pattern.

42 Broken Fabric Pattern

No. 42 Broken Fabric Pattern 2 sts.
See note below No. 40.
1st row: (right side) *K.1, yarn forward, sl.1, yarn back; rep. from * to end.
2nd row: *P.1, k.1; rep. from * to end.
3rd row: *Sl.1, yarn forward, k.1, yarn back; rep. from * to end.
4th row: *K.1, p.1; rep. from * to end.
These 4 rows form the pattern.

No. 43 Broken Fabric Pattern reversed 2 sts.
This pattern is worked as No. 42 but with the 1st and following alternate rows set as the wrong side of the work. Both sides of the pattern are equally attractive.

43 Broken Fabric Pattern reversed

No. 44 Scalloped Waves 4 sts. plus 2
1st and 3rd rows: (right side) K. to end.
2nd and 4th rows: P.
5th row: *P.2, sl. 2 sts. purlwise carrying yarn loosely
across slipped sts.; rep. from * to last 2 sts., p.2.
6th row: P. to end.
7th row: As 5th row.
8th row: P. to end.
These 8 rows form the pattern.

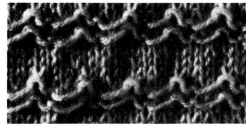

44 Scalloped Waves

No. 45 Shadow Stocking Stitch 6 sts. plus 4
1st row: *K.4, sl. 2 purlwise keeping yarn back; rep.
from * to last 4 sts., k.4.
2nd row and foll. alt. rows: P. to end.
3rd, 5th, 7th and 9th rows: As 1st row.
11th row: K.1, *keeping yarn back sl. 2 purlwise, k.4;
rep. from * to last 3 sts., keeping yarn back sl.2, k.1.
13th, 15th, 17th and 19th rows: As 11th row.
20th row: P. to end.
These 20 rows form the pattern.

45 Shadow Stocking Stitch

No. 46 Slip Stitch Fabric Pattern Plain 2 sts. plus 1
1st row: (right side) K. to end.
2nd row: K.1, *sl. 1 purlwise, k.1; rep. from * to end.
3rd row: K. to end.
4th row: Sl. 1 purlwise, *k.1, sl. 1 purlwise; rep. from *
to end.
These 4 rows form the pattern.

46 Slip Stitch Fabric Pattern Plain

No. 47 Little Waffle Pattern 4 sts. plus 3
1st row: K.3, *k.1 winding yarn twice round needle, k.3;
rep. from * to end.
2nd row: P.3, *sl. 1 purlwise dropping extra loop, p.3;
rep. from * to end.
3rd row: K.3, *sl. 1 purlwise, k.3; rep. from * to end.
4th row: K.
These 4 rows form the pattern.

47 Little Waffle Pattern

48 Alternating Waffle Pattern

No. 48 Alternating Waffle Pattern 4 sts. plus 3
1st row: *K.3, k.1 winding yarn 3 times round needle; rep. from * to last 3 sts., k.3.
2nd row: *P.3, sl. 1 dropping extra loops; rep. from * to last 3 sts., p.3.
3rd row: *K.3, sl.1; rep. from * to last 3 sts., k.3.
4th row: K. to end.
5th row: K.1, *k.1 winding yarn 3 times round needle, k.3; rep. from * to last 2 sts., k.1 winding yarn 3 times round needle, k.1.
6th row: P.1, *sl. 1 dropping extra loops, p.3; rep. from * to last 2 sts., sl. 1 dropping extra loops, p.1.
7th row: K.1, *sl.1, k.3; rep. from * to last 2 sts., sl.1, k.1.
8th row: K. to end.
These 8 rows form the pattern.

49 Hawthorn Pattern

No. 49 Hawthorn Pattern 4 sts. plus 2
K. 2 T., k. 2 twice thus: insert needle in each st. as if to knit, wind yarn twice round needle then k. in usual way.
Sl. 2 L., slip 2 long sts. thus: sl. 2 sts. purlwise dropping the extra loops thus forming 2 long sts.
1st row: K.1, *p.2, k. 2 T.; rep. from * to last st., k.1.
2nd row: K.1, *yarn forward, sl. 2 L., yarn back, k.2; rep. from * to last st., k.1.
3rd row: K.1, *p.2, yarn back, sl.2, yarn forward; rep. from * to last st., yarn back, k.1.
4th row: K.1, *yarn forward, sl.2, yarn back, k.2; rep. from * to last st., k.1.
5th row: K.1, *k. 2 T., p.2; rep. from * to last st., k.1.
6th row: K.1, *k.2, yarn forward, sl. 2 L., yarn back; rep. from * to last st., k.1.
7th row: K.1, *yarn back, sl.2, yarn forward, p.2; rep. from * to last st., yarn back, k.1.
8th row: K.1, *k.2, yarn forward, sl.2, yarn back; rep. from * to last st., k.1.
These 8 rows form the pattern.

50 Corn Cob Pattern

No. 50 Corn Cob Pattern 3 sts. plus 2
1st row: (right side) K.1, *k.1, sl. 1 purlwise, k.1, yarn forward to make a st., pass the sl. st. over the made st. and k.1; rep. from * to last st., k.1.
2nd row: P.1, *p.1, sl. 1 purlwise, p.1, yarn forward to make a st., pass sl. st. over the made st. and p.1; rep. from * to last st., p.1.
These 2 rows form the pattern.

No. 51 Goldcrest Pattern Even number of sts.
1st row: (wrong side) *Sl. 1 purlwise, yarn round needle
to make a st.; rep. from * to last st., k.1.
2nd row: Sl.1, *k. 2 tog. t.b.l.; rep. from * to end.
These 2 rows form the pattern.

51 Goldcrest Pattern

No. 52 Perigord Pattern 4 sts.
In this pattern it is the loops formed by winding yarn
round needle that are slipped over existing stitches.
1st row: K. to end.
2nd row: P.3, *y.r.n., p.2, pass the y.r.n. over the p.2,
p.2; rep. from * to last st., p.1.
3rd row: K. to end.
4th row: P.1, *y.r.n., p.2, pass the y.r.n. over the p.2,
p.2; rep. from * to end, ending p.1 instead of p.2.
These 4 rows form the pattern.

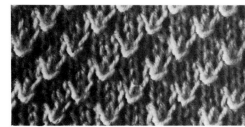

52 Perigord Pattern

No. 53 Ladder Pattern 8 sts. plus 1
1st and 3rd rows: *K.5, yarn forward, sl. 3 sts. purlwise,
yarn back; rep. from * to last st., k.1.
2nd row: P.1, *yarn back, sl. 3 purlwise, yarn forward,
p.5; rep. from * to end.
4th row: P. to end.
5th and 7th rows: K.1, *yarn forward, sl. 3 purlwise,
yarn back, k.5; rep. from * to end.
6th row: *P.5, yarn back, sl. 3 purlwise, yarn forward;
rep. from * to last st., p.1.
8th row: P. to end.
These 8 rows form the pattern.

53 Ladder Pattern

No. 54 Skye Pattern 4 sts. plus 2
1st row: P.2, *k.2, p.2; rep. from * to end.
2nd row: K.2, *p.2, k.2; rep. from * to end.
3rd row: P.2, *keeping yarn in front, sl. 2 purlwise, p.2;
rep. from * to end.
4th row: K.2, *keeping yarn in back, sl. 2 purlwise, k.2;
rep. from * to end.
5th and 6th rows: As 1st and 2nd rows.
7th row: P.2, *insert right hand needle under the 2
strands from 3rd and 4th rows and k. tog. with next st.,
k.1, p.2; rep. from * to end.
8th row: As 2nd row.
9th to 14th rows: As 1st to 6th rows.

54 Skye Pattern

15th row: P.2, *k.1, insert right hand needle under 2 strands from 11th and 12th rows and k. tog. with next st., p.2; rep. from * to end.
16th row: As 2nd row.
These 16 rows form the pattern.

No. 55 Cellular Pattern 2 sts. plus 2
This pattern, with its eyelet construction, is suitable for shawls and blankets. It has, however, a tendency to bias, and it is advisable to use yarn that can be pressed into shape, so check the instructions for pressing on the yarn ball band.
1st row: (right side) P. to end.
2nd row: K. to end.
3rd row: K.2, *sl. 1 purlwise, k.1; rep. from * to end.
4th row: *K.1, sl. 1 purlwise; rep. from * to last 2 sts., k.2.
5th row: K.1, *yarn forward, k. 2 tog.; rep. from * to last st., k.1.
6th row: P. to end.
These 6 rows form the pattern.

55 Cellular Pattern

No. 56 Tweed Weave Pattern 4 sts.
1st row: K.2, *sl. 1 knitwise, y.r.n., k.1; rep. from * to end.
2nd row: (right side) *K.1, k. the made st. and sl. st. tog. t.b.l.; rep. from * to last 2 sts., k.2.
3rd row: *K.1, sl. 1 knitwise, y.r.n.; rep. from * to last 2 sts., k.2.
4th row: K.2, *k. the made st. and sl. st. tog. t.b.l., k.1; rep. from * to end.
These 4 rows form the pattern.

56 Tweed Weave Pattern

No. 57 Inca Pattern 6 sts. plus 3
See note below No. 52.
1st row: K. to end.
2nd row: P. to end.
3rd row: K.3, *yarn forward, k.3, pass the yarn forward loop over the last k.3, k.3; rep. from * to end.
4th row: P. to end.
5th row: K.6, *yarn forward, k.3, pass the yarn forward loop over last k.3, k.3; rep. from * ending last rep., k.6, instead of k.3.
6th row: P. to end.
Rows 3 to 6 inclusive form the pattern.

57 Inca Pattern

No. 58 Quilt Pattern 8 sts. plus 10

1st row: K. to end.

2nd row: P.4, *p.2 winding yarn twice round needle for
each st., p.6; rep. from * ending last rep., p.4, instead of
p.6.

3rd row: K.1, *slip next 3 sts. to back on cable needle, k.
long st. dropping extra loop, k. 3 from cable needle, slip
next long st. to front on cable needle dropping extra
loop, k.3, k. 1 from cable needle; rep. from * to last st.,
k.1.

4th row: P. to end.

5th row: K. to end.

6th row: P.1, *p.1 winding yarn twice as before, p.6, p.1
winding yarn twice as before; rep. from * to last st., p.1.

7th row: K.1, *slip next long st. to front on cable needle
dropping extra loop, k.3, k. 1 from cable needle, slip
next 3 sts. to back on cable needle, k. long st. dropping
extra loop, k. 3 from cable needle; rep. from * to last st.,
k.1.

8th row: P. to end.

These 8 rows form the pattern.

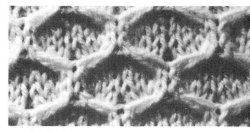

58 Quilt Pattern

No. 59 Cross Slip Stitch Pattern 4 sts. plus 2

1st row: (wrong side) Sl.1, *p.1 winding yarn twice
round needle; rep. from * to last st., p.1.

2nd row: K.1, *sl. next 4 sts. on to right-hand needle
dropping extra loops, return these long sts. to left-hand
needle and, with right needle point, lift 3rd and 4th sts.
over 1st and 2nd sts. and k. each st. in this order –
called cross 4; rep. from * to last st., k.1.

3rd row: As 1st row.

4th row: K.3, *cross 4; rep. from * to last 3 sts., k.3.

These 4 rows form the pattern.

59 Cross Slip Stitch Pattern

No. 60 Crossed Loop Ridges 2 sts. plus 1

1st row: K. to end.

2nd row: P. to end.

3rd row: K.1, *yarn forward, sl. 1 purlwise, yarn over
needle k.1; rep. from * to end.

4th row: *K.1, k. tog. the slipped st. and crossed over
loop; rep. from * to last st., k.1.

These 4 rows form the pattern.

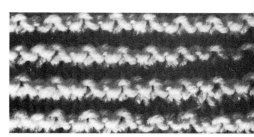

60 Crossed Loop Ridges

61 Diagonal Mesh

62 Slip Stitch Pattern

63 Cross Stitch Fabric

No. 61   Diagonal Mesh 4 sts. plus 2
1st row: K.1, *yarn forward, sl.1, k.3, pass the slipped st. over the k.3; rep. from * to last st., k.1.
2nd row: P. to end.
3rd row: K.3, *yarn forward, sl.1, k.3, pass the slipped st. over the k.3; rep. from * to last 3 sts., k.3.
4th row: P. to end.
These 4 rows form the pattern.

No. 62   Slip Stitch Pattern 4 sts. plus 1
M.1, make 1 thus: pick up loop lying between sts. and k. it.
1st row: (right side) K.1, *sl. 1 purlwise, M.1, sl. 1 purlwise, k.1, pass first slipped st. over last 3 sts., k.1; rep. from * to end.
2nd row: Sl. 1 purlwise, p. to last st., sl. 1 purlwise.
3rd row: K.3, *sl. 1 purlwise, M.1, sl. 1 purlwise, k.1, pass first slipped st. over the last 3, k.1; rep. from * to last 2 sts., k.2.
4th row: As 2nd row.
These 4 rows form the pattern.

TWIST AND CROSS STITCH PATTERNS
Continuing the all-over fabric patterns, the following samples are achieved by slipping and lifting stitches in small neat sequences. Again, even the beginner will find them easy to work but it is recommended that a large test piece be made before attempting a whole garment.

No. 63   Cross Stitch Fabric 2 sts. plus 2
1st row: K.2, *yarn forward, k.2; rep. from * to end.
2nd row: P.1, *sl. next st. on to right hand needle dropping the extra loop then sl. the st. back on to left hand needle, miss this st., p. in second st. on left hand needle then p. the missed st.; rep. from * to last st., p.1.
These 2 rows form the pattern.

No. 64 Spiral Pattern even number of sts.
This pattern requires one needle two sizes thicker than
normal (A) and one needle three sizes thicker than A –
needle B.
1st row: With B needle, K.1, p. to last st., k.1.
2nd row: With A needle, K.1, *lift the second st. on left
hand needle over the first st. and k. it, then k. the first
st.; rep. from * to last st., k.1.
These 2 rows form the pattern.

64 Spiral Pattern

No. 65 Simple Twist Stitch Pattern 2 sts.
This pattern has a tendency to bias and should only be
worked in a yarn that can be pressed straight. Check the
yarn ball band for pressing instructions. It requires the
same needle combination as No. 64.
1st row: (wrong side) With B needle, p. to end.
2nd row: With A needle, K.1, *twist 2 sts. by k. into
second st. on left hand needle then into first st on left
hand needle and slip both loops off together; rep. from
* to last st., k.1.
These 2 rows form the pattern.

65 Simple Twist Stitch Pattern

No. 66 Stocking Stitch with Cross Stitches 4 sts.
1st row: (wrong side) P. to end.
2nd row: K. to end.
3rd row: P. to end.
4th row: K.1, *insert the needle purlwise in first st. on
left hand needle, k. second st. pulling it through first st.
then k. in back of first st. and slip both loops off
together – called Cr. 2, k.1; rep. from * to last 3 sts., Cr.
2, k.1.
5th, 6th and 7th rows: As 1st, 2nd and 3rd rows.
8th row: K.3, *Cr. 2, k.2; rep. from * to last st., k.1.
These 8 rows form the pattern.

66 Stocking Stitch with Cross Stitches

No. 67 Ribbon Pattern 2 sts. plus 4
This pattern requires two pairs of needles; one pair in
the normal size for the yarn (A), and one pair two sizes
thicker (B).
1st row: With B needle, K.1, *sl. 1 purlwise, k.1, yarn
forward, pass the slipped st. over the k.1 and the yarn
forward; rep. from * to last st., k.1.
2nd row: With B needle, *p. in front of second st. on left
hand needle but do not slip loop off, p. in front of first
st. and slip both loops off together; rep. from * to end.
3rd row: With A needle, k. to end.
4th row: With A needle, p. to end.
These 4 rows form the pattern.

67 Ribbon Pattern

68 Crossed Purl Pattern

69 Risotto Pattern

70 Twisted Fabric

71 Twist Moss Stitch Pattern

No. 68   Crossed Purl Pattern Even number of sts.
1st row: K. to end.
2nd row: (wrong side) *P. 2 tog. leaving loops on left hand needle, p. the first of these loops again and slip both loops off left hand needle together – called Cross 2 purlwise; rep. from * to end.
3rd row: As 1st row.
4th row: P.1, *Cross 2 purlwise; rep. from * to last st., p.1.
These 4 rows form the pattern.

No. 69   Risotto Pattern Even number of sts.
1st and 3rd rows: K. to end.
2nd row: K.1, *p. 2 tog. without dropping the loops k. tog. the same sts.; rep. from * to last st., k.1.
4th row: K.1, p.1, *p. 2 tog. then k. same 2 sts. tog. as before; rep. from * to last 2 sts., p.1, k.1.
These 4 rows form the pattern.

No. 70   Twisted Fabric 2 sts.
1st row: (right side) K. to end.
2nd row: P. to end.
3rd row: K.1, *sl.1, k.1, p.s.s.o., but k. in back of the slip st. before slipping it off the needle; rep. from * to last st., k.1.
4th row: P. to end.
5th row: K.2, *rep. from * of 3rd pattern row to last 2 sts., k.2.
The 2nd to 5th rows form the pattern.

No. 71   Twist Moss Stitch Pattern 2 sts. plus 2
1st row: K.1, *yarn forward, k.2; rep. from * to last st., yarn forward, k.1.
2nd row: P.1, drop yarn forward loop, *p. in front of second st. on left hand needle then in front of first st. and slip both loops off together, drop yarn forward loop; rep. from * to last st., p.1.
These 2 rows form the pattern.

No. 72 Rowan Pattern 3 sts. plus 1
1st row: K. to end.
2nd row: K.1, *p. 2 tog. leaving loops on left hand
needle, then p. in first st. and slip both loops off needle,
k.1; rep. from * to end.
3rd row: K. to end.
4th row: K.2, *p. 2 tog. leaving loops as before, k. first
st. and slip both loops off, k.1; rep. from * to last 2 sts.,
k.2.
5th row: K. to end.
6th row: K.3, *p. 2 tog. leaving loops as before, k. in
first st., slip loops off needle, k.1; rep. from * to last st.,
k.1.
These 6 rows form the pattern.

72 Rowan Pattern

No. 73 Textured Twist Pattern 4 sts. plus 2
Tw. 2 K., twist 2 sts. k. thus: k. in front of second st.
on left hand needle then k. in first st. and slip both
loops off together.
1st row: P.2, *k.2, p.2; rep. from * to end.
2nd row: K.2, *p.2, k.2; rep. from * to end.
3rd row: P.2, *Tw. 2 k., p.2; rep. from * to end.
4th and 5th rows: As 2nd row.
6th row: As 1st row.
7th row: Tw. 2 k., *p.2, Tw. 2 k.; rep. from * to end.
8th row: P.2, *k.2, p.2; rep. from * to end.
These 8 rows form the pattern.

73 Textured Twist Pattern

No. 74 Single Row Twist 6 sts.
1st row: K.2, *yarn round needle, p. 2 tog., k.4; rep.
from * to last 4 sts., yarn round needle, p. 2 tog., k.2.
This row forms the pattern.

74 Single Row Twist

No. 75 Zigzag Twists 4 sts. plus 2
Tw. 2 F., twist 2 front thus: k. in front of second st. on
left hand needle, then in front of first st. and slip both
loops off together.
Tw. 2 B., twist 2 back thus: passing needle behind first
st. on left hand needle, k. in front of second st., then k.
in front of first st. and slip both loops off together.
1st row: K.2, *Tw. 2 F., k.2; rep. from * to end.
2nd row: P. to end.

75 Zigzag Twists

33

3rd row: K.2, *Tw. 2 B., k.2; rep. from * to end.
4th row: P. to end.
These 4 rows form the pattern.

No. 76   Raised Ladder Pattern 7 sts. plus 2
1st row: (right side) P.2, *k. 1 t.b.l., p.3, k. 1 t.b.l., p.2;
rep. from * to end.
2nd row: K.2, *p. 1 t.b.l., k.3, p. 1 t.b.l., k.2; rep. from
* to end.
3rd row: P.2, *k. 1 t.b.l., k.3, k. 1 t.b.l., p.2; rep. from *
to end.
4th row: K.2, *p. 1 t.b.l., p.3, p. 1 t.b.l., k.2; rep. from *
to end.
These 4 rows form the pattern.

76 Raised Ladder Pattern

No. 77   Lovat Pattern 8 sts. plus 7
1st row: P.3, *k. in front and back of next st., p.7; rep.
from *, ending last rep., p.3 instead of p.7.
2nd row: K.3, *k. 2 tog. t.b.l., k.7; rep. from * ending
last rep., k.3 instead of k.7.
3rd row: P.2, *k. in front and back of next st., p.1, k. in
front and back of next st., p.5; rep. from * ending last
rep., p.2 instead of p.5.
4th row: K.2, *k. 2 tog. t.b.l., k.1, k. 2 tog. t.b.l., k.5;
rep. from * ending last rep., k.2 instead of k.5.
These 4 rows form the pattern.

77 Lovat Pattern

No. 78   Twisted Ringwood Pattern 2 sts. plus 1
1st row: K. in back of all sts. to end.
2nd row: K.1, *p.1, k.1; rep. from * to end.
These 2 rows form the pattern.

78 Twisted Ringwood Pattern

No. 79   Broad Twist Pattern 5 sts. plus 1
1st row: (wrong side) *K.2, p.2, k.1; rep. from * to last
st., k.1.
2nd row: K.1, *k.1, k. in back of second st. on left hand
needle, then in front of first st. and slip both loops off
together, k.1, p.1; rep. from * ending last rep., k.2
instead of k.1, p.1.
These 2 rows form the pattern.

79 Broad Twist Pattern

No. 80 Cross and Moss Stitch Pattern 5 sts. plus 3

Cr. 2 k., cross 2 knitwise thus: k. in back of second st. on left hand needle, then in front of first st. and slip both loops off together.

Cr. 2 p., cross 2 purlwise thus: p. in second st. on left hand needle, then p. in first st. and slip both loops off together.

1st row: P.1, k.1, p.1, *Cr. 2 k., p.1, k.1, p.1; rep. from * to end.

2nd row: P.1, k.1, p.1, *Cr. 2 p., p.1, k.1, p.1; rep. from * to end.

These 2 rows form the pattern.

80 *Cross and Moss Stitch Pattern*

No. 81 Corded Pattern 2 sts. plus 3.

1st row: (right side) P.1, *p.1, k. in front and back of next st.; rep. from * to last 2 sts., p.1, k.1.

2nd row: K.1, *k.1, p. 2 tog.; rep. from * to last 2 sts., k.2.

These 2 rows form the pattern.

81 *Corded Pattern*

No. 82 Glovers Fabric 2 sts.

1st row: *K.1 t.b.l., p.1; rep. from * to end.

2nd row: *K.1, p. 1 t.b.l.; rep. from * to end.

3rd row: As 1st row.

4th row: P. to end.

5th row: K. to end.

6th row: P. to end.

7th row: *P.1, k. 1 t.b.l.; rep. from * to end.

8th row: *P. 1 t.b.l., k.1; rep. from * to end.

9th row: As 7th row.

10th row: P. to end.

11th and 12th rows: As 5th and 6th rows.

These 12 rows form the pattern.

82 *Glovers Fabric*

No. 83 Checkered Pattern 4 sts. plus 2

1st, 3rd and 5th rows: P.2, *k. in back and front of each of next 2 sts., p.2; rep. from * to end.

2nd, 4th and 6th rows: K.2, *p. 2 tog. twice, k.2; rep. from * to end.

7th, 9th and 11th rows: *K. in back and front of each of next 2 sts., p.2; rep. from * to last 2 sts., k. in back and front of each st.

8th, 10th and 12th rows: *P. 2 tog. twice, k.2; rep. from * to last 4 sts., p. 2 tog. twice.

These 12 rows form the pattern.

83 *Checkered Pattern*

84 Husky Twist Rib Checks

85 Slip Stitch Checks

86 Twist Stitch Bricks

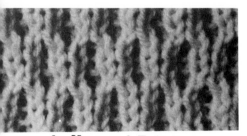

87 Honeycomb Twist Pattern

No. 84   Husky Twist Rib Checks 4 sts. plus 2
1st row: K.2, *p. 2 t.b.l., k.2; rep. from * to end.
2nd row: P.2, *k. 2 t.b.l., p.2; rep. from * to end.
3rd to 6th rows: Rep. last 2 rows twice more.
7th row: P. 2 t.b.l., *k.2, p. 2 t.b.l.; rep. from * to end.
8th row: K. 2 t.b.l., *p.2, k. 2 t.b.l.; rep. from * to end.
9th to 12th rows: Rep. last 2 rows twice more.
These 12 rows form the pattern.

No. 85   Slip Stitch Checks 4 sts. plus 3
1st row: K.1, *yarn forward to make a st., sl. 1 purlwise, k.3; rep. from * to last 2 sts., yarn forward, sl.1, k.1.
2nd row: K.1, *k. tog. the sl. st. and the made st. of the previous row, p.3; rep. from * to last 3 sts., k. 2 tog. as before, k.1.
3rd row: As 1st row.
4th row: As 2nd row.
5th and 6th rows: As 1st and 2nd rows.
7th row: K.3, *yarn forward, sl.1, k.3; rep. from * to end.
8th row: K.1, p.2, *k. tog. the sl. st. and the made st. of the previous row, p.3; rep. from * to last 5 sts., k. 2 tog. as before, p.2, k.1.
9th to 12th rows: Rep. 7th and 8th rows twice.
These 12 rows form the pattern.

No. 86   Twist Stitch Bricks 6 sts.
1st row: (wrong side) *K.3, p.1 t.b.l., k.2; rep. from * to end.
2nd row: *P.2, k. 1 t.b.l., p.3; rep. from * to end.
3rd row: As 1st row.
4th row: As 2nd row.
5th and 6th rows: As 1st and 2nd rows.
7th row: *P. 1 t.b.l., k.5; rep. from * to end.
8th row: *P.5, k. 1 t.b.l.; rep. from * to end.
9th to 12th rows: Rep. last 2 rows twice more.
These 12 rows form the pattern.

No. 87   Honeycomb Twist Pattern 4 sts. plus 2
Tw. 2 F., twist 2 front thus: k. in front of second st. on left hand needle, then k. in front of first st. and slip both loops off together.
Tw. 2 B., twist 2 back thus: k. in back of second st. on left hand needle, then k. in front of first st. and slip both loops off together.
1st row: (right side) Sl.1, *Tw. 2 F., Tw. 2 B.; rep. from * to last st., k.1.

2nd row: Sl.1, p.1, *k.2, p.2; rep. from * to end.
3rd row: Sl.1, k.1, *p.2, k.2; rep. from * to end.
4th row: As 2nd row.
5th row: Sl.1, *Tw. 2 B., Tw. 2 F.; rep. from * to last st., p.1.
6th row: As 3rd row.
7th and 8th rows: As 2nd and 3rd rows.
These 8 rows form the pattern.

No. 88   Taffy Twist 4 sts. plus 1
1st row: P.1, *miss next st., k. in front of second st., k. missed st. and slip both loops off together, k.1, p.1; rep. from * to end.
2nd row: *K.1, p.3; rep. from * to last st., k.1.
3rd row: P.1, *k.1, with needle at back of work k. in back of second st., k. the missed st. and slip both loops off together, p.1; rep. from * to end.
4th row: As 2nd row.
These 4 rows form the pattern.

88 Taffy Twist

No. 89   Broken Twist Rib 4 sts. plus 1
1st row: K.1, *k. 1 t.b.l., p.1; rep. from * to last 2 sts., k. 1 t.b.l., k.1.
2nd row: *K. 1 t.b.l., p. 1 t.b.l.; rep. from * to last st., k. 1 t.b.l.
3rd row: As 1st row.
4th row: As 2nd row.
5th row: K.1, *p.1, k. 1 t.b.l.; rep. from * to last 2 sts., p.1, k.1.
6th row: K.2, *p. 1 t.b.l., k. 1 t.b.l.; rep. from * to last st., k.1 t.b.l.
These 6 rows form the pattern.

89 Broken Twist Rib

No. 90   Garter Stitch Diamonds 15 sts. plus 3
Tw. 2 B.P., twist 2 back purl thus: slip next st. to back on cable needle, k. 1 t.b.l., then p.1 from cable needle.
Tw. 2 F.P., twist 2 front purl thus: slip next st. to front on cable needle, p.1, then k. 1 t.b.l. from cable needle.
Tw. 2 B.K., twist 2 back knit thus: slip next st. to back on cable needle, k. 1 t.b.l., then k. 1 from cable needle.
Tw. 2 F.K., twist 2 front knit thus: slip next st. to front on cable needle, k.1, then k. 1 t.b.l. from cable needle.
1st row: P.3, *k.4, Tw. 2 B.P., Tw. 2 F.P., k.4, p.3; rep. from * to end.
2nd row and foll. alt. row: P. to end.
3rd row: P.3, *k.3, Tw. 2 B.P., p.2, Tw. 2 F.P., k.3, p.3; rep. from * to end.

90 Garter Stitch Diamonds

5th row: P.3, *k.2, Tw. 2 B.P., p.4, Tw. 2 F.P., k.2, p.3; rep. from * to end.

7th row: P.3, *k.1, Tw. 2 B.P., p.6, Tw. 2 F.P., k.1, p.3; rep. from * to end.

9th row: P.3, *k.2, p.8, k.2, p.3; rep. from * to end.

11th row: P.3, *k.1, Tw. 2 F.K., p.6, Tw. 2 B.K., k.1, p.3; rep. from * to end.

13th row: P.3, *k.2, Tw. 2 F.K., p.4, Tw. 2 B.K., k.2, p.3; rep. from * to end.

15th row: P.3, *k.3, Tw. 2 F.K., p.2, Tw. 2 B.K., k.3, p.3; rep. from * to end.

17th row: P.3, *k.4, Tw. 2 F.K., Tw. 2 B.K., k.4, p.3; rep. from * to end.

19th row: P.3, *k.5, Tw. 2 F.K., k.5, p.3; rep. from * to end.

20th row: As 2nd row.

These 20 rows form the pattern.

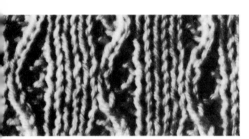

91 Wave Rib Welt

No. 91 Wave Rib Welt 6 sts. plus 1

This pattern, although a flat fabric, is sometimes used as a fancy rib welt on traditional Aran sweaters.

L.Tw., left twist thus: k. t.b.l. the second st. on left hand needle, k. first and second sts. together t.b.l. and slip both loops off together.

R.Tw., right twist thus: k. second st. on left hand needle, then k. first st. and slip both loops off together.

1st row: (right side) K. to end.

2nd row: P.2, *k.2, p.4; rep. from * ending last rep., p.3.

3rd row: K.2, *L.Tw., k.4; rep. from * ending last rep., k.3.

4th row: P.2, *k.1, p.1, k.1, p.3; rep. from * ending last rep., p.2.

5th row: K.3, *L.Tw., k.4; rep. from * ending last rep., k.2.

6th row: P.3, *k.2, p.4; rep. from * ending last rep., p.2.

7th row: K. to end.

8th row: As 6th row.

9th row: K.3, *R.Tw., k.4; rep. from * ending last rep., k.2.

10th row: As 4th row.

11th row: K.2, *R.Tw., k.4; rep. from * ending last rep., k.3.

12th row: As 2nd row.

These 12 rows form the pattern.

No. 92 Twist Stitch Zigzag 12 sts.

L.Tw., left twist thus: p. t.b.l. in second st. on left hand needle, k. first st. and slip both loops off together.
R.Tw., right twist thus: k. second st. on left hand needle, p. first st. and slip both loops off together.

1st row: (right side) P.1, (L.Tw.) twice, p.7.
2nd row: K.6, (L.Tw.) twice, k.2.
3rd row: P.3, (L.Tw.) twice, p.5.
4th row: K.4, (L.Tw.) twice, k.4.
5th row: P.5, (L.Tw.) twice, p.3.
6th row: K.2, (L.Tw.) twice, k.6.
7th row: P.7, (L.Tw.) twice, p.1.
8th row: K. the k. sts. and p. the p. sts. as they present themselves.
9th row: P.7, (R.Tw.) twice, p.1.
10th row: K.2, (R.Tw.) twice, k.6.
11th row: P.5, (R.Tw.) twice, p.3.
12th row: K.4, (R.Tw.) twice, k.4.
13th row: P.3, (R.Tw.) twice, p.5.
14th row: K.6, (R.Tw.) twice, k.2.
15th row: P.1, (R.Tw.) twice, p.7.
16th row: As 8th row.
These 16 rows form the pattern.

92 Twist Stitch Zigzag

No. 93 Knot Stitch 12 sts. plus 9

1st row: K. to end.
2nd row: P. to end.
3rd to 6th rows: Rep. last 2 rows twice more.
7th row: K.9, *p. 3 tog. leaving loops on left hand needle, k. the same 3 loops tog. then p. the same 3 loops tog. – making 3 sts, out of 3 sts., k.9; rep. from * to end.
8th row: P. to end.
9th to 14th rows: As 1st and 2nd rows.
15th row: K.3, *in next 3 sts. p. 3 tog.-k. 3 tog.-p. 3 tog. as 7th row, k.9; rep. from * ending last rep., k.3 instead of k.9.
16th row: P. to end.
These 16 rows form the pattern.

93 Knot Stitch

No. 94 Herringbone Rib Pattern 6 sts. plus 4

This pattern, despite its name, is a flat weave without the elasticity we expect from patterns termed rib.

Note that all sts. are slipped purlwise in this pattern.
1st row: (wrong side) Sl.1, *p.2, yarn back, sl. 4 sts., yarn forward and round needle to make a st.; rep. from * to last 3 sts., p.2, k.1.
2nd row: Sl.1, *yarn forward, sl. 2 sts., yarn back, drop made st. off needle, k.4; rep. from * to last 3 sts., yarn

94 Herringbone Rib Pattern

forward, sl.2, yarn back, k.1.

3rd row: As 1st row.

4th row: As 2nd row.

5th row: As 1st row.

6th row: Sl.1, *yarn forward, sl. 2 sts., yarn back, drop made loop, k.1, with point of right hand needle pick up lowest of three dropped strands lying across front of work and carry it behind the other two strands, k.1 from left hand needle and pass the raised loop over the k.1 – called RK.1 –, k.2; rep. from * to last 3 sts., yarn forward, sl.2, yarn back, k.1.

7th row: As 1st row.

8th row: As 6th row.

9th row: As 1st row.

10th row: As 6th row.

11th row: As 1st row.

12th row: Sl.1, *yarn forward, sl.2, yarn back, drop made loop, k.2, RK.1, k.1; rep. from * to last 3 sts., yarn forward, sl.2, yarn back, k.1.

13th row: As 1st row.

14th row: As 12th row.

15th row: As 1st row.

16th row: As 12th row.

17th row: As 1st row.

The 6th to 17th rows form the pattern.

No. 95 Arrowhead Twist Stitch Pattern 10 sts. plus 11

Tw. 2 B., twist 2 back thus: k. in back of second st. on left hand needle, then k. in front of first st., and slip both loops off together.

Tw. 2 F., twist 2 sts. front thus: k. in front of second st. on left hand needle, then k. in front of first st. and slip both loops off together.

1st row: P.3, *Tw. 2 F., p.1, Tw. 2 B., p.5; rep. from * ending p.3 instead of p.5.

2nd row: K.3, *p.2, k.1, p.2, k.5; rep. from * ending k.3 instead of k.5.

3rd row: P.2, *Tw. 2 F., k.1, p.1, k.1, Tw. 2 B., p.3; rep. from * ending p.2 instead of p.3.

4th row: K.2, *p.3, k.1, p.3, k.3; rep. from * ending k.2 instead of k.3.

5th row: *P.1, Tw. 2 F., k.2, p.1, k.2, Tw. 2 B.; rep. from * to last st., p.1.

6th row: *K.1, p.4; rep. from * to last st., k.1.

These 6 rows form the pattern.

95 *Arrowhead Twist Stitch Pattern*

EYELET AND LACE PATTERNS

THREE

Not all patterns with eyelet holes are knitted lace. Some of the simplest examples are little more than solid fabric with eyelets to break the possible heaviness. Other, larger, patterns are very elaborate, and are used mainly for formal garments, such as christening robes, wedding gowns etc.

It is not difficult to turn a classic sweater or cardigan pattern from plain stocking stitch into a lace patterned one. The less experienced knitter might prefer to use the lace pattern as an insertion, alternating it with one of the plainer patterns and allowing the shaping to be set within the plain pattern rows.

Do not limit yourself to working in fine yarns. The photographs on page 189 show how different a pattern can look when worked in a variety of yarns. Always work a large test sample before beginning a garment: this will help you to become accustomed to the pattern and will provide a useful tension sample. Patterns with eyelets, generally speaking, have a wider tension than the equivalent stocking stitch tension. Cast on the number of stitches for the sample tension when working a complete garment, allowing for the extra width.

The patterns here range from tiny eyelets to large and intricate designs, most of them well loved and many of great antiquity.

No. 96 Lambstail Pattern 6 sts. plus 5
1st row: P.2, *yarn round needle, p. 2 tog., p.4; rep. from * to last 3 sts., yarn round needle, p. 2 tog., p.1.
2nd row: K.2, *p.1, k.5; rep. from * to last 3 sts., p.1, k.2.
3rd row: P.2, *k.1, p.5; rep. from * to last 3 sts., k.1, p.2.

96 Lambstail Pattern

4th row: As 2nd row.
5th row: As 3rd row.
6th row: As 2nd row.
7th row: P.5, *yarn round needle, p. 2 tog., p.4; rep. from * to end.
8th row: K.5, *p.1, k.5; rep. from * to end.
9th row: P.5, *k.1, p.5; rep. from * to end.
10th row: As 8th row.
11th row: As 9th row.
12th row: As 8th row.
These 12 rows form the pattern.

No. 97   Eiffel Tower Pattern   8 sts. plus 2

1st row: K.1, *yarn round needle, p. 2 tog., p.6; rep. from * to last st., k.1.
2nd, 4th and 6th rows: K.1, *k.7, p.1; rep. from * to last st., k.1.
3rd, 5th and 7th rows: K.1, *k.1, p.7; rep. from * to last st., k.1.
8th row: P. to end.
9th row: K.1, *p.4, yarn round needle, p. 2 tog., p.2; rep. from * to last st., k.1.
10th, 12th and 14th rows: K.1, *k.3, p.1, k.4; rep. from * to last st., k.1.
11th, 13th and 15th rows: K.1, *p.4, k.1, p.3; rep. from * to last st., k.1.
16th row: P. to end.
These 16 rows form the pattern.

97 Eiffel Tower Pattern

No. 98   Droplet Pattern   6 sts. plus 5

1st row: (right side) P.5, *k.1, yarn round needle, p.5; rep. from * to end.
2nd row: K.5, *p.2, k.5; rep. from * to end.
3rd row: P.5, *k.2, p.5; rep. from * to end.
4th and 5th rows: As 2nd and 3rd rows.
6th row: K.5, *p. 2 tog., k.5; rep. from * to end.
7th row: P.2, *k.1, yarn round needle, p.5; rep. from * to last 3 sts., k.1, yarn round needle, p.2.
8th row: K.2, *p.2, k.5; rep. from * to last 4 sts., p.2, k.2.
9th row: P.2, *k.2, p.5; rep. from * to last 4 sts., k.2, p.2.
10th and 11th rows: As 8th and 9th rows.
12th row: K.2, *p. 2 tog., k.5; rep. from * to last 4 sts., p. 2 tog., k.2.
These 12 rows form the pattern.

98 Droplet Pattern

No. 99   Sandalwood Lace 6 sts. plus 5

1st row: (right side) P.4, *k.3, p.3; rep. from * to last st., p.1.

2nd row: K.4, *p.3, k.3; rep. from * to last st., k.1.

3rd row: P.4, *yarn round needle, p. 3 tog., yarn round needle, p.3; rep. from * to last st., p.1.

4th row: As 2nd row.

5th row: K.4, *p.3, k.3; rep. from * to last st., k.1.

6th row: P.4, *k.3, p.3; rep. from * to last st., p.1.

7th row: K.1, *yarn round needle, p. 3 tog., yarn round needle p.3; rep. from * ending last rep. k.1 instead of p.3.

8th row: As 6th row.

These 8 rows form the pattern.

99 Sandalwood Lace

No. 100   Milano Lace 6 sts. plus 8

1st row: (right side) K.1, yarn forward, k. 2 tog. t.b.l., *k.2, k. 2 tog., yarn forward, k. 2 tog. t.b.l.; rep. from * to last 5 sts., k.2, k. 2 tog., yarn forward, k.1.

2nd row: K.1, p.5* p. in front and back of the yarn forward of the previous row, p.4; rep. from * to last 2 sts., p.1, k.1.

3rd row: K.2, *k. 2 tog., yarn forward, k. 2 tog. t.b.l., k.2; rep. from * to end.

4th row: K.1, p.2; *p. in front and back of yarn forward of previous row, p.4; rep. from * to last 4 sts., p. in front and back of yarn forward, p.2, k.1.

These 4 rows form the pattern.

100 Milano Lace

No. 101   Layette Lace 4 sts. plus 2

1st row: K.1, *yarn forward, sl.1, k. 2 tog., p.s.s.o., yarn forward, k.1; rep. from * to last st., k.1.

2nd row: P. to end.

3rd row: K.3, *yarn forward, sl.1, k. 2 tog., p.s.s.o., yarn forward, k.1; rep. from * to last 3 sts., k.3.

4th row: P. to end.

These 4 rows form the pattern.

101 Layette Lace

No. 102   Picot Stripes 2 sts. plus 2

1st row: P.1, *yarn round needle, p. 2 tog.; rep. from * to last st., k.1.

2nd row: *P.1, p. 1 t.b.l.; rep. from * to end.

3rd row: K. to end.

4th row: P. to end.

5th row: P.1, *p. 2 tog., yarn round needle; rep. from * to last st., p.1.

6th row: *P. 1 t.b.l., p.1; rep. from * to end.

102 Picot Stripes

7th row: K. to end.
8th row: P. to end.
These 8 rows form the pattern.

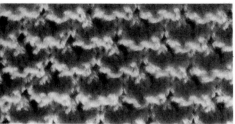

103 Rose Lace

No. 103 Rose Lace 8 sts. plus 1
1st row: (right side) K. to end.
2nd row: P. to end.
3rd and 4th rows: *K.2, yarn forward, k. 2 tog.; rep.
from * to last st., k.1.
5th row: K. to end.
6th row: P. to end.
7th and 8th rows: K.4, *yarn forward, k. 2 tog., k.2; rep.
from * to last st., k.1.
These 8 rows form the pattern.

No. 104 Shamrock Pattern 4 sts. plus 2
1st row: Sl. 1 purlwise, *k. loosely in front, back, then in
front again of next st., k. 3 tog.; rep. from * to last st.,
k.1.
This row forms the pattern.

104 Shamrock Pattern

No. 105 Faggotted Rib Simple 4 sts. plus 1
A variation on faggotted lace pattern, a truly antique
stitch much used in Victorian 'white work'.
1st row: (wrong side) P. to end.
2nd row: K.1, *yarn forward, sl.1, k. 2 tog., p.s.s.o.,
yarn forward, k.1; rep. from * to end.
These 2 rows form the pattern.

105 Faggotted Rib Simple

No. 106 Zigzag Mesh 2 sts. plus 1
1st row: (wrong side) P. to end.
2nd row: K.1, *yarn forward, k. 2 tog.; rep. from * to
end.
3rd row: P. to end.
4th row: *Sl.1, k.1, p.s.s.o., yarn forward; rep. from * to
last st., k.1.
These 4 rows form the pattern.

106 Zigzag Mesh

No. 107 Trinity or Blackberry Pattern 4 sts. plus 2
1st row: (right side) P. to end.
2nd row: K.1, *(k.1, p.1, k.1) all in next st., p. 3 tog.;
rep. from * to last st., k.1.
3rd row: P. to end.
4th row: K.1, *p. 3 tog., (k.1, p.1, k.1) all in next st.;
rep. from * to last st., k.1.
These 4 rows form the pattern.

107 Trinity or Blackberry Pattern

No. 108 Puff Stitch 6 sts. plus 1
1st row: (right side) P.3, k.1, *p.5, k.1; rep. from * to
last 3 sts., p.3.
2nd row: Sl.1, k. 2 tog., p.s.s.o., *yarn forward, (k.1,
p.1, k.1) all in next st., yarn forward, k. 3 tog., k. 2 tog.,
pass second st. on right hand needle over first st. and off
needle; rep. from * to last 4 sts., yarn forward, (k.1, p.1,
k.1) all in next st., yarn forward, k. 3 tog.
3rd row: P. to end.
4th row: P.1, *k.5, p.1; rep. from * to end.
5th row: K.1, *p.5, k.1; rep. from * to end.
6th row: K. twice in first st., *yarn forward, k. 3 tog., k.
2 tog., pass second st. on right hand needle over first st.
and off needle, yarn forward, (k.1, p.1, k.1) all in next
st.; rep. from * to last 6 sts., yarn forward, k. 3 tog., k. 2
tog., pass second st. over first as before, yarn forward,
k. twice in last st.
7th row: P. to end.
8th row: K.3, p.1, *k.5, p.1; rep. from * to last 3 sts.,
k.3.
These 8 rows form the pattern.

108 Puff Stitch

No. 109 Puff Stitch reversed 6 sts. plus 1
This is worked in the same way as No. 108, having the
1st and following alternate rows as the wrong side.

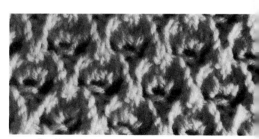

109 Puff Stitch reversed

110 Picot Pattern

111 Ripple Stitch

112 Faggotted Lace Alternating

113 Gathered Eyelet Pattern

No. 110   Picot Pattern 2 sts.

As this pattern has a tendency to bias, care should be taken to use a yarn that can be pressed. Check the pressing instructions on the yarn ball band.

1st row: P. to end.

2nd row: As 1st row.

3rd row: K.1, *yarn forward, k. 2 tog.; rep. from * to last st., k.1.

4th row: P. to end.

These 4 rows form the pattern.

No. 111   Ripple Stitch 4 sts. plus 2

1st row: (wrong side) K.1, p. to last st., k.1.

2nd row: K.1, *pick up and k. loop lying before next st., k.1, pick up and k. loop lying before next st. – called M.k.M., k. 3 tog.; rep. from * to last st., k.1.

3rd row: As 1st row.

4th row: K. to end.

5th row: As 1st row.

6th row: K.1, *k. 3 tog., M.k.M.; rep. from * to last st., k.1.

7th row: As 1st row.

8th row: K. to end.

These 8 rows form the pattern.

No. 112   Faggotted Lace Alternating 8 sts. plus 4

1st row: (right side) *P.4, k.2, yarn round needle, p. 2 tog.; rep. from * to last 4 sts., p.4.

2nd row: *K.4, p.2, yarn over needle, k. 2 tog.; rep. from * to last 4 sts., k.4.

3rd to 8th rows: Rep. last 2 rows 3 times more.

9th row: *K.2, yarn round needle, p. 2 tog., p.4; rep. from * to last 4 sts., k.2, yarn round needle, p. 2 tog.

10th row: *P.2, yarn over needle, k. 2 tog., k.4; rep. from * to last 4 sts., p.2, y.o.n., k. 2 tog.

11th to 16th rows: Rep. last 2 rows 3 times more.

These 16 rows form the pattern.

No. 113   Gathered Eyelet Pattern 6 sts. plus 8

K.H.B., yarn back, knit in hole 4 rows below.

1st row: (wrong side) K.3, *k. 2 tog., yarn forward, k.4; rep. from * to last 5 sts., k. 2 tog., yarn forward, k.3.

2nd row: P. to end.

3rd row: K. to end.

4th row: P.3, *K.H.B., p.5; rep. from * to last 5 sts., K.H.B., p.4.

5th row: K. to end.

6th row: P. to end.

7th row: K.6, *k. 2 tog., yarn forward, k.4; rep. from * to last 8 sts., k. 2 tog., yarn forward, k.6.

8th row: P. to end.

9th row: K. to end.

10th row: P.6, *K.H.B., p.5; rep. from * to last 8 sts., K.H.B., p.7.

11th row: K. to end.

12th row: P. to end.

These 12 rows form the pattern.

No. 114   Bethany Lace Pattern 8 sts. plus 5

1st row: *K. 2 tog., yarn forward, k.1, yarn forward, k. 2 tog. t.b.l., k.3; rep. from * to last 5 sts., k. 2 tog., yarn forward, k.1, yarn forward, k. 2 tog. t.b.l.

2nd row: P. to end.

3rd row: K.1, *k. 2 tog., yarn forward, k.6; rep. from * to last 4 sts., k. 2 tog., yarn forward, k.2.

4th row: P.1, *k.3, p.5; rep. from * ending last rep. p.1 instead of p.5.

5th row: K.1, *p.3, k.5; rep. from * ending last rep., k.1 instead of k.5.

6th row: As 4th row.

7th row: K.4, *k. 2 tog., yarn forward, k.1, yarn forward, k. 2 tog. t.b.l., k.3; rep. from * to last st., k.1.

8th row: P. to end.

9th row: K.5, *k. 2 tog., yarn forward, k.6; rep. from * to end.

10th row: *P.5, k.3; rep. from * to last 5 sts., p.5.

11th row: K.5, *p.3, k.5; rep. from * to end.

12th row: As 10th row.

These 12 rows form the pattern.

114 Bethany Lace Pattern

No. 115   Daisy Pattern 6 sts. plus 8

1st row: (right side) P. to end.

2nd row: K. to end.

3rd row: P. to end.

4th row: K. to end.

5th row: P.1, *count 4 p. ridges below second st. on left hand needle, insert right needle point through the loop immediately below the 4th ridge in line with the second st., yarn round needle and draw a loop through, now k. the first st. on left hand needle and pass the loop over, (insert needle again into same space and draw loop through, k. next st. on left hand needle and pass loop over) twice – called 1 daisy, p.3; rep. from * to last st., p.1.

115 Daisy Pattern

6th row: K.4, *p.3, k.3; rep. from * to last 4 sts., p.3, k.1.

7th row: P. to end.

8th row: K. to end.

9th row: K.1, *p.3, work 1 daisy; rep. from * to last st., p.1.

10th row: K.1, *p.3, k.3; rep. from * to last st., p.1.

The 3rd to 10th rows form the pattern.

No. 116 Eyelet Garter Stripes 3 sts.

1st and 2nd rows: K. to end.

3rd row: Winding yarn twice round needle for each st., k. to end.

4th row: *Slip 3 sts. on to right hand needle dropping extra loops, slip these 3 sts. back on to left hand needle, (k.1, p.1, k.1) all in back of 3 long sts. tog. making 3 sts. out of 3 long sts.; rep. from * to end.

5th and 6th rows: K. to end.

These 6 rows form the pattern.

116 Eyelet Garter Stripes

No. 117 Ripple Wave Pattern 6 sts. plus 7

1st row: K.2, *yarn forward, sl.1, k. 2 tog., p.s.s.o., yarn forward, k.3; rep. from * ending last rep., k.2 instead of k.3.

2nd row: P. to end.

3rd and 4th rows: Rep. 1st and 2nd rows

5th to 8th rows: K. to end.

These 8 rows form the pattern.

117 Ripple Wave Pattern

No. 118 Lace and Stocking Stitch Stripes 3 sts. plus 1

1st row: K. to end.

2nd row: P. to end.

3rd to 6th rows: Rep. last 2 rows twice more.

7th row: K. to end.

8th row: K. in back of each st. to end.

9th row: K.1, *yarn over needle, k. 2 tog., k.1; rep. from * to end.

10th row: P. to end.

11th row: *K.1, k. 2 tog., yarn over needle; rep. from * to last st., k.1.

12th row: P. to end.

13th row: As 9th row.

14th row: P. to end.

15th row: As 11th row.

118 Lace and Stocking Stitch Stripes

16th row: K. in back of first st., *k.1, k. in back of each of next 2 sts; rep. from * to end.
These 16 rows form the pattern.

No. 119   Dorothy Lace   5 sts. plus 2

1st row: K.1, *yarn forward to make 1, k.1; rep. from * to last st., k.1.
2nd row: K.1, *p.1, drop made loop; rep. from * to last st., k.1.
3rd row: K.1, *k. 4 tog., (k.1, p.1, k.1, p.1) all in next st.; rep. from * to last st., k.1.
4th row: P. to end.
5th row: As 1st row.
6th row: As 2nd row.
7th row: K.1, *(k.1, p.1, k.1, p.1) all in next st., k. 4 tog.; rep. from * to last st., k.1.
8th row: P. to end.
These 8 rows form the pattern.

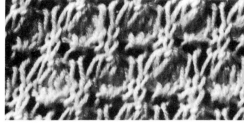

119 Dorothy Lace

No. 120   Moss and Lace Rib   6 sts. plus 2

1st row: *K.1, p.1, k. 2 tog., (yarn forward) twice, k. 2 tog. t.b.l.; rep. from * to last 2 sts., k.1, p.1.
2nd row: *P.1, k.1, p.1, p. in front of first yarn forward and p. in back of second yarn forward of previous row, p.1; rep. from * to last 2 sts., p.1, k.1.
3rd row: *K.1, p.1, yarn over needle, k. 2 tog. t.b.l., k. 2 tog., yarn forward; rep. from * to last 2 sts., k.1, p.1.
4th row: *P.1, k.1, p.4; rep. from * to last 2 sts., p.1, k.1.
These 4 rows form the pattern.

120 Moss and Lace Rib

No. 121   Eyelet Lace Simple   3 sts.

1st row and foll. alt. rows: (right side) P. to end.
2nd row: K.2, *yarn forward, sl.1, k.2, pass the sl. st. over the k.2; rep. from * to last st., k.1.
4th row: K. to end.
6th row: K.1, *sl.1, k.2, pass the sl. st. over the k.2, yarn forward; rep. from * to last 2 sts., k.2.
8th row: K. to end.
These 8 rows form the pattern.

121 Eyelet Lace Simple

49

122 Eyelet Lace Simple reversed

No. 122   Eyelet Lace Simple reversed 3 sts.
The reverse side of No. 121 is as attractive as the commonly used side, especially for baby garments. It is worked in the same way as 121, having the 1st and following alternate rows as the wrong side of the work.

123 Bubble Pattern

No. 123   Bubble Pattern 4 sts. plus 3
1st row: (right side) K.2, *(p. 3 tog., k. 3 tog., p. 3 tog.) all in next 3 sts., k.1; rep. from * to last st., k.1.
2nd row: P. to end.
These 2 rows form the pattern.

124 Flat Faggoting Stitch

No. 124   Flat Faggoting Stitch 2 sts. plus 1
The basic pattern of this kind. Notice that it has sideways stretch, and allow for this when adapting patterns.
1st row: K.1, *yarn forward, k. 2 tog.; rep. from * to end.
This row forms the pattern.

125 Faggoting Variation

No. 125   Faggoting Variation 2 sts. plus 1
1st row: *Sl.1, k.1, p.s.s.o., yarn forward; rep. from * to last st., k.1.
2nd row: *P. 2 tog., yarn round needle; rep. from * to last st., p.1.
These 2 rows form the pattern.

126 Vandyke Lace Rib

No. 126   Vandyke Lace Rib 6 sts. plus 1
1st row: (wrong side) P. to end.
2nd row: K.1, *yarn forward, k.1, sl.1, k. 2 tog., p.s.s.o., k.1, yarn forward, k.1; rep. from * to end.
These 2 rows form the pattern.

No. 127 Eyelet Panels 10 sts. plus 3

1st row: (wrong side) *P.3, k.1, p.5, k.1; rep. from * to last 3 sts., p.3.
2nd row: *K.3, p.1, k. 2 tog., yarn forward, k.1, yarn forward, sl.1, k.1, p.s.s.o., p.1; rep. from * to last 3 sts., k.3.
3rd row: As 1st row.
4th row: *K.3, p.1, k.5, p.1; rep. from * to last 3 sts., k.3.
These 4 rows form the pattern.

127 Eyelet Panels

No. 128 Feathered Lace Rib 6 sts. plus 1

1st row: K.1, *p.5, k.1; rep. from * to end.
2nd row: P.1, *k.2, yarn forward, k. 2 tog. t.b.l., k.1, p.1; rep. from * to end.
3rd row: As 1st row.
4th row: P.1, *k.1, yarn forward, sl.1, k. 2 tog., p.s.s.o., yarn forward, k.1, p.1; rep. from * to end.
5th row: As 1st row.
6th row: As 2nd row.
These 6 rows form the pattern.

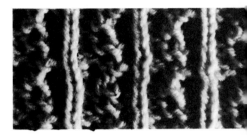

128 Feathered Lace Rib

No. 129 Wisteria Lace Rib 7 sts. plus 2

1st row: P.2, *k. 2 tog., yarn forward, k.1, yarn forward, sl.1, k.1, p.s.s.o., p.2; rep. from * to end.
2nd row: K.2, *p.5, k.2; rep. from * to end.
3rd row: P.2, *k.5, p.2; rep. from * to end.
4th row: As 2nd row.
These 4 rows form the pattern.

129 Wisteria Lace Rib

No. 130 Swiss Ribbons 9 sts. plus 2

1st row: *P.2, sl.1, k.1, p.s.s.o., yarn forward, k.3, yarn forward, k. 2 tog.; rep. from * to last 2 sts., p.2.
2nd row: K.2, *p.7, k.2; rep. from * to end.
3rd row: *P.2, k.2, yarn forward, sl.1, k.2 tog., p.s.s.o., yarn forward, k.2; rep. from * to last 2 sts., p.2.
4th row: As 2nd row.
These 4 rows form the pattern.

130 Swiss Ribbons

131 Reeded Rib Lace

No. 131   Reeded Rib Lace 4 sts. plus 1
1st row: P. to end.
2nd row: K.1, *yarn forward, sl.2, k.1, pass the 2 sl. sts. over the k.1, yarn forward, k.1; rep. from * to end.
These 2 rows form the pattern.

132 Robin Lace

No. 132   Robin Lace 5 sts. plus 2
1st row: (right side) P.2, *k.3, p.2; rep. from * to end.
2nd row: K.2, *p.3, k.2; rep. from * to end.
3rd row: P.2, *yarn round needle, p. 3 tog., yarn round needle, p.2; rep. from * to end.
4th row: As 2nd row.
These 4 rows form the pattern.

133 Nosegay Lace

No. 133   Nosegay Lace 4 sts. plus 5
1st row: Sl.1, k.1, *p.1, yarn over needle, sl.1, k. 2 tog., p.s.s.o., yarn round needle; rep. from * to last 3 sts., p.1, k.2.
2nd row: Sl.1, p.1, *k.1, p.3; rep. from * to last 3 sts., k.1, p.2.
3rd row: Sl.1, k.1, *p.1, k.3; rep. from * to last 3 sts., p.1, k.2.
4th row: As 2nd row.
These 4 rows form the pattern.

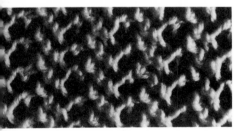

134 Spinel Lace

No. 134   Spinel Lace 4 sts. plus 2
1st row: K.1, *yarn forward, sl.1, k. 2 tog., p.s.s.o., yarn forward, k.1; rep. from * to last st., k.1.
2nd row: P. to end.
3rd row: K.2, *yarn forward, sl.1, k. 2 tog., p.s.s.o., yarn forward, k.1; rep. from * to end.
4th row: P. to end.
These 4 rows form the pattern.

No. 135   Picot Lace 6 sts. plus 2
1st row: K.1, *yarn forward, k. 3 tog. t.b.l., yarn
forward, k.3; rep. from * to last st., k.1.
2nd row: P. to end.
3rd row: K.1, *k.3, yarn forward, k. 3 tog. t.b.l., yarn
forward; rep. from * to last st., k.1.
4th row: As 2nd row.
These 4 rows form the pattern.

135 Picot Lace

No. 136   Shawl Lace Pattern 4 sts. plus 1
1st row: (right side) *K.1, yarn forward, sl.1, k. 2 tog.,
p.s.s.o., yarn forward; rep. from * to last st., k.1.
2nd row: P. to end.
3rd row: K. to end.
4th row: P. to end.
5th row: K. 2 tog., yarn forward, *k.1, yarn forward,
sl.1, k. 2 tog., p.s.s.o., yarn forward; rep. from * to last
3 sts., k.1, yarn forward, k. 2 tog. t.b.l.
6th row: P. to end.
7th and 8th rows: As 3rd and 4th rows.
These 8 rows form the pattern.

136 Shawl Lace Pattern

No. 137   Oleander Pattern 4 sts. plus 2
1st row: K.1, *p.1, k.2, p.1; rep. from * to last st., k.1.
2nd row: K.1, *k.1, p.2, k.1; rep. from * to last st., k.1.
3rd row: K.1, *k. 2 tog. wrap yarn round needle twice,
sl.1, k.1, p.s.s.o.; rep. from * to last st., k.1.
4th row: K.1, *p.1, k. in back of first made st., then in
front of second made st., p.1; rep. from * to last st., k.1.
5th row: K.1, *k.1, p.2, k.1; rep. from * to last st., k.1.
6th row: K.1, *p.1, k.2, p.1; rep. from * to last st., k.1.
7th row: K.1, yarn forward, *sl.1, k.1, p.s.s.o., k. 2 tog.,
wrap yarn round needle twice; rep. from * to last 5 sts.,
sl.1, k.1, p.s.s.o., k. 2 tog., yarn forward, k.1.
8th row: K.2, *p.2, k. in back of first made st., then in
front of second made st.; rep. from * to last 4 sts., p.2,
k.2.
These 8 rows form the pattern.

137 Oleander Pattern

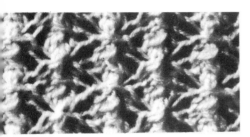

138 Cashmere Lace

No. 138   Cashmere Lace 8 sts. plus 11

1st row: (right side) K.1, k. 2 tog., *k.2, yarn forward, k.1, yarn forward, k.2, sl.1, k. 2 tog., p.s.s.o.; rep. from * to last 8 sts., k.2, yarn forward, k.1, yarn forward, k.2, k. 2 tog., k.1.

2nd row: K.1, p. 2 tog., *p.1, yarn round needle, p.3, yarn round needle, p.1, p. 3 tog.; rep. from * to last 8 sts., p.1, yarn round needle, p.3, yarn round needle, p.1, p. 2 tog., k.1.

3rd row: K.1, k. 2 tog., *yarn forward, k.5, yarn forward, sl.1, k. 2 tog., p.s.s.o.; rep. from * to last 8 sts., yarn forward, k.5, yarn forward, k. 2 tog., k.1.

4th row: K.1, p.1, *yarn round needle, p.2, p. 3 tog., p.2, yarn round needle, p.1; rep. from * to last st., k.1.

5th row: *K.3, yarn forward, k.1, sl.1, k. 2 tog., p.s.s.o., k.1, yarn forward; rep. from * to last 3 sts., k.3.

6th row: K.1, *p.3, yarn round needle, p. 3 tog., yarn round needle, p.2; rep. from * to last 2 sts., p.1, k.1.

These 6 rows form the pattern.

No. 139   Cashmere Lace reversed 8 sts. plus 11.
The reverse side of No. 138 is too pretty to go unnoticed. To work it, simply use pattern No. 138, having the 1st row and following alternate rows as the wrong side of the work.

139 Cashmere Lace reversed

140 Broad Rib Lace

No. 140   Broad Rib Lace 9 sts. plus 3

1st row: K.1, *k.1, yarn forward, sl.1, k.1, p.s.s.o., k.4, k. 2 tog., yarn forward; rep. from * to last 2 sts., k.2.

2nd row: K.1, *p.3, k.4, p.2; rep. from * to last 2 sts., p.1, k.1.

3rd row: K.1, *k.2, yarn forward, sl.1, k.1, p.s.s.o., k.2, k. 2 tog., yarn forward, k.1; rep. from * to last 2 sts., k.2.

4th row: K.1, *p.4, k.2, p.3; rep. from * to last 2 sts., p.1, k.1.

These 4 rows form the pattern.

No. 141   Shetland Lace 6 sts. plus 1

1st row: K.1, *yarn forward, sl.1, k.1, p.s.s.o., k.1, k. 2 tog., yarn forward, k.1; rep. from * to end.

2nd row: P. to end.

3rd row: K.2, *yarn forward, sl.1, k. 2 tog., p.s.s.o., yarn forward, k.3; rep. from * ending last rep., k.2 instead of k.3.

4th row: P. to end.

These 4 rows form the pattern.

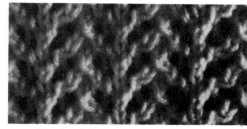
141 Shetland Lace

No. 142   Honeysuckle Lace 7 sts. plus 2

1st row: (right side) P.2, *yarn over needle, k. 2 tog. t.b.l., k.1, k. 2 tog., yarn round needle, p.2; rep. from * to end.

2nd row: K.2, *p.1, k.3, p.1, k.2; rep. from * to end.

3rd row: P.2, *k.1, yarn forward, k. 3 tog. t.b.l., yarn forward, k.1, p.2; rep. from * to end.

4th row: K.2, *p.2, k.1, p.2, k.2; rep. from * to end.

These 4 rows form the pattern.

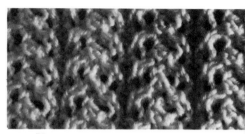
142 Honeysuckle Lace

No. 143   Honeysuckle Lace reversed 7 sts. plus 2

Honeysuckle lace is another pattern which is attractive on both sides. The reverse side is useful where a lightweight ribbed pattern stitch is required. Work the pattern in the same way as No. 142, having the first and following alternate rows as the wrong side of the work.

143 Honeysuckle Lace reversed

No. 144   Candystick Pattern 7 sts. plus 6

Tw. 3., twist 3 thus: k. in front of third st. on left hand needle, then in front of first and second sts. and slip three loops off together.

1st row: (right side) K.1, *k. 2 tog., yarn forward and then round needle to make 2 sts., sl.1, k.1, p.s.s.o., k.3; rep. from * to last 5 sts., k. 2 tog., make 2 as before, sl.1, k.1, p.s.s.o., k.1.

2nd row: K.1, *k.1, work k.1 t.b.l. and k.1 into the 2 made sts. of the previous row, k.1, p.3; rep. from * to last 5 sts., k.1, work k.1 t.b.l., and k.1 into the 2 made sts., k.2.

3rd row: K.1, *k. 2 tog., make 2 as before, sl.1, k.1, p.s.s.o., Tw.3; rep. from * to last 5 sts., k. 2 tog., make 2 as before, sl.1, k.1, p.s.s.o., k.1.

4th row: As 2nd row.

These 4 rows form the pattern.

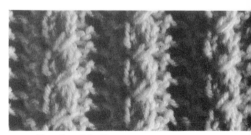
144 Candystick Pattern

145 Shetland Panels

No. 145 Shetland Panels 9 sts.
1st row: *(right side) K.2, k. 2 tog., yarn forward, k.1, yarn forward, sl.1, k.1, p.s.s.o., k.2; rep. from * to end.
2nd row and foll. alt. rows: P. to end.
3rd row: *K.1, k. 2 tog., yarn forward, k.3, yarn forward, sl.1, k.1, p.s.s.o., k.1; rep. from * to end.
5th row: *K.1, yarn forward, sl.1, k.1, p.s.s.o., yarn forward, sl. 2 sts. knitwise, k.1, pass the 2 slipped sts. over the k.1, yarn forward, k. 2 tog., yarn forward, k.1; rep. from * to end.
7th row: *K.3, yarn forward, sl. 2 knitwise, k.1, pass the 2 slipped sts. over the k.1, yarn forward, k.3; rep. from * to end.
8th row: As 2nd row.
These 8 rows form the pattern.

146 Pimpernel Lace Pattern

No. 146 Pimpernel Lace Pattern 6 sts, plus 9
1st row: (right side) K.1, *k.1, yarn forward, k. 2 tog. t.b.l., k.1, k. 2 tog., yarn forward; rep. from * to last 2 sts., k.2.
2nd row: K.1, p.2, *yarn round needle, p. 3 tog., yarn round needle, p.3; rep. from * ending p.2, k.1 instead of p.3.
3rd row: K. to end.
4th row: K.1, *p.1, p. 2 tog. t.b.l., yarn round needle, p.1, yarn round needle, p. 2 tog.; rep. from * to last 2 sts., p.1, k.1.
5th row: K.1, k. 2 tog., *yarn forward, k.3, yarn forward, k. 3 tog.; rep. from * to last 6 sts., yarn forward k.3, yarn forward, k. 2 tog. t.b.l., k.1.
6th row: P. to end.
These 6 rows form the pattern.

147 Small Diamond Lace

No. 147 Small Diamond Lace 6 sts. plus 3
1st row: (right side) K.2, *yarn round needle, sl.1, k.1, p.s.s.o., k.1, k. 2 tog., yarn round needle, k.1; rep. from * to last st., k.1.
2nd row and foll. alt. rows: P. to end.
3rd row: K.3, *yarn round needle, sl.1, k. 2 tog., p.s.s.o., yarn round needle, k.3; rep. from * to end.
5th row: K.2, *k. 2 tog., yarn round needle, k.1, yarn round needle, sl.1, k.1, p.s.s.o., k.1; rep. from * to last st., k.1.
7th row: K.1, k. 2 tog., *yarn round needle, k.3, yarn round needle, sl.1, k. 2 tog., p.s.s.o.; rep. from * to last 6 sts., yarn round needle, k.3, yarn round needle, sl.1, k.1, p.s.s.o., k.1.

8th row: P.
These 8 rows form the pattern.

No. 148 Diamond Leaves 6 sts. plus 1
1st row and foll. alt. rows: (wrong side) P. to end.
2nd row: K.1, *yarn forward, sl.1, k.1, p.s.s.o., k.1, k. 2
tog., yarn forward, k.1; rep. from * to end.
4th row: K.1, *yarn forward, k.1, sl.1, k. 2 tog., p.s.s.o.,
k.1, yarn forward, k.1; rep. from * to end.
6th row: K.1, *k. 2 tog., yarn forward, k.1, yarn
forward, sl.1, k.1, p.s.s.o., k.1; rep. from * to end.
8th row: K. 2 tog., *k.1, yarn forward, k.1, yarn
forward, k.1, sl.1, k. 2 tog., p.s.s.o.; rep. from * to last 5
sts., (k.1, yarn forward) twice, k.1, sl.1, k.1, p.s.s.o.
These 8 rows form the pattern

148 Diamond Leaves

No. 149 Alternating Diamond Lace 6 sts. plus 5
1st row: K.2, *k.1, yarn forward, sl.1, k.1, p.s.s.o., k.1,
k. 2 tog., yarn forward; rep. from * to last 3 sts., k.3.
2nd row and foll. alt. rows: P. to end.
3rd row: K.4, *yarn forward, k.3; rep. from * to last st.,
k.1.
5th row: K.2, k. 2 tog., *yarn forward, sl.1, k.1, p.s.s.o.,
k.1, k. 2 tog., yarn forward, sl. 2 knitwise, k.1, pass the
2 slipped sts. over the k.1; rep. from * ending last rep.,
sl.1, k.1, p.s.s.o., k.2.
7th row: K.2, *k.1, k. 2 tog., yarn forward, k.1, yarn
forward, sl.1, k.1, p.s.s.o.; rep. from * to last 3 sts., k.3.
9th row: As 3rd row.
11th row: K.2, *k.1, k. 2 tog., yarn forward, sl. 2
knitwise, k.1, pass the 2 slipped sts. over the k.1, yarn
forward, sl.1, k.1, p.s.s.o.; rep. from * to last 3 sts., k.3.
12th row: P. to end.
These 12 rows form the pattern.

149 Alternating Diamond Lace

No. 150 Frosted Diamonds 11 sts. plus 4
1st row: K.2, *k.3, k. 2 tog., yarn forward, k.1, yarn
forward, k. 2 tog. t.b.l., k.3; rep. from * to last 2 sts.,
k.2.
2nd row: K.2, *k.2, p. 2 tog. t.b.l., yarn round needle,
p.3, yarn round needle, p. 2 tog., k.2; rep. from * to last
2 sts., k.2.
3rd row: K.2, *k.1, (k. 2 tog., yarn forward) twice, k.1,
(yarn forward, k. 2 tog. t.b.l.) twice, k.1; rep. from * to
last 2 sts., k.2.
4th row: K.2, *p. 2 tog. t.b.l., yarn round needle, p. 2
tog. t.b.l., yarn over needle, k.3, (yarn round needle, p.

150 Frosted Diamonds

2 tog.) twice; rep. from * to last 2 sts., k.2.

5th row: K.2, *k.1, (yarn forward, k. 2 tog. t.b.l.) twice, k.1, (k. 2 tog., yarn forward) twice, k.1; rep. from * to last 2 sts., k.2.

6th row: K.2, *k.2, yarn round needle, p. 2 tog., yarn round needle, p. 3 tog., yarn round needle, p. 2 tog. t.b.l., yarn over needle, k.2; rep. from * to last 2 sts., k.2.

7th row: K.2, *k.3, yarn forward, k. 2 tog. t.b.l., k.1, k. 2 tog., yarn forward, k.3; rep. from * to last 2 sts., k.2.

8th row: K.2, *k.4, yarn round needle, p. 3 tog., yarn over needle, k.4; rep. from * to last 2 sts., k.2.

These 8 rows form the pattern.

151 Ampulla Pattern

No. 151   Ampulla Pattern 7 sts. plus 2

1st row: K.1, *k.2, k. 2 tog., yarn forward, k.3; rep. from * to last st., k.1.

2nd row: K.1, *p.1, p. 2 tog. t.b.l., yarn round needle, p.1, yarn round needle, p. 2 tog., p.1; rep. from * to last st., k.1.

3rd row: K.1, *k. 2 tog., yarn forward, k.3, yarn forward, sl.1, k.1, p.s.s.o.; rep. from * to last st., k.1.

4th row: P. to end.

5th row: K.1, *yarn forward, sl.1, k.1, p.s.s.o., k.5; rep. from * to last st., k.1.

6th row: K.1, *yarn round needle, p. 2 tog., p.2, p. 2 tog. t.b.l., yarn round needle, p.1; rep. from * to last st., k.1.

7th row: K.1, *k.2, yarn forward, sl.1, k.1, p.s.s.o., k. 2 tog., yarn forward k.1; rep. from * to last st., k.1.

8th row: As 4th row.

These 8 rows form the pattern.

152 Clover Lace

No. 152   Clover Lace 10 sts. plus 3

1st row: K.2, *yarn forward, sl.1, k.1, p.s.s.o., k.5, k. 2 tog., yarn forward, k.1; rep. from * to last st., k.1.

2nd row: K.1, p.2, *yarn round needle, p. 2 tog., p. 3, p. 2 tog. t.b.l., yarn round needle, p. 3; rep. from * ending last rep., p.2, k.1 instead of p.3.

3rd row: K.4, *yarn forward, sl.1, k.1, p.s.s.o., k.1, k. 2 tog., yarn forward, k.5; rep. from * ending last rep., k.4 instead of k.5.

4th row: K.1, p.4, *yarn round needle, p. 3 tog., yarn round needle, p.2, p. 2 tog., yarn round needle, p.3; rep. from * to last 8 sts., yarn round needle, p. 3 tog., yarn round needle, p.4, k.1.

5th row: K.4, *k. 2 tog., yarn forward, k.1, yarn

forward, sl.1, k.1, p.s.s.o., k.5; rep. from * ending last rep., k.4 instead of k.5.

6th row: K.1, p.2, *p. 2 tog. t.b.l., yarn round needle, p.3, yarn round needle, p. 2 tog., p.3; rep. from * ending last rep., p.2, k.1 instead of p.3.

7th row: K.2, *k. 2 tog., yarn forward, k.5, yarn forward, sl.1, k.1, p.s.s.o., k.1; rep. from * ending last rep., k.2 instead of k.1.

8th row: K.1, p. 2 tog., *yarn round needle, p.2, p. 2 tog., yarn round needle, p.3, yarn round needle, p. 3 tog.; rep. from * to last 10 sts., yarn round needle, p.2, p. 2 tog., yarn round needle, p.3, yarn round needle, p. 2 tog., k.1.

These 8 rows form the pattern.

No. 153 Garter Stitch Diamonds 6 sts. plus 1

1st row: (right side) K.1, *k. 2 tog., yarn forward, k.1, yarn forward, k. 2 tog. t.b.l., k.1; rep. from * to end.

2nd row: K.1, *p.1, k.3, p.1, k.1; rep. from * to end.

3rd row: K. 2 tog., *yarn forward, k.3, yarn forward, sl.1, k. 2 tog., p.s.s.o.; rep. from * to last 5 sts., yarn forward, k.3, yarn forward, k. 2 tog. t.b.l.

4th row: P.1, *k.5, p.1; rep. from * to end.

5th row: K.1, *yarn forward, k. 2 tog. t.b.l., k.1, k. 2 tog., yarn forward, k.1; rep. from * to end.

6th row: *K.2, (p.1, k.1) twice; rep. from * to last st., k.1.

7th row: *K.2, yarn forward, sl.1, k. 2 tog., p.s.s.o., yarn forward, k.1; rep. from * to last st., k.1.

8th row: *K.3, p.1, k.2; rep. from * to last st., k.1.

These 8 rows form the pattern.

153 Garter Stitch Diamonds

No. 154 Chevron Pattern Lace 12 sts. plus 1

1st row: K.1, *yarn forward, k.1, sl.1, k.1, p.s.s.o., k.5, k. 2 tog., k.1, yarn forward, k.1; rep. from * to end.

2nd row and foll. alt. rows: P. to end.

3rd row: K.1, *k.1, yarn forward, k.1, sl.1, k.1, p.s.s.o., k.3, k. 2 tog., k.1, yarn forward, k.2; rep. from * to end.

5th row: K.1, *k.2, yarn forward, k.1, sl.1, k.1, p.s.s.o., k.1, k. 2 tog., k.1, yarn forward, k.3; rep. from * to end.

7th row: K.1, *k. 3, yarn forward, k.1, sl.1, k. 2 tog., p.s.s.o., k.1, yarn forward, k.4; rep. from * to end.

8th row: P. to end.

These 8 rows form the pattern.

154 Chevron Pattern Lace

155 Leaf Border Pattern

No. 155 Leaf Border Pattern 10 sts. plus 4

Although this is termed a border pattern, repeating the rows forms a beautiful all-over lace pattern.

1st row: (right side) K.2, *yarn forward, sl.1, k.1, p.s.s.o., k.8; rep. from * to last 2 sts., k.2.

2nd row: P.2, *yarn round needle, p. 2 tog., p.5, p. 2 tog. t.b.l., yarn round needle, p.1; rep. from * to last 2 sts., p.2.

3rd row: K.4, *yarn forward, sl.1, k.1, p.s.s.o., k.3, k. 2 tog., yarn forward, k.3; rep. from * to end.

4th row: P.4, *yarn round needle, p. 2 tog., p.1, p.2 tog. t.b.l., yarn round needle, p.5; rep. from * to end.

5th row: K.6, *yarn forward, sl.1, k. 2 tog., p.s.s.o., yarn forward, k.7; rep. from * ending last rep., k.5 instead of k.7.

6th row: P.2, *p.3, p. 2 tog. t.b.l., yarn round needle; rep. from * to last 2 sts., p.2.

7th row: K.3, *yarn forward, sl.1, k.1, p.s.s.o., k.3; rep. from * to last st., k.1.

8th row: P.3, *p. 2 tog. t.b.l., yarn round needle, p.3; rep. from * to last st., p.1.

9th row: K.5, *yarn forward, sl.1, k.1, p.s.s.o., k.3; rep. from * to last 4 sts., yarn forward, sl.1, k.1, p.s.s.o., k.2.

10th row: P.1, *p. 2 tog. t.b.l., yarn round needle, p.3; rep. from * to last 3 sts., p.3.

11th row: K.2, *yarn forward, sl.1, k.1, p.s.s.o., k.3; rep. from * to last 2 sts., k.2.

12th to 15th rows: As 2nd to 5th rows.

16th row: P.3, *p.3, yarn round needle, p. 2 tog.; rep. from * to last st., p.1.

17th row: K.5, *k. 2 tog., yarn forward, k.3; rep. from * to last 4 sts., k. 2 tog., yarn forward, k.2.

18th row: P.3, *yarn round needle, p. 2 tog., p.3; rep. from * to last st., p.1.

19th row: K.3, *k. 2 tog., yarn forward, k.3; rep. from * to last st., k.1.

20th row: P.2, *p.3, yarn round needle, p. 2 tog.; rep. from * to last 2 sts., p.2.

21st row: K.1, *k. 2 tog., yarn forward, k.3; rep. from * to last 3 sts., k.3.

22nd to 25th rows: As 2nd to 5th rows.

26th row: P. to end.

These 26 rows form the pattern.

No. 156 Grapevine Pattern 8 sts. plus 6

As the number of stitches varies from row to row on this pattern, it is advisable to take a stitch count only after a 12th pattern row has been worked.

1st row and foll. alt. rows: (wrong side) P.

2nd row: K.2, *k. 2 tog., k.1, yarn forward, k.1, sl.1, k.1, p.s.s.o., k.2; rep. from * ending last rep., k.6.

4th row: K.1, k. 2 tog., k.1, yarn forward, *k.1, yarn forward, k.1, sl.1, k.1, p.s.s.o., k. 2 tog., k.1, yarn forward; rep. from * ending k.2.

6th row: K.3, yarn forward, *k.3, yarn forward, k.1, sl.1, k.1, p.s.s.o., k.1, yarn forward; rep. from * ending k.3.

8th row: K.5, *k. 2 tog., k.1, yarn forward, k.1, sl.1, k.1, p.s.s.o., k.2; rep. from * ending k.4.

10th row: K.4, *k. 2 tog., k.1, (yarn forward, k.1) twice, sl.1, k.1, p.s.s.o.; rep. from * ending k.3.

12th row: K.3, k. 2 tog., *k.1, yarn forward, k.3, yarn forward, k.1, k. 2 tog.; rep. from * ending k.2.

These 12 rows form the pattern.

156 Grapevine Pattern

No. 157 Almond Lace 4 sts. plus 2

1st row: K.1, *yarn forward, sl. 1 knitwise, k.1, p.s.s.o., k.2; rep. from * to last st., k.1.

2nd row: K.1, p.1, *p. 2 tog. t.b.l., yarn round needle, p.2; rep. from * to last 4 sts., p. 2 tog. t.b.l., yarn round needle, p.1, k.1.

3rd row: K.1, *yarn forward, k. 2 tog., yarn forward, sl.1, k.1, p.s.s.o.; rep. from * to last st., k.1.

4th row: K.1, p.3, *p. 2 tog. t.b.l., yarn round needle, p.2; rep. from * to last 6 sts., p. 2 tog. t.b.l., yarn round needle, p.3, k.1.

5th row: K.1, *k.2, k. 2 tog., yarn forward; rep. from * to last st., k.1.

6th row: K.1, p.1, *yarn round needle, p. 2 tog., p.2; rep. from * to last 4 sts., yarn round needle, p. 2 tog., p.1, k.1.

7th row: K.1, *k. 2 tog., yarn forward, k.2; rep. from * to last st., k.1.

8th row: K.1, p.3, *yarn round needle, p. 2 tog., p.2; rep. from * to last 6 sts., yarn round needle, p. 2 tog., p.3, k.1.

These 8 rows form the pattern.

157 Almond Lace

158 Inverness Pattern

No. 158   Inverness Pattern 6 sts. plus 3

1st row: K.2, *k. 2 tog., yarn forward, k.1, yarn forward, sl.1, k.1, p.s.s.o., k.1; rep. from * to last st., k.1.

2nd row and foll. alt. rows: P. to end.

3rd row: As 1st row.

5th row: K.2, *yarn forward, sl.1, k.1, p.s.s.o., k.1, k. 2 tog., yarn forward, k.1; rep. from * to last st., k.1.

7th row: K.3, *yarn forward, sl.1, k. 2 tog., p.s.s.o., yarn forward, k.3; rep. from * to end.

8th row: P. to end.

These 8 rows form the pattern.

159 Lavender Lace Pattern

No. 159   Lavender Lace Pattern 10 sts. plus 3

1st row: K.3, *yarn over needle, k. 2 tog. t.b.l., k.3, k. 2 tog., yarn over needle, k.3; rep. from * to end.

2nd row and foll. alt. rows: P. to end.

3rd row: K.4, *yarn over needle, k. 2 tog. t.b.l., k.1, k. 2 tog., yarn over needle, k.5; rep. from * ending last rep., k.4 instead of k.5.

5th row: K.5, *yarn over needle, sl.1, k. 2 tog., p.s.s.o., yarn over needle, k.7; rep. from * ending last rep., k.5 instead of k.7.

7th row: K.2, *yarn over needle, k. 2 tog. t.b.l., k. 2 tog., yarn over needle, k.1; rep. from * ending last rep. k. 2 instead of k.1.

9th to 12th rows: Rep. last 2 rows twice more.

These 12 rows form the pattern.

160 Candle and Chevron Pattern

No. 160   Candle and Chevron Pattern 10 sts. plus 3

1st row: K.2, *k. 2 tog., k.2, yarn forward, k.1, yarn forward, k.2, sl.1, k.1, p.s.s.o., k.1; rep. from * to last st., k.1.

2nd row and foll. alt. rows: P. to end.

3rd, 5th, 7th and 9th rows: As 1st row.

11th row: K.2, *yarn forward, sl.1, k.1, p.s.s.o., k.5, k. 2 tog., yarn forward, k.1; rep. from * to last st., k.1.

13th row: K.3, *yarn forward, sl.1, k.1, p.s.s.o., k.3, k. 2 tog., yarn forward, k.3; rep. from * to end.

15th row: K.4, *yarn forward, sl.1, k.1, p.s.s.o., k.1, k. 2 tog., yarn forward, k.5; rep. from * ending last rep., k.4.

17th row: K.5, *yarn forward, sl.1, k. 2 tog., p.s.s.o., yarn forward, k.7; rep. from * to end, ending last rep. k.5 instead of k.7.

19th, 21st, 23rd, 25th and 27th rows: K.2, *yarn forward, k.2, sl.1, k.1, p.s.s.o., k.1, k. 2 tog., k.2, yarn forward, k.1; rep. from * to last st., k.1.

29th row: K.4, *k. 2 tog., yarn forward, k.1, yarn forward, sl.1, k.1, p.s.s.o., k.5; rep. from * to end, ending last rep., k.4 instead of k.5.

31st row: K.3, *k. 2 tog., yarn forward, k.3, yarn forward, sl.1, k.1, p.s.s.o., k.3; rep. from * to end.

33rd row: K.2, *k. 2 tog., yarn forward, k.5, yarn forward, sl.1, k.1, p.s.s.o., k.1; rep. from * to last st., k.1.

35th row: K.1, k. 2 tog., *yarn forward, k.7, yarn forward, sl.1, k. 2 tog., p.s.s.o.; rep. from * ending last rep., sl.1, k.1, p.s.s.o., k.1.

36th row: P. to end.

These 36 rows form the pattern.

No. 161   Broad Chevron Lace   12 sts. plus 1

1st row: (wrong side) P. to end.

2nd row: K.1, *yarn forward, k.4, sl.1, k. 2 tog., p.s.s.o., k.4, yarn forward, k.1; rep. from * to end.

These 2 rows form the pattern.

161 Broad Chevron Lace

No. 162   Candlelight Lace   12 sts. plus 1

1st row: K.1, *yarn forward, sl.1, k.1, p.s.s.o., k.7, k. 2 tog., yarn forward, k.1; rep. from * to end.

2nd row and foll. alt. rows: P. to end.

3rd row: K.1, *yarn forward, k.1, sl.1, k.1, p.s.s.o., k.5, k. 2 tog., k.1, yarn forward, k.1; rep. from * to end.

5th row: K.1, *yarn forward, k.2, sl.1, k.1, p.s.s.o., k.3, k. 2 tog., k.2, yarn forward, k.1; rep. from * to end.

7th row: K.1, *yarn forward, k.3, sl.1, k.1, p.s.s.o., k.1, k. 2 tog., k.3, yarn forward, k.1; rep. from * to end.

9th row: K.1, *yarn forward, k.4, sl.1, k. 2 tog., p.s.s.o., k.4, yarn forward, k.1; rep. from * to end.

11th row: K.1, *k.3, k. 2 tog., yarn forward, k.1, yarn forward, sl.1, k.1, p.s.s.o., k.4; rep. from * to end.

13th row: K.1, *k.2, k. 2 tog., k.1, (yarn forward, k.1) twice, sl.1, k.1, p.s.s.o., k.3; rep. from * to end.

15th row: K.1, *k.1, k. 2 tog., k.2, yarn forward, k.1, yarn forward, k.2, sl.1, k.1, p.s.s.o., k.2; rep. from * to end.

17th row: K.1, *k. 2 tog., k.3, yarn forward, k.1, yarn forward, k.3, sl.1, k.1, p.s.s.o., k.1; rep. from * to end.

19th row: Sl.1, k.1, p.s.s.o., *k.4, yarn forward, k.1, yarn forward, k.4, sl.1, k. 2 tog., p.s.s.o.; rep. from * ending last rep., sl.1, k.1, p.s.s.o.

20th row: P. to end.

These 20 rows form the pattern.

162 Candlelight Lace

163 Diamond Shadow Lace

No. 163 Diamond Shadow Lace 14 sts. plus 15

1st row: K.6, *yarn forward, k. 3 tog., yarn forward, k. 11; rep. from * to last 9 sts., yarn forward, k. 3 tog., yarn forward, k.6.

2nd row and foll. alt. rows: P. to end.

3rd row: K.5, *yarn forward, k. 2 tog., k.1, k. 2 tog., yarn forward, k.9; rep. from * to last 10 sts., yarn forward, k. 2 tog., k.1, k. 2 tog., yarn forward, k.5.

5th row: K.4, *yarn forward, k. 2 tog., yarn forward, k. 3 tog., yarn forward, k. 2 tog., yarn forward, k.7; rep. from * ending last rep., k.4 instead of k.7.

7th row: K.3, *(yarn forward, k. 2 tog.) twice, k.1, (k. 2 tog., yarn forward) twice, k.5; rep. from * ending k.3 instead of k.5.

9th row: K.2, *(yarn forward, k. 2 tog.) twice, yarn forward, k. 3 tog., (yarn forward, k. 2 tog.) twice, yarn forward, k.3; rep. from * ending last rep., k.2 instead of k.3.

11th row: K.1, *(yarn forward, k. 2 tog.) 3 times, k.1, (k. 2 tog., yarn forward) 3 times, k.1; rep. from * to end.

13th row: As 9th row.

15th row: As 7th row.

17th row: As 5th row.

19th row: As 3rd row.

20th row: P. to end.

These 20 rows form the pattern.

No. 164 Double Diamond Lace 19 sts. plus 2

1st row: (right side) K.1, *k.7, k. 2 tog., yarn forward, k.1, yarn forward, k. 2 tog. t.b.l., k.7; rep. from * to last st., k.1.

2nd row and foll. alt. rows: P. to end.

3rd row: K.1, *k.6, k. 2 tog., yarn forward, k.3, yarn forward, k. 2 tog. t.b.l., k.6; rep. from * to last st., k.1.

5th row: K.1, *k.5, (k. 2 tog., yarn forward) twice, k.1, (yarn forward, k. 2 tog. t.b.l.) twice, k.5; rep. from * to last st., k.1.

7th row: K.1, *k.4, (k. 2 tog., yarn forward) twice, k.3, (yarn forward, k. 2 tog. t.b.l.) twice, k.4; rep. from * to last st., k.1.

9th row: K.1, *k.3, (k. 2 tog., yarn forward) 3 times, k.1, (yarn forward, k. 2 tog. t.b.l.) 3 times, k.3; rep. from * to last st., k.1.

11th row: K.1, *k.2, (k. 2 tog., yarn forward) 3 times, k.3, (yarn forward, k. 2 tog. t.b.l.) 3 times, k.2; rep. from * to last st., k.1.

13th row: K.1, *k.1, (k. 2 tog., yarn forward) 3 times,

164 Double Diamond Lace

k.5, (yarn forward, k. 2 tog. t.b.l.) 3 times, k.1; rep. from * to last st., k.1.

15th row: K.1, *k.2, (yarn forward, k. 2 tog. t.b.l.) 3 times, k.3, (k. 2 tog., yarn forward) 3 times, k.2; rep. from * to last st., k.1.

17th row: K.1, *k.3, (yarn forward, k. 2 tog. t.b.l.) 3 times, k.1, (k. 2 tog., yarn forward) 3 times, k.3; rep. from * to last st., k.1.

19th row: K.1, *k.4, (yarn forward, k. 2 tog. t.b.l.) twice, yarn forward, sl.1, k. 2 tog., p.s.s.o., yarn forward, (k. 2 tog., yarn forward) twice, k.4; rep. from * to last st., k.1.

21st row: K.1, *k.5, (yarn forward, k. 2 tog. t.b.l.) twice, k.1, (k. 2 tog., yarn forward) twice, k.5; rep. from * to last st., k.1.

23rd row: K.1, *k.6, yarn forward, k. 2 tog. t.b.l., yarn forward, sl.1, k. 2 tog., p.s.s.o., yarn forward, k. 2 tog., yarn forward, k.6; rep. from * to last st., k.1.

25th row: K.1, *k.7, yarn forward, k. 2 tog. t.b.l., k.1, k. 2 tog., yarn forward, k.7; rep. from * to last st., k.1.

27th row: K.1, *k.8, yarn forward, sl.1, k. 2 tog., p.s.s.o., yarn forward, k.8; rep. from * to last st., k.1.

28th row: P. to end.

29th row: K. to end.

30th row: P. to end.

These 30 rows form the pattern.

No. 165 **Diamond Eyelet Lace** 12 sts. plus 3

1st row: *K.5, k. 2 tog., yarn round needle, p.1, yarn over needle, sl.1, k.1, p.s.s.o., k.2; rep. from * to last 3 sts., k.3.

2nd row: *P.6, k.2, k. 1 t.b.l., p.3; rep. from * to last 3 sts., p.3.

3rd row: *K.4, k. 2 tog., yarn round needle, p.3, yarn over needle, sl.1, k.1, p.s.s.o., k.1; rep. from * to last 3 sts., k.3.

4th row: *P.5, k.4, k. 1 t.b.l., p.2; rep. from * to last 3 sts., p.3.

5th row: *K.3, k. 2 tog., yarn round needle, p.5, yarn over needle, sl.1, k.1, p.s.s.o.; rep. from * to last 3 sts., k.3.

6th row: *P.4, k.6, k. 1 t.b.l., p.1; rep. from * to last 3 sts., p.3.

7th row: K.1, *k.1, k. 2 tog., yarn round needle, p.7, yarn over needle, sl.1, k.1, p.s.s.o.; rep. from * to last 2 sts., k.2.

8th row: *P.3, k.8, k. 1 t.b.l.; rep. from * to last 3 sts., p.3.

165 Diamond Eyelet Lace

9th row: K.1, k. 2 tog., *yarn round needle, p.9, yarn over needle, sl.1, k. 2 tog., p.s.s.o.; rep. from * to last 12 sts., yarn round needle, p.9, yarn over needle, sl.1, k.1, p.s.s.o., k.1.

10th row: P.1, *p.1, k.10, k. 1 t.b.l.; rep. from * to last 2 sts., p.2.

11th row: K.1, *k.1, p.11; rep. from * to last 2 sts., k.2.

12th row: P.1, *p.1, k.11; rep. from * to last 2 sts., p.2.

13th row: K.1, *k.1, yarn round needle, p. 2 tog., p.7; p. 2 tog., yarn over needle; rep. from * to last 2 sts., k.2.

14th row: *P.3, k.9; rep. from * to last 3 sts., p.3.

15th row: *K.3, yarn round needle, p. 2 tog., p.5, p. 2 tog., yarn over needle; rep. from * to last 3 sts., k.3.

16th row: *P.4, k.7, p.1; rep. from * to last 3 sts., p.3.

17th row: *K.4, yarn round needle, p. 2 tog., p.3, p. 2 tog., yarn over needle, k.1; rep. from * to last 3 sts., k.3.

18th row: *P.5, k.5, p.2; rep. from * to last 3 sts., p.3.

19th row: *K.5, yarn round needle, p. 2 tog., p.1, p. 2 tog., yarn over needle, k.2; rep. from * to last 3 sts., k.3.

20th row: *P.6, k.3, p.3; rep. from * to last 3 sts., p.3.

21st row: *K.6, yarn round needle, sl.1, k. 2 tog., p.s.s.o., yarn over needle, k.3; rep. from * to last 3 sts., k.3.

22nd row: *P.7, k.1, p.4; rep. from * to last 3 sts., p.3.

23rd row: *K.7, p.1, k.4; rep. from * to last 3 sts., k.3.

24th row: *P.7, k.1, p.4; rep. from * to last 3 sts., p.3.

These 24 rows form the pattern.

No. 166   Trellis Lace   15 sts. plus 2

1st row: P.1, *k.1, yarn forward, sl.1, k.1, p.s.s.o., k.2, yarn forward, sl.1, k.1, p.s.s.o., k.1, k. 2 tog., yarn forward, k.2, k. 2 tog., yarn forward, k.1; rep. from * to last st., k.1.

2nd row and foll. alt. rows: P. to end.

3rd row: P.1, *k.2, yarn forward, sl.1, k.1, p.s.s.o., k.2, yarn forward, sl.1, k. 2 tog., p.s.s.o., yarn forward, k.2, k. 2 tog., yarn forward, k.2; rep. from * to last st., p.1.

5th row: P.1, *k.3, yarn forward, sl.1, k.1, p.s.s.o., k.1, k. 2 tog., yarn forward, k.2, k. 2 tog., yarn forward, k.3; rep. from * to last st., k.1.

7th row: P.1, k.4, yarn forward, sl.1, k. 2 tog., p.s.s.o., yarn forward, k.2, k. 2 tog., yarn forward, k.4; rep. from * to last st., p.1.

9th row: P.1, *k.4, k. 2 tog., yarn forward, k.2, k. 2 tog., yarn forward, k.5; rep. from * to last st., p.1.

11th row: P.1, *k.3, k. 2 tog., yarn forward, k.2, k. 2 tog., yarn forward, k.1, yarn forward, sl.1, k.1, p.s.s.o.,

166 Trellis Lace

k.3; rep. from * to last st., p.1.

13th row: P.1, *(k.2, k. 2 tog., yarn forward) twice, k.3, yarn forward, sl.1, k.1, p.s.s.o., k.2; rep. from * to last st., p.1.

15th row: P.1, *k.1, k. 2 tog., yarn forward, k.2, k. 2 tog., yarn forward, k.1, yarn forward, si.1, k.1, p.s.s.o., k.2, yarn forward, sl.1, k.1, p.s.s.o., k.1; rep. from * to last st., p.1.

17th row: P.1, *k. 2 tog., yarn forward, k.2, k. 2 tog., yarn forward, k.3, yarn forward, sl.1, k.1, p.s.s.o., k.2, yarn forward, sl.1, k.1, p.s.s.o.; rep. from * to last st., p.1.

18th row: P. to end.

These 18 rows form the pattern.

No. 167 Fleurette Lace 8 sts. plus 8

1st row: (wrong side) P. to end.

2nd row: K. to end.

3rd row and foll. alt. rows: As 1st row.

4th row: K.3, *yarn forward, k. 2 tog. t.b.l., k.6; rep. from * ending last rep., k.3 instead of k.6.

6th row: K.1, *k. 2 tog., yarn forward, k.1, yarn forward, k. 2 tog. t.b.l., k.3; rep. from * ending last rep., k.2 instead of k.3.

8th row: As 4th row.

10th row: K. to end.

12th row: K.7, *yarn forward, k. 2 tog. t.b.l., k.6; rep. from * to last st., k.1.

14th row: K.5, *k. 2 tog., yarn forward, k.1, yarn forward, k. 2 tog. t.b.l., k.3; rep. from * to last 3 sts., k.3.

16th row: As 12th row.

These 16 rows form the pattern.

167 Fleurette Lace

No. 168 Open Diamond Lace 8 sts. plus 7

Note that all slipped sts. on this pattern must be slipped knitwise.

1st row: (wrong side) P. to end.

2nd row: K.7, *yarn forward, sl.1, k.1, p.s.s.o., k.6; rep. from * to end.

3rd row and foll. alt. rows: As 1st row.

4th row: K.5, *k. 2 tog., yarn forward, k.1, yarn forward, sl.1, k.1, p.s.s.o., k.3; rep. from * to last 2 sts., k.2.

6th row: K.4, *k. 2 tog., yarn forward, k.3, yarn forward, sl.1, k.1, p.s.s.o., k.1; rep. from * to last 3 sts., k.3.

168 Open Diamond Lace

8th row: K.6, *yarn forward, sl.1, k. 2 tog., p.s.s.o., yarn forward, k.5; rep. from * to last st., k.1.

10th row: K.3, *yarn forward, sl.1, k.1, p.s.s.o., k.6; rep. from * to last 4 sts., yarn forward, sl.1, k.1, p.s.s.o., k.2.

12th row: K.1, *k. 2 tog., yarn forward, k.1, yarn forward, sl.1, k.1, p.s.s.o., k.3; rep. from * to last 6 sts., k. 2 tog., yarn forward, k.1, yarn forward, sl.1, k.1, p.s.s.o., k.1.

14th row: *K. 2 tog., yarn forward, k.3, yarn forward, sl.1, k.1, p.s.s.o., k.1; rep. from * to end, omitting k.1 at end of last repeat.

16th row: K.2, *yarn forward, sl.1, k. 2 tog., p.s.s.o., yarn forward, k.5; rep. from * to last 5 sts., yarn forward, sl.1, k. 2 tog., p.s.s.o., yarn forward, k.2.
These 16 rows form the pattern.

169 Nottingham Lace Pattern

No. 169   Nottingham Lace Pattern 6 sts. plus 5

1st row: K. to end.

2nd row and foll. alt. rows: P. to end.

3rd row: *K.1, k. 2 tog., yarn forward, k.3; rep. from * ending last rep., k.2 instead of k.3.

5th row: *K. 2 tog., yarn forward, k.1, yarn forward, k. 2 tog. t.b.l., k.1; rep. from * omitting k.1 at end of last repeat.

7th row: K. to end.

9th row: *K.4, k. 2 tog., yarn forward; rep. from * to last 5 sts., k.5.

11th row: K.3, *k. 2 tog., yarn forward, k.1, yarn forward, k. 2 tog. t.b.l., k.1; rep. from * to last 2 sts., k.2.

12th row: P. to end.
These 12 rows form the pattern.

170 French Lace Pattern

No. 170   French Lace Pattern 12 sts. plus 5

1st row: (wrong side) P. to end.

2nd row: K.1, *k.1, yarn forward, k.3, k. 2 tog., k.1, sl.1, k.2, p.s.s.o., k.3, yarn forward; rep. from * to last 3 sts., k.3.

3rd row and foll. alt. rows: As 1st row.

4th row: As 2nd row.

6th row: K.2, *k.1, sl.1, k.1, p.s.s.o., k.3, yarn forward, k.1, yarn forward, k.3, k. 2 tog.; rep. from * to last 3 sts., k.3.

8th row: As 6th row.
These 8 rows form the pattern.

No. 171   Cellular Open Mesh 4 sts. plus 2

1st row: (right side) P.2, *k.2, p.2; rep. from * to end.
2nd row: K.2, *p.2, k.2; rep. from * to end.
3rd row: K.1, *k. 2 tog., yarn forward, sl.1, k.1, p.s.s.o.; rep. from * to last st., k.1.
4th row: P.2, *k.1, then p.1 both in next st., p.2; rep. from * to end.
5th row: K.2, *p.2, k.2; rep. from * to end.
6th row: P.2, *k.2, p.2; rep. from * to end.
7th row: K.1, yarn forward, *sl.1, k.1, p.s.s.o., k. 2 tog., yarn forward; rep. from * to last st., k.1.
8th row: P.1, k.1, *p.2, k.1, then p.1 both in next st.; rep. from * to last 4 sts., p.2, k.1, p.1.
These 8 rows form the pattern.

171 Cellular Open Mesh

No. 172   Broad Leaf Lace 19 sts. plus 2

1st row: (right side) P.2, *yarn over needle, k.7, p. 3 tog., k.7, yarn round needle, p.2; rep. from * to end.
2nd row and foll. alt. rows: K.2, *p.17, k.2; rep. from * to end.
3rd row: P.2, *k.1, yarn forward, k.6, p. 3 tog., k.6, yarn forward, k.1, p.2; rep. from * to end.
5th row: P.2, *k.2, yarn forward, k.5, p. 3 tog., k.5, yarn forward, k.2, p.2; rep. from * to end.
7th row: P.2, *k.3, yarn forward, k.4, p. 3 tog., k.4, yarn forward, k.3, p.2; rep. from * to end.
9th row: P.2, *k.4, yarn forward, k.3, p. 3 tog., k.3, yarn forward, k.4, p.2; rep. from * to end.
11th row: P.2, *k.5, yarn forward, k.2, p. 3 tog., k.2, yarn forward, k.5, p.2; rep. from * to end.
13th row: P.2, *k.6, yarn forward, k.1, p. 3 tog., k.1, yarn forward, k.6, p.2; rep. from * to end.
15th row: P.2, *k.7, yarn round needle, p. 3 tog., yarn over needle, k.7, p.2; rep. from * to end.
16th row: As 2nd row.
These 16 rows form the pattern.

172 Broad Leaf Lace

No. 173   Fern Frond Lace 11 sts. plus 2

1st row: P.2, *yarn over needle, k.3, p. 3 tog., k.3, yarn round needle, p.2; rep. from * to end.
2nd row and foll. alt. rows: K.2, *p.9, k.2; rep. from * to end.
3rd row: P.2, *k.1, yarn over needle, k.2, p. 3 tog., k.2, yarn over needle, k.1, p.2; rep. from * to end.
5th row: P.2, *k.2, yarn over needle, k.1, p. 3 tog., k.1, yarn over needle, k.2, p.2; rep. from * to end.
7th row: P.2, *k.3, yarn round needle, p. 3 tog., yarn

173 Fern Frond Lace

over needle, k.3, p.2; rep. from * to end.
8th row: As 2nd row.
These 8 rows form the pattern.

174 Horseshoe Print

No. 174   Horseshoe Print   10 sts. plus 1
1st row: (wrong side) P. to end.
2nd row: K.1, *yarn forward, k.3, sl.1, k. 2 tog., p.s.s.o., k.3, yarn forward, k.1; rep. from * to end.
3rd row: As 1st row.
4th row: P.1, *k.1, yarn forward, k.2, sl.1, k. 2 tog., p.s.s.o., k.2, yarn forward, k.1, p.1; rep. from * to end.
5th row: K.1, *p.9, k.1; rep. from * to end.
6th row: P.1, *k.2, yarn forward, k.1, sl.1, k. 2 tog., p.s.s.o., k.1, yarn forward, k.2, p.1; rep. from * to end.
7th row: As 5th row.
8th row: P.1, *k.3, yarn forward, sl.1, k. 2 tog., p.s.s.o., yarn forward, k.3, p.1; rep. from * to end.
These 8 rows form the pattern.

No. 175   Snowdrop Lace   8 sts. plus 1
1st row: (right side) K.1, *yarn forward, k.2, sl.1, k. 2 tog., p.s.s.o., k.2, yarn forward, k.1; rep. from * to end.
2nd row and foll. alt. rows: P. to end.
3rd row: K.2, *yarn forward, k.1, sl.1, k. 2 tog., p.s.s.o., k.1, yarn forward, k.3; rep. from * ending k.2.
5th row: K.3, *yarn forward, sl.1, k. 2 tog., p.s.s.o., yarn forward, k.5; rep. from * ending k.3.
6th row: P. to end.
These 6 rows form the pattern.

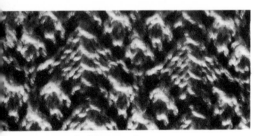

175 Snowdrop Lace

No. 176   Minster Lace   10 sts. plus 1
1st row: K.1, *yarn forward, k.3, sl.1, k. 2 tog., p.s.s.o., k.3, yarn forward, k.1; rep. from * to end.
2nd row and foll. alt. rows: P. to end.
3rd row: K.1, *k.1, yarn forward, k.2, sl.1, k. 2 tog., p.s.s.o., k.2, yarn forward, k.2; rep. from * to end.
5th row: K. 2 tog., yarn forward, k.1, *yarn forward, k.1, sl.1, k. 2 tog., p.s.s.o., k.1, yarn forward, k.1, yarn forward, sl.1, k. 2 tog., p.s.s.o., yarn forward, k.1; rep. from * to last 8 sts., yarn forward, k.1, sl.1, k. 2 tog., p.s.s.o., k.1, yarn forward, k.1, yarn forward, sl.1, k.1, p.s.s.o.
7th row: K.1, *k.3, yarn forward, sl.1, k. 2 tog., p.s.s.o., yarn forward, k.4; rep. from * to end.
9th row: K.1, *yarn forward, sl.1, k. 2 tog., p.s.s.o., yarn forward, k.3, yarn forward, sl.1, k. 2 tog., p.s.s.o., yarn forward, k.1; rep. from * to end.

176 Minster Lace

10th row: P. to end.
These 10 rows form the pattern.

No. 177   Matinee Lace 8 sts. plus 1
1st row: K.1, *k. 2 tog., k.1, (yarn forward, k.1) twice, k.
2 tog. t.b.l., k.1; rep. from * to end.
2nd row: P. to end.
These 2 rows form the pattern.

177 Matinee Lace

No. 178   Lace Swirl Pattern 10 sts. plus 1
1st row: (right side) P.1, *yarn round needle, p.3, p. 3
tog., p.3, yarn round needle, p.1; rep. from * to end.
2nd row and foll. alt. rows: P. to end.
3rd row: P.1, *k.1, yarn round needle, p.2, p. 3 tog., p.2,
yarn over needle, k.1, p.1; rep. from * to end.
5th row: P.1, *k.2, yarn round needle, p.1, p. 3 tog., p.1,
yarn over needle, k.2, p.1; rep. from * to end.
7th row: P.1, *k.3, yarn round needle, p. 3 tog., yarn
over needle, k.3, p.1; rep. from * to end.
8th row: P. to end.
These 8 rows form the pattern

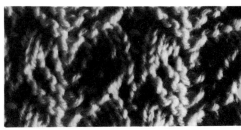

178 Lace Swirl Pattern

No. 179   Waterfall Lace Pattern 11 sts. plus 2
1st row: *P.2, yarn over needle, k.3, sl.1, k. 2 tog.,
p.s.s.o., k.3, yarn round needle; rep. from * to last 2
sts., p.2.
2nd row and foll. alt. rows: P. to end.
3rd row: *P.2, k.1, yarn forward, k.2, sl.1, k. 2 tog.,
p.s.s.o., k.2, yarn forward, k.1; rep. from * to last 2 sts.,
p.2.
5th row: *P.2, k.2, yarn forward, k.1, sl.1, k. 2 tog.,
p.s.s.o., k.1, yarn forward, k.2; rep. from * to last 2 sts.,
p.2.
7th row: *P.2, k.3, yarn forward, sl.1, k. 2 tog., p.s.s.o.,
yarn forward, k.3; rep. from * to last 2 sts., p.2.
8th row: P. to end.
These 8 rows form the pattern.

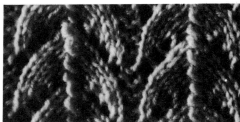

179 Waterfall Lace Pattern

180 Feather Lace

No. 180   Feather Lace 8 sts. plus 5
1st row: K.1, *yarn forward, sl.1, k. 2 tog., p.s.s.o., yarn forward, k.5; rep. from * to last 4 sts., yarn forward, sl.1, k. 2 tog., p.s.s.o., yarn forward, k.1.
2nd row and foll. alt. rows: P. to end.
3rd row: As 1st row.
5th row: K.1, *k.3, yarn forward, sl.1, k.1, p.s.s.o., k.1, k. 2 tog., yarn forward; rep. from * to last 4 sts., k.4.
7th row: K.1, *yarn forward, sl.1, k. 2 tog., p.s.s.o., yarn forward, k.1; rep. from * to end.
8th row: P. to end.
These 8 rows form the pattern.

181 Aubretia Pattern

No. 181   Aubretia Pattern 7 sts. plus 1
1st row: (wrong side) P. to end.
2nd row: K.1, *yarn forward, k.1, sl.1, k.1, p.s.s.o., k. 2 tog., k.1, yarn forward, k.1; rep. from * to end.
These 2 rows form the pattern.

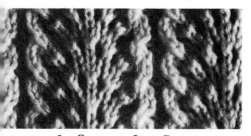

182 Spectrum Lace Pattern

No. 182   Spectrum Lace Pattern 15 sts. plus 2
1st row: K.1, *p.1, k.13, p.1; rep. from * to last st., k.1.
2nd row: P.1, *k.1, p.13, k.1; rep. from * to last st., p.1.
3rd row: K.1, *p.1, sl. next 2 sts. knitwise together, k. 2 tog., pass the 2 slipped sts. over the k. 2 tog., (yarn forward, k.1) 5 times, yarn forward, sl. next 2 sts. as before, k. 2 tog., pass 2 sl. sts. over the k. 2 tog., p.1; rep. from * to last st., k.1.
4th row: As 2nd row.
These 4 rows form the pattern.

183 Vine Lace

No. 183   Vine Lace 9 sts. plus 4
1st row: (wrong side) P. to end.
2nd row: K.3, *yarn forward, k.2, sl.1, k.1, p.s.s.o., k. 2 tog., k.2, yarn forward, k.1; rep. from * to last st., k.1.
3rd row: As 1st row.
4th row: K.2, *yarn forward, k.2, sl.1, k.1, p.s.s.o., k. 2 tog., k.2, yarn forward, k.1; rep. from * to last 2 sts., k.2.
These 4 rows form the pattern.

No. 184 Harebell Lace 13 sts. plus 3

1st row: K. to end.
2nd row: P. to end.
3rd row: K.1, p.1, *(k. 2 tog.) twice, (yarn forward, k.1) 4 times, (k. 2 tog.) twice, p.1; rep. from * to last st., k.1.
4th row: P. to end.
These 4 rows form the pattern.

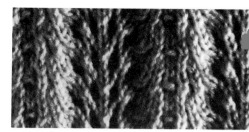

184 Harebell Lace

No. 185 Celtic Lace Pattern 13 sts. plus 2

1st row: K.1, *(k. 2 tog., yarn round needle) twice, k.1, yarn round needle, (k. 2 tog.) twice, k.2, yarn round needle, k. 2 tog., yarn round needle; rep. from * to last st., k.1.
2nd row: P. to end.
3rd row: K.1, *(yarn round needle, k. 2 tog.) twice, yarn round needle, k.2, (k. 2 tog.) twice, yarn round needle, k.1, yarn round needle, k. 2 tog.; rep. from * to last st., k.1.
4th row: P. to end.
These 4 rows form the pattern.

185 Celtic Lace Pattern

No. 186 Glamis Lace 8 sts. plus 1

1st row: K.1, *yarn forward, k.2, sl.1, k. 2 tog., p.s.s.o., k.2, yarn forward, k.1; rep. from * to end.
2nd row and foll. alt. rows: P. to end.
3rd row: K.2, *yarn forward, k.1, sl.1, k.2 tog., p.s.s.o., k.1, yarn forward, k.3; rep. from * to last 7 sts., yarn forward, k.1, sl.1, k. 2 tog., p.s.s.o., k.1, yarn forward, k.2.
5th row: K. 2 tog., *yarn forward, k.1, yarn forward, sl.1, k. 2 tog., p.s.s.o.; rep. from * to last 3 sts., yarn forward, k.1, yarn forward, sl.1, k.1, p.s.s.o.
6th row: P. to end.
These 6 rows form the pattern.

186 Glamis Lace

No. 187 Diamond Point Lace 8 sts. plus 1

1st row: K.3, *yarn round needle, sl.1, k. 2 tog., p.s.s.o., yarn round needle, k.5; rep. from * to end, ending last rep., k.3 instead of k.5.
2nd row and foll. alt. rows: P. to end.
3rd row: K.1, k. 2 tog., *yarn round needle, k.3, yarn round needle, sl.1, k.1, p.s.s.o., k.1, k. 2 tog.; rep. from * to last 6 sts., yarn round needle, k.3, yarn round needle, sl.1, k.1, p.s.s.o., k.1.
5th row: K. 2 tog., *yarn round needle, k.5, yarn round

187 Diamond Point Lace

73

needle, sl.1, k. 2 tog., p.s.s.o.; rep. from * to last 7 sts., yarn round needle, k.5, yarn round needle, sl.1, k.1, p.s.s.o.

7th row: K.2, *yarn round needle, sl.1, k.1, p.s.s.o., k.1, k. 2 tog., yarn round needle, k.3; rep. from * ending last rep., k.2 instead of k.3.

8th row: P. to end.

These 8 rows form the pattern.

No. 188   Leaf Arches Pattern 18 sts.

1st row: *Sl.1, k. 2 tog., p.s.s.o., k.4, yarn forward, k.1, yarn round needle, p.2, yarn over needle, k.1, yarn forward, k.4, k. 3 tog.; rep. from * to end.

2nd row and foll. alt. rows: *P.8, k.2, p.8; rep. from * to end.

3rd row: *Sl.1, k. 2 tog., p.s.s.o., k.3, (yarn forward, k.1) twice, p.2, (k.1, yarn forward) twice, k.3, k. 3 tog.; rep. from * to end.

5th row: *Sl.1, k. 2 tog., p.s.s.o., k.2, yarn forward, k.1, yarn forward, k.2, p.2, k.2, yarn forward, k.1, yarn forward, k.2, k. 3 tog.; rep. from * to end.

7th row: *Sl.1, k. 2 tog., p.s.s.o., k.1, yarn forward, k.1, yarn forward, k.3, p.2, k.3, (yarn forward, k.1) twice, k. 3 tog.; rep. from * to end.

9th row: *Sl.1, k. 2 tog., p.s.s.o., yarn forward, k.1, yarn forward, k.4, p.2, k.4, yarn forward, k.1, yarn forward, k. 3 tog.; rep. from * to end.

10th row: As 2nd row.

These 10 rows form the pattern.

188 Leaf Arches Pattern

No. 189   Twig Pattern 11 sts. plus 2

1st row: K.1, *k.2, k. 2 tog., (k.1, yarn forward) twice, k.1, sl.1, k.1, p.s.s.o., k.2; rep. from * to last st., k.1.

2nd row and foll. alt. rows: P. to end.

3rd row: K.1, *k.1, k. 2 tog., k.1, yarn forward, k.3, yarn forward, k.1, sl.1, k.1, p.s.s.o., k.1; rep. from * to last st., k.1.

5th row: K.1, *k. 2 tog., k.1, yarn forward, k.5, yarn forward, k.1, sl.1, k.1, p.s.s.o.; rep. from * to last st., k.1.

7th row: K.1, *k. 2 tog., yarn forward, k.7, yarn forward, k. 2 tog.; rep. from * to last st., k.1.

8th row: P. to end.

These 8 rows form the pattern.

189 Twig Pattern

No. 190   Blossom and Twig Pattern   11 sts. plus 2

This pattern will form blossoms above the twig pattern of No. 189. Repeat the 8 rows of No. 189 as required then work the following pattern rows.

1st row: K.1, *k. 2 tog., yarn forward, k.2, k. 2 tog., yarn forward, k.3, yarn forward, k. 2 tog.; rep. from * to last st., k.1.

2nd row and foll. alt. rows: P. to end.

3rd row: K.1, *k.1, yarn forward, sl.1, k. 2 tog., p.s.s.o., yarn forward, k.3, yarn forward, k. 3 tog., yarn forward, k.1; rep. from * to last st., k.1.

5th row: K.1, *k.2, sl.1, k.1, p.s.s.o., k.1, yarn forward, k.1, yarn forward, k. 3 tog., yarn forward, k.2; rep. from * to last st., k.1.

7th row: K.1, *k.3, yarn forward, sl.1, k.1, p.s.s.o., k.1, k. 2 tog., yarn forward, k.3; rep. from * to last st., k.1.

9th row: K.1, *k.4, yarn forward, sl.1, k. 2 tog., p.s.s.o., yarn forward, k.4; rep. from * to last st., k.1.

10th row: P. to end.

These 10 rows form the pattern.

190 Blossom and Twig Pattern

No. 191   Open Fan Pattern   18 sts. plus 2

There are many patterns based on the traditional Shetland lace knitting. Some of the following variations have been handed down for generations using their genuine names, while the names of other, equally old stitches, have become corrupted and may not be instantly recognisable by the name given here.

1st row: K.1, *sl.1, k.1, p.s.s.o., (yarn forward, k. 2 tog.) 3 times, yarn forward, k.2, (yarn forward, k. 2 tog.) 4 times; rep. from * to last st., k.1.

2nd row: K. to end.

3rd row: K.1, *sl.1, k.1, p.s.s.o., k.6, yarn forward, k.2, yarn forward, k.6, k. 2 tog.; rep. from * to last st., k.1.

4th row: P.1, *p.8, k.2, p.8; rep. from * to last st., p.1.

5th row: As 3rd row.

6th row: K. to end.

These 6 rows form the pattern.

191 Open Fan Pattern

No. 192   Miniature Shell Pattern   6 sts. plus 1

1st row: K.1, *yarn round needle, p.1, p. 3 tog., p.1, yarn forward, k.1; rep. from * to end.

2nd row: P. to end.

3rd row: K. to end.

4th row: P. to end.

These 4 rows form the pattern.

192 Miniature Shell Pattern

193 Old Shale Pattern

No. 193 Old Shale Pattern 18 sts.

1st row: (right side) K. to end.
2nd row: P. to end.
3rd row: ★(K. 2 tog.) 3 times, (yarn forward, k.1) 6 times, (k. 2 tog.) 3 times; rep. from ★ to end.
4th row: K. to end.
These 4 rows form the pattern.

194 Feather and Fan Pattern

No. 194 Feather and Fan Pattern 15 sts. plus 4

1st row: (wrong side) P.4, ★k.11, p.4; rep. from ★ to end.
2nd row: K.4, ★p.11, k.4; rep. from ★ to end.
3rd row: P.2, ★p. 2 tog., p.11, p. 2 tog. t.b.l.; rep. from ★ to last 2 sts., p.2.
4th row: K.2, ★sl.1, k.1, p.s.s.o., k.9, k. 2 tog.; rep. from ★ to last 2 sts., k.2.
5th row: P.2, ★p. 2 tog., p.7, p. 2 tog. t.b.l.; rep. from ★ to last 2 sts., p.2.
6th row: K.4, ★(yarn forward, k.1) 5 times, yarn forward, k.4; rep. from ★ to end.
These 6 rows form the pattern.

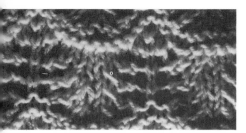

195 Feather and Fan Variation

No. 195 Feather and Fan Variation 12 sts. plus 1

1st row: K. to end.
2nd, 3rd and 4th rows: As 1st row.
5th row: (right side) K.1, ★(k. 2 tog.) twice, (yarn forward, k.1) 3 times, yarn forward, (sl.1, k.1, p.s.s.o.) twice, k.1; rep. from ★ to end.
6th row: P. to end.
7th, 9th and 11th rows: As 5th row.
8th, 10th and 12th rows: As 6th row.
These 12 rows form the pattern.

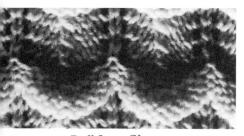

196 Puff Lace Chevron

No. 196 Puff Lace Chevron 10 sts. plus 11

1st row: K. 2 tog., ★k.3, yarn forward, k.1, yarn forward, k.3, sl.1, k. 2 tog., p.s.s.o.; rep. from ★ ending last rep., k. 2 tog. instead of sl.1, k. 2 tog., p.s.s.o.
2nd row: P. to end.
3rd to 10th rows: Rep. 1st and 2nd rows 4 times more.
11th row: P. to end.
12th row: K. to end.
13th and 14th rows: Rep. 11th and 12th rows once more.
These 14 rows form the pattern.

No. 197 Victoriana Lace 6 sts. plus 7

1st row: (right side) K.2, *(k.1 winding yarn 3 times round needle) 3 times, k.3; rep. from * to last 5 sts., (k.1, winding yarn round needle 3 times) 3 times, k.2.
2nd row: K.2, sl. next 3 sts. on to right hand needle dropping extra loops to make 3 long sts., then slip these 3 long sts. back on to left hand needle – called long 3 – yarn round needle, p. 3 tog., yarn over needle, *k.3, long 3, yarn round needle, p. 3 tog., yarn over needle; rep. from * to last 2 sts., k.2.
3rd row: K.5, *(k.1 winding yarn 3 times round needle) 3 times, k.3; rep. from * to last 2 sts., k.2.
4th row: K.5, *long 3, yarn round needle, p. 3 tog., yarn over needle, k.3; rep. from * to last 2 sts., k.2.
These 4 rows form the pattern.

197 Victoriana Lace

No. 198 Cross Lace Checks 4 sts. plus 2

Cr. sts., cross stitches thus: slip next 4 sts. purlwise on to right hand needle dropping the yarn round needle of previous row, slip the 4 sts. back on to left hand needle, inserting point of right hand needle through all loops and counting these 4 sts. as one, (p.1, k.1) twice into them, making 4 sts. out of 4 together.
1st row: K.1, *k.1, wrapping yarn 3 times round needle; rep. from * to last st., k.1.
2nd row: K.1, Cr. sts.; rep. from * to last st., k.1.
3rd row: K. to end.
4th row: As 3rd row.
These 4 rows form the pattern.

198 Cross Lace Checks

No. 199 Reversible Lace Pattern 4 sts. plus 4

You will need one pair of needles one size thicker than normal for the yarn (A) and one pair four times finer than A needles (B).
1st row: With B needles, P.2, *yarn round needle, p. 4 tog.; rep. from * to last 2 sts., p.2.
2nd row: With A needles, K.2, *k.1, (k.1, p.1, k.1) all in made st. of previous row; rep. from * to last 2 sts., k.2.
3rd row: With A needles, k. to end.
These 3 rows form the pattern.

199 Reversible Lace Pattern

200 Cocktail Lace

No. 200 Cocktail Lace 8 sts. plus 1
1st row: P.1, *yarn round needle, p.2, p. 3 tog., p.2,
yarn round needle, p.1; rep. from * to end.
2nd row and foll. alt. rows: P. to end.
3rd row: P.1, *k.1, yarn round needle, p.1, p. 3 tog., p.1,
yarn round needle, k.1, p.1; rep. from * to end.
5th row: P.1, *k.2, yarn round needle, p. 3 tog., yarn
round needle, k.2, p.1; rep. from * to end.
6th row: As 2nd row.
These 6 rows form the pattern.

No. 201 Diamond and Faggot Lace Panel 17 sts.
plus 2
1st row: (wrong side) *P.2, yarn round needle, p. 2 tog.,
p.11, yarn round needle, p. 2 tog.; rep. from * to last 2
sts., p.2.
2nd row: *K.2, yarn forward, sl.1, k.1, p.s.s.o., k.2, k. 2
tog., yarn forward, k.1, yarn forward, sl.1, k.1, p.s.s.o.,
k.4, yarn forward, sl.1, k.1, p.s.s.o.; rep. from * to last 2
sts., k.2.
3rd row and foll. alt. rows: As 1st row.
4th row: *K.2, yarn forward, sl.1, k.1, p.s.s.o., k.1, k. 2
tog., yarn forward, k.3, yarn forward, sl.1, k.1, p.s.s.o.,
k.3, yarn forward, sl.1, k.1, p.s.s.o.; rep. from * to last 2
sts., k.2.
6th row: *K.2, yarn forward, sl.1, k.1, p.s.s.o., k. 2 tog.,
yarn forward, k.5, yarn forward, sl.1, k.1, p.s.s.o., k.2,
yarn forward, sl.1, k.1, p.s.s.o.; rep. from * to last 2 sts.,
k.2.
8th row: *K.2, yarn forward, sl.1, k.1, p.s.s.o., k.1, yarn
forward, k.2, sl.1, k. 2 tog., p.s.s.o., k.2, yarn forward,
k.3, yarn forward, sl.1, k.1, p.s.s.o.; rep. from * to last 2
sts., k.2.
10th row: *K.2, yarn forward, sl.1, k.1, p.s.s.o., k.2,
yarn forward, k.1, sl.1, k. 2 tog., p.s.s.o., k.1, yarn
forward, k.4, yarn forward, sl.1, k.1, p.s.s.o.; rep. from *
to last 2 sts., k.2.
12th row: *K.2, yarn forward, sl.1, k.1, p.s.s.o., k.3,
yarn forward, sl.1, k. 2 tog., p.s.s.o., yarn forward, k.5,
yarn forward, sl.1, k.1, p.s.s.o.; rep. from * to last 2 sts.,
k.2.
These 12 rows form the pattern.

*201 Diamond and Faggot Lace
Panel*

No. 202 Scalloped Lace Pattern 8 sts. plus 1

1st row: K.1, *yarn forward, k.2, sl.1, k. 2 tog., p.s.s.o.,
k.2, yarn forward, k.1; rep. from * to end.

2nd row: P. to end.

3rd to 6th rows: Rep. 1st and 2nd rows twice more.

7th row: K. 2 tog., *k.2, yarn forward, k.1, yarn
forward, k.2, sl.1, k. 2 tog., p.s.s.o.; rep. from * ending
last rep., sl.1, k.1, p.s.s.o. instead of sl.1, k. 2 tog.,
p.s.s.o.

8th row: P. to end.

9th to 12th rows: Rep. 7th and 8th rows twice more.
These 12 rows form the pattern.

202 Scalloped Lace Pattern

No. 203 Autumn Leaves 22 sts. plus 7

1st row: (right side) *K.2, (yarn forward, k.1) 3 times,
yarn forward, k.2, k. 2 tog., yarn forward, k.1, sl.1, k.1,
p.s.s.o., k.5, k. 2 tog., k.1, yarn forward, sl.1, k.1,
p.s.s.o.; rep. from * to last 7 sts., k.2, (yarn forward,
k.1) 3 times, yarn forward, k.2.

2nd row and foll. alt. rows: P. to end.

3rd row: *K.1, k. 2 tog., yarn forward, k.2, yarn
forward, k.1, yarn forward, k.2, yarn forward, sl.1, k.1,
p.s.s.o., k.1, k. 2 tog., yarn forward, k.1, sl.1, k.1,
p.s.s.o., k.3, k. 2 tog., k.1, yarn forward, sl.1, k.1,
p.s.s.o.; rep. from * to last 11 sts., k.1, k. 2 tog., yarn
forward, k.2, yarn forward, k.1, yarn forward, k.2, yarn
forward, sl.1, k.1, p.s.s.o., k.1.

5th row: *K.1, k. 2 tog., yarn forward, k.3, yarn
forward, k.1, yarn forward, k.3, yarn forward, sl.1, k.1,
p.s.s.o., k.1, k. 2 tog., yarn forward, k.1, sl.1, k.1,
p.s.s.o., k.1, k. 2 tog., k.1, yarn forward, sl.1, k.1,
p.s.s.o.; rep. from * to last 13 sts., k.1, k. 2 tog., yarn
forward, k.3, yarn forward, k.1, yarn forward, k.3, yarn
forward, sl.1, k.1, p.s.s.o., k.1.

7th row: *K.1, k. 2 tog., yarn forward, k.4, yarn
forward, k.1, yarn forward, k.4, yarn forward, sl.1, k.1,
p.s.s.o., k.1, k. 2 tog., yarn forward, k.1, sl.1, k. 2 tog.,
p.s.s.o., k.1, yarn forward, sl.1, k.1, p.s.s.o.; rep. from *
to last 15 sts., k.1, k. 2 tog., yarn forward, k.4, yarn
forward, k.1, yarn forward, k.4, yarn forward, sl.1, k.1,
p.s.s.o., k.1.

9th row: *K.1, k. 2 tog., yarn forward, k.1, sl.1, k.1,
p.s.s.o., k.5, k. 2 tog., k.1, yarn forward, sl.1, k.1,
p.s.s.o., k.1, k. 2 tog., yarn forward, sl.1, k. 2 tog.,
p.s.s.o., yarn forward, sl.1, k.1, p.s.s.o.; rep. from * to
last 17 sts., k.1, k. 2 tog., yarn forward, k.1, sl.1, k.1,

203 Autumn Leaves

p.s.s.o., k.5, k. 2 tog., k.1, yarn forward, sl.1, k.1, p.s.s.o., k.1.

11th row: *K.1, k. 2 tog., yarn forward, k.1, sl.1, k.1, p.s.s.o., k.3, k. 2 tog., k.1, yarn forward, sl.1, k.1, p.s.s.o., k.2, (yarn forward, k.1) 3 times, yarn forward, k.1; rep. from * to last 15 sts., k.1, k. 2 tog., yarn forward, k.1, sl.1, k.1, p.s.s.o., k.3, k. 2 tog., k.1, yarn forward, sl.1, k.1, p.s.s.o., k.1.

13th row: *K.1, k. 2 tog., yarn forward, k.1, sl.1, k.1, p.s.s.o., k.1, k. 2 tog., k.1, yarn forward, sl.1, k.1, p.s.s.o., k.1, k. 2 tog., yarn forward, k.2, yarn forward, k.1, yarn forward, k.2, yarn forward, sl.1, k.1, p.s.s.o.; rep. from * to last 13 sts., k.1, k. 2 tog., yarn forward, k.1, sl.1, k.1, p.s.s.o., k.1, k. 2 tog., k.1, yarn forward, sl.1, k.1, p.s.s.o.

15th row: *K.1, k. 2 tog., yarn forward, k.1, sl.1, k. 2 tog., p.s.s.o., k.1, yarn forward, sl.1, k.1, p.s.s.o., k.1, k. 2 tog., yarn forward, k.3, yarn forward, k.1, yarn forward, k.3, yarn forward, sl.1, k.1, p.s.s.o.; rep. from * to last 11 sts., k.1, k. 2 tog., yarn forward, k.1, sl.1, k. 2 tog., p.s.s.o., k.1, yarn forward, sl.1, k.1, p.s.s.o., k.1.

17th row: *K.1, k. 2 tog., yarn forward, sl.1, k. 2 tog., p.s.s.o., yarn forward, sl.1, k.1, p.s.s.o., k.1, k. 2 tog., yarn forward, k.4, yarn forward, k.1, yarn forward, k.4, yarn forward, sl.1, k.1, p.s.s.o.; rep. from * to last 9 sts., k.1, k. 2 tog., yarn forward, sl.1, k. 2 tog., p.s.s.o., yarn forward, sl.1, k.1, p.s.s.o., k.1.

18th row: P. to end.

These 18 rows form the pattern.

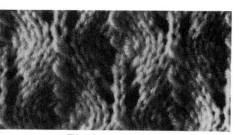

204 Fir Cone Pattern

No. 204 Fir Cone Pattern 10 sts. plus 1

1st row: (right side) K.1, *yarn forward, k.3, sl.1, k. 2 tog., p.s.s.o., k.3, yarn forward, k.1; rep. from * to end.

2nd row: P. to end.

3rd to 8th rows: Rep. last 2 rows 3 times more.

9th row: K. 2 tog., *k.3, yarn forward, k.1, yarn forward, k.3, sl.1, k. 2 tog., p.s.s.o.; rep. from * to last 9 sts., k.3, yarn forward, k.1, yarn forward, k.3, sl.1, k.1, p.s.s.o.

10th row: P. to end.

11th to 16th rows: Rep. last 2 rows 3 times more.

These 16 rows form the pattern.

No. 205 Elm Leaf Pattern 15 sts. plus 1

1st row: (right side) *K.1, yarn forward, k.1, sl.1, k.1,
p.s.s.o., p.1, k. 2 tog., k.1, yarn forward, p.1, sl.1, k.1,
p.s.s.o., p.1, k. 2 tog., yarn forward, k.1, yarn forward;
rep. from * to last st., k.1.

2nd row: P.1, *p.4, k.1, p.1, k.1, p.3, k.1, p.4; rep. from
* to end.

3rd row: *K.1, yarn forward, k.1, sl.1, k.1, p.s.s.o., p.1,
k. 2 tog., k.1, p.1, sl.1, k. 2 tog., p.s.s.o., yarn forward,
k.3, yarn forward; rep. from * to last st., k.1.

4th row: P.1, *p.6, k.1, p.2, k.1, p.4; rep. from * to end.

5th row: *(k.1, yarn forward) twice, sl.1, k.1, p.s.s.o.,
p.1, (k. 2 tog.) twice, yarn forward, k.5, yarn forward;
rep. from * to last st., k.1.

6th row: P.1, *p.7, k.1, p.1, k.1, p.5; rep. from * to end.

7th row: *K.1, yarn forward, k.3, yarn forward, sl.1, k. 2
tog., p.s.s.o., p.1, yarn round needle, k.1, sl.1, k.1,
p.s.s.o., p.1, k. 2 tog., k.1, yarn forward; rep. from * to
last st., k.1.

8th row: P.1 *(p.3, k.1) twice, p.7; rep. from * to end.

9th row: *K.1, yarn forward, k.5, yarn forward, sl.1, k.1,
p.s.s.o., k.1, sl.1, k.1, p.s.s.o., p.1, k. 2 tog., k.1, yarn
forward; rep. from * to last st., k.1.

10th row: P.1, *p.3, k.1, p.2, k.1, p.8; rep. from * to
end.

These 10 rows form the pattern.

205 Elm Leaf Pattern

No. 206 Crown of Glory 14 sts. plus 5

This is a very old Shetland lace pattern. It requires
careful working as the stitches vary from row to row and
may only be counted after the 7th to 12th rows.

1st row: (right side) K.3, *sl.1, k.1, p.s.s.o., k.9, k. 2
tog., k.1; rep. from * to last 2 sts., k.2.

2nd row: P.2, *p.1, p. 2 tog., p.7, p. 2 tog. t.b.l.; rep.
from * to last 3 sts., p.3.

3rd row: K.3, *sl.1, k.1, p.s.s.o., k.2, wrap yarn 3 times
round needle, k.3, k. 2 tog., k.1; rep. from * to last 2
sts., k.2.

4th row: P.2, *p.1, p. 2 tog., p.2, (k.1, p.1, k.1, p.1, k.1)
all into yarn round needle 3 times, thus making 5 sts.,
p.1, p. 2 tog. t.b.l.; rep. from * to last 3 sts., p.3.

5th row: K.3, *sl.1, k.1, p.s.s.o., k.6, k. 2 tog., k.1; rep.
from * to last 2 sts., k.2.

6th row: P.2, *p.1, p. 2 tog., p.6; rep. from * ending last
rep., p.3 instead of p.6.

7th row: K.3, *k.1, (yarn forward, k.1) 6 times, k.1; rep.
from * to last 2 sts., k.2.

206 Crown of Glory

8th row: P. to end.
9th and 10th rows: K. to end.
11th row: P. to end.
12th row: K. to end.
These 12 rows form the pattern.

207 Spanish Lace

No. 207 Spanish Lace 34 sts. plus 2

Another very old, classical lace pattern. It looks beautiful in any type of yarn and is not complicated to knit since many of the rows repeat.

1st row: (right side) K.1, *k.3, k. 2 tog., k.4, yarn round needle, p.2, (k.2, yarn forward, sl.1, k.1, p.s.s.o.) 3 times, p.2, yarn over needle, k.4, sl.1, k.1, p.s.s.o., k.3; rep. from * to last st., k.1.

2nd row: K.1, *p.2, p. 2 tog. t.b.l., p.4, yarn round needle, p.1, k.2, (p.2, yarn round needle, p. 2 tog.) 3 times, k.2, p.1, yarn round needle, p.4, p. 2 tog., p.2; rep. from * to last st., k.1.

3rd row: K.1, *k.1, k. 2 tog., k.4, yarn forward, k.2, p.2, (k.2, yarn forward, sl.1, k.1, p.s.s.o.) 3 times, p.2, k.2, yarn forward, k.4, sl.1, k.1, p.s.s.o., k.1; rep. from * to last st., k.1.

4th row: K.1, *p. 2 tog. t.b.l., p.4, yarn round needle, p.3, k.2, (p.2, yarn round needle, p. 2 tog.) 3 times, k.2, p.3, yarn round needle, p.4, p. 2 tog.; rep. from * to last st., k.1.

5th to 12th rows: Rep. 1st to 4th rows twice more.

13th row: K.1, *yarn forward, sl.1, k.1, p.s.s.o., k.2, yarn forward, sl.1, k.1, p.s.s.o., p.2, yarn over needle, k.4, sl.1, k.1, p.s.s.o., k.6, k. 2 tog., k.4, yarn round needle, p.2, k.2, yarn forward, sl.1, k.1, p.s.s.o., k.2; rep. from * to last st., k.1.

14th row: K.1, *yarn round needle, p. 2 tog., p.2, yarn round needle, p. 2 tog., k.2, p.1, yarn round needle, p.4, p. 2 tog., p.4, p. 2 tog. t.b.l., p.4, yarn round needle, p.1, k.2, p.2, yarn round needle, p. 2 tog., p.2; rep. from * to last st., k.1.

15th row: K.1, *yarn forward, sl.1, k.1, p.s.s.o., k.2, yarn forward, sl.1, k.1, p.s.s.o., p.2, k.2, yarn forward, k.4, sl.1, k.1, p.s.s.o., k.2, k. 2 tog., k.4, yarn forward, k.2, p.2, k.2, yarn forward, sl.1, k.1, p.s.s.o., k.2; rep. from * to last st., k.1.

16th row: K.1, *yarn round needle, p. 2 tog., p.2, yarn round needle, p. 2 tog., k.2, p.3, yarn round needle, p.4, p. 2 tog., p. 2 tog. t.b.l., p.4, yarn round needle, p.3, k.2, p.2, yarn round needle, p. 2 tog., p.2; rep. from * to last st., k.1.

17th to 24th rows: Rep. 13th to 16th rows twice more.
These 24 rows form the pattern.

No. 208   Madeira Lace 20 sts. plus 5

1st row: (right side) P. to end.

2nd row: K. to end.

3rd row: K.2, *k.1, yarn forward, k.8, sl.1, k. 2 tog.,
p.s.s.o., k.8, yarn forward; rep. from * to last 3 sts., k.3.

4th row and foll. alt. rows to 18th row: P. to end.

5th row: K.2, *k.2, yarn forward, k.7, sl.1, k. 2 tog.,
p.s.s.o., k.7, yarn forward, k.1; rep. from * to last 3 sts.,
k.3.

7th row: K.2, k. 2 tog., *yarn forward, k.1, yarn
forward, k.6, sl.1, k. 2 tog., p.s.s.o., k.6, yarn forward,
k.1, yarn forward, sl.1, k. 2 tog., p.s.s.o.; rep. from * to
last 4 sts., ending last rep., yarn forward, sl.1, k.1,
p.s.s.o., k.2 instead of yarn forward, sl.1, k. 2 tog.,
p.s.s.o.

9th row: K.2, *k.4, yarn forward, k.5, sl.1, k. 2 tog.,
p.s.s.o., k.5, yarn forward, k.3; rep. from * to last 3 sts.,
k.3.

11th row: K.2, *k.1, yarn forward, sl.1, k. 2 tog.,
p.s.s.o., yarn forward, k.1, yarn forward, k.4, sl.1, k. 2
tog., p.s.s.o., k.4, yarn forward, k.1, yarn forward, sl.1,
k. 2 tog., p.s.s.o., yarn forward; rep. from * to last 3
sts., k.3.

13th row: K.2, *k.6, yarn forward, k.3, sl.1, k. 2 tog.,
p.s.s.o., k.3, yarn forward, k.5; rep. from * to last 3 sts.,
k.3.

15th row: K.2, k. 2 tog., *yarn forward, k.1, yarn
forward, sl.1, k. 2 tog., p.s.s.o., yarn forward, k.1, yarn
forward, k.2, sl.1, k. 2 tog., p.s.s.o., k.2, (yarn forward,
k.1, yarn forward, sl.1, k. 2 tog., p.s.s.o.) twice; rep.
from * to last 4 sts., ending last rep., yarn forward, sl.1,
k.1, p.s.s.o., k.2 instead of yarn forward, sl.1, k. 2 tog.,
p.s.s.o.

17th row: K.2, *k.8, yarn forward, k.1, sl.1, k. 2 tog.,
p.s.s.o., k.1, yarn forward, k.7; rep. from * to last 3 sts.,
k.3.

18th row: P. to end.

19th row: K.2, *(k.1, yarn forward, sl.1, k. 2 tog.,
p.s.s.o., yarn forward) 5 times; rep. from * to last 3 sts.,
k.3.

20th row: K. to end.

These 20 rows form the pattern.

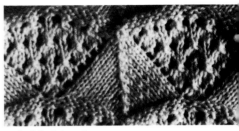

208 Madeira Lace

209 Imperial Lace Pattern

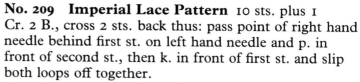

No. 209   Imperial Lace Pattern 10 sts. plus 1

Cr. 2 B., cross 2 sts. back thus: pass point of right hand needle behind first st. on left hand needle and p. in front of second st., then k. in front of first st. and slip both loops off together.

Cr. 2 F., cross 2 sts. front thus: k. in front of second st. on left hand needle then p. in first st. and slip both loops off together.

1st row: (right side) P.1, *k.1, (yarn forward, k. 2 tog.) 4 times, p.1; rep. from * to end.

2nd row: K.1, *p.9, k.1; rep. from * to end.

3rd row: P.1, *Cr. 2 B., k.5, Cr. 2 F., p.1; rep. from * to end.

4th row: K.2, *Cr. 2 F., p.3, Cr. 2 B., k.3; rep. from * ending last rep., k.2 instead of k.3.

5th row: P.3, *Cr. 2 B., k.1, Cr. 2 F., p.5; rep. from * ending last rep., p.3 instead of p.5.

6th row: K.4, *p.1, k.1, p.1, k.7; rep. from * ending last rep. k.4 instead of k.7.

7th row: K.1, yarn forward, k. 2 tog., yarn forward, k. 2 tog., *p.1, k.1, (yarn forward, k. 2 tog.) 4 times; rep. from * to last 6 sts., p.1, k.1, yarn forward, k. 2 tog., yarn forward, k. 2 tog.

8th row: P.5, *k.1, p.9; rep. from * ending p.5 instead of p.9.

9th row: K.3, *Cr. 2 F., p.1, Cr. 2 B., k.5; rep. from * ending k.3 instead of k.5.

10th row: P.2, *Cr. 2 B., k.3, Cr. 2 F., p.3; rep. from * ending last rep., p.2 instead of p.3.

11th row: K.1, *Cr. 2 F., p.5, Cr. 2 B., k.1; rep. from * to end.

12th row: K.1, *p.1, k.7, p.1, k.1; rep. from * to end.

These 12 rows form the pattern.

No. 210   Travelling Vine 8 sts. plus 4

A very old pattern of great elegance. Care must be taken when shaping in this pattern, since there is a gain in the number of stitches on the right side rows which is compensated for on the following wrong side rows.

1st row: K.2, *yarn forward, k. 1 t.b.l., yarn forward, k. 2 tog. t.b.l., k.5; rep. from * to last 2 sts., k.2.

2nd row: P.2, *p.4, p. 2 tog. t.b.l., p.3; rep. from * to last 2 sts., p.2.

3rd row: K.2, *yarn forward, k. 1 t.b.l., yarn forward, k.2, k. 2 tog. t.b.l., k.3; rep. from * to last 2 sts., k.2.

4th row: P.2, *p.2, p. 2 tog. t.b.l., p.5; rep. from * to last 2 sts., p.2.

5th row: K.2, *k. 1 t.b.l., yarn forward, k.4, k. 2 tog.

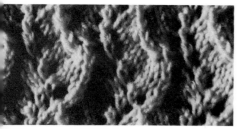

210 Travelling Vine

84

t.b.l., k.1, yarn forward; rep. from * to last 2 sts., k.2.

6th row: P.2, *p.1, p. 2 tog. t.b.l., p.6; rep. from * to last 2 sts., p.2.

7th row: K.2, *k.5, k. 2 tog., yarn forward, k. 1 t.b.l., yarn forward; rep. from * to last 2 sts., k.2.

8th row: P.2, *p.3, k. 2 tog., p.4; rep. from * to last 2 sts., p.2.

9th row: K.2, *k.3, k. 2 tog., k.2, yarn forward, k. 1 t.b.l., yarn forward; rep. from * to last 2 sts., k.2.

10th row: P.2, *p.5, p. 2 tog., p.2; rep. from * to last 2 sts., p.2.

11th row: K.2, *yarn forward, k.1, k. 2 tog., k.4, yarn forward, k. 1 t.b.l.; rep. from * to last 2 sts., k.2.

12th row: P.2, *p.6, p. 2 tog., p.1; rep. from * to last 2 sts., p.2.

These 12 rows form the pattern.

No. 211   Cockleshell Pattern   19 sts. plus 2

1st row: K. to end.

2nd row: As 1st row.

3rd row: K.1, *k.1, (yarn round needle) twice, p. 2 tog. t.b.l., k.13, p. 2 tog., (yarn round needle) twice, k.1; rep. from * to last st., k.1.

4th row: K.1, *k.1, (k.1 then p.1) into the double loop, k.15, (p.1 then k.1) into the double loop, k.1; rep. from * to last st., k.1.

5th and 6th rows: K. to end.

7th row: K.1, *k.1, (make double loop as 3rd row, p. 2 tog. t.b.l.) twice, k.11, (p. 2 tog., make double loop) twice, k.1; rep. from * to last st., k.1.

8th row: K.1, *(k.1, then k.1 and p.1 into double loop) twice, k.13, (p.1 and k.1 into double loop, k.1) twice; rep. from * to last st., k.1.

9th row: K. to end.

10th row: K.1, *k.6, (make double loop as 3rd row, k.1) 14 times, k.5; rep. from * to last st., k.1.

11th row: K.1, *k.1, (make double loop, p. 2 tog. t.b.l.) twice, yarn round needle twice to make double loop, then slip next 15 sts. on to right hand needle dropping extra loops, slip these long sts. back on to left hand needle and p.15 long loops tog., (make double loop, p. 2 tog. t.b.l.) twice, make double loop, k.1; rep. from * to last st., k.1.

12th row: K.1, *(k.1, then p.1 and k.1 into double loops) 3 times, k.1, (k.1 and p.1 into double loops, k.1) 3 times; rep. from * to last st., k.1.

These 12 rows form the pattern.

211 Cockleshell Pattern

212 Palladian Lace

No. 212 Palladian Lace 18 sts. plus 1
C. 3 B., cable 3 back thus: sl. next 2 sts. to back on cable needle, k.1, then p.2 from cable needle.
C. 3 F., cable 3 front thus: sl. next st. to front on cable needle, p.2, then k.1 from cable needle.
1st row: P.1, *k.8, p.1; rep. from * to end.
2nd row: K.1, *p.8, k.1; rep. from * to end.
3rd row: P.1, *k.5, C. 3 B., p.1, C. 3 F., k.5, p.1; rep. from * to end.
4th row: K.1, *p.6, k.5, p.6, k.1; rep. from * to end.
5th row: P.1, *k.3, C. 3 B., p.5, C. 3 F., k.3, p.1; rep. from * to end.
6th row: K.1, *p.4, k.9, p.4, k.1; rep. from * to end.
7th row: P.1, *C. 3 F., k.1, p.1, (yarn round needle, p. 2 tog.) 4 times, k.1, C. 3 B., p.1; rep. from * to end.
8th row: K.3, *p.6, k.1, p.6, k.5; rep. from * ending k.3 instead of k.5.
9th row: P.3, *C. 3 F., k.3, p.1, k.3, C. 3 B., p.5; rep. from * ending p.3 instead of p.5.
10th row: K.5, *p.4, k.1, p.4, k.9; rep. from * ending k.5 instead of k.9.
11th row: P.1, (yarn round needle, p. 2 tog.) twice, *k.1, C. 3 B., p.1, C. 3 F., k.1, p.1, (yarn round needle, p. 2 tog.) 4 times; rep. from * ending (yarn round needle, p. 2 tog.) twice instead of 4 times.
12th row: K.1, *p.6, k.5, p.6, k.1; rep. from * to end.
The 5th to 12th rows form the pattern.

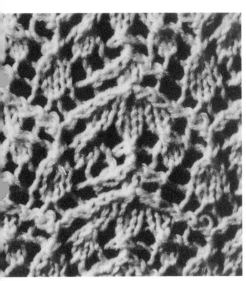

213 Breton Lace

No. 213 Breton Lace 10 sts. plus 3
1st row: K.1, k. 2 tog., *yarn forward, k.3, yarn forward, k. twice in next st., yarn forward, k.3, yarn forward, sl.1, k. 2 tog., p.s.s.o.; rep. from * ending sl.1, k.1, p.s.s.o., k.1 instead of sl.1, k. 2 tog., p.s.s.o.
2nd row and foll. alt. rows: P. to end
3rd row: K.1, k. 2 tog., *yarn forward, k. 3 tog., yarn forward, k. 2 tog., yarn forward, sl.1, k.1, p.s.s.o., yarn forward, sl.2, k.1, pass the 2 slipped sts. over the k.1, yarn forward, sl.1, k. 2 tog., p.s.s.o.; rep. from * ending sl.1, k.1, p.s.s.o., k.1, instead of sl.1, k. 2 tog., p.s.s.o.
5th row: K.4, *k. 2 tog., yarn forward, k.1, yarn forward, sl.1, k.1, p.s.s.o., k.5; rep. from * ending k.4 instead of k.5.
7th row: K.3, *k. 2 tog., yarn forward, k.3, yarn forward, sl.1, k.1, p.s.s.o., k.3; rep. from * to end.
9th row: K.1, k. 3 tog., *yarn forward, k.1, yarn forward, k.3, yarn forward, k.1, yarn forward, sl.2, k.1, pass the 2 sl. sts. over the k.1 and off the needle, now

slip the k. st. back on to left hand needle, pass the first and second sts. on left hand needle over this k. st. and off the needle, then pass the k. st. back on to right hand needle; rep. from * to last 9 sts., yarn forward, k.1, yarn forward, k.3, yarn forward, k.1, yarn forward, sl.2, k.1, pass the 2 sl. sts. over the k.1.

11th row: K.2, *k. 2 tog., yarn forward, k.1, yarn forward, sl.1, k. 2 tog., p.s.s.o., yarn forward, k.1, yarn forward, sl.1, k.1, p.s.s.o., k.1; rep. from * to last st., k.1.

12th row: P. to end.

These 12 rows form the pattern.

No. 214 Lace Diamond Insertion 11 sts. plus 2
The diamonds of this pattern may be worked as a border, or between stocking stitch by omitting 13th to 18th rows.

1st row: K. to end.

2nd row: P. to end.

3rd row: K.1, *k.3, k. 2 tog., yarn forward, k.1, yarn forward, sl.1, k.1, p.s.s.o., k.3; rep. from * to last st., k.1.

214 Lace Diamond Insertion

4th row: P.1, *p.2, p. 2 tog. t.b.l., yarn round needle, p.3, yarn round needle, p. 2 tog., p.2; rep. from * to last st., p.1.

5th row: K.1, *k.1, then (k. 2 tog., yarn forward) twice, k.1, then (yarn forward, sl.1, k.1, p.s.s.o.) twice, k.1; rep. from * to last st., k.1.

6th row: P.1, *(p. 2 tog., yarn round needle) twice, p.3, (yarn round needle, p. 2 tog.) twice; rep. from * to last st., k.1.

7th row: K.1, *k.1, (yarn forward, sl.1, k.1, p.s.s.o.) twice, (k.1, p.1) 3 times in next st., (k. 2 tog., yarn forward) twice, k.1; rep. from * to last st., k.1.

8th row: P.1, *p.2, yarn round needle, p. 2 tog., yarn round needle, p. 8 tog., yarn round needle, p. 2 tog. t.b.l., yarn round needle, p.2; rep. from * to last st., p.1.

9th row: K.1, *k.3, yarn forward, sl.1, k.1, p.s.s.o., k.1, k. 2 tog., yarn forward, k.3; rep. from * to last st., k.1.

10th row: P.1, *p.4, yarn round needle, p. 3 tog., yarn round needle, p.4; rep. from * to last st., p.1.

11th row: K. to end.

12th row: P. to end.

13th to 18th rows: Beg. p. row, work 6 rows reversed stocking stitch – p. is right side of work.

These 18 rows form the pattern.

215 Hyacinth Pattern

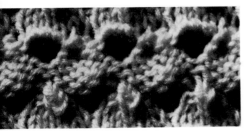

216 Tricorne Lace

217 Cable Lacettes

No. 215 Hyacinth Pattern 4 sts. plus 2

1st row: (wrong side) P.1, *p. 3 tog., (k.1, p.1, k.1) all in next st.; rep. from * to last st., p.1.

2nd row: P. to end.

3rd row: P.1, *(k.1, p.1, k.1) all in next st., p. 3 tog.; rep. from * to last st., p.1.

4th row: As 2nd row.

5th row: K. to end winding yarn 3 times round needle on each st.

6th row: P. to end dropping extra loops to form long sts.

These 6 rows form the pattern.

No. 216 Tricorne Lace 5 sts. plus 2

This pattern is reversible.

1st row: (right side) K. to end.

2nd row: P. to end.

3rd row: K.1, *yarn forward, k.5; rep. from * to last st., k.1.

4th row: K.1, *p.5, (k.1, p.1, k.1, p.1) into made st.; rep. from * to last st., k.1.

5th row: K.1, *p.4, sl next 3 sts. as if to k. 3 tog., k. 2 tog. and pass the 3 slipped sts. over the k. 2 tog.; rep. from * to last st., k.1.

6th to 10th rows: As 1st to 5th rows.

These 10 rows form the pattern.

No. 217 Cable Lacettes 6 sts. plus 2

1st row: (right side) P.2, *sl. next 2 sts. to front on cable needle, k.2, then k.2 from cable needle, p.2; rep. from * to end.

2nd row: K.2, *p.2, yarn round needle, p. 2 tog., k.2; rep. from * to end.

3rd row: P.2, *k.2, yarn forward, k. 2 tog. t.b.l., p.2; rep. from * to end.

4th row: As 2nd row.

5th to 12th rows: Rep. 3rd and 4th rows 4 times.

These 12 rows form the pattern.

No. 218 Open and Closed Diamonds 12 sts. plus 1

1st row: (wrong side) P. to end.

2nd row: K.1, *yarn forward, sl.1, k.1, p.s.s.o., k.7, k. 2 tog., yarn forward, k.1; rep. from * to end.

3rd row and foll. alt. rows: As 1st row.

4th row: K.1, *k.1, yarn forward, sl.1, k.1, p.s.s.o., k.5, k. 2 tog., yarn forward, k.2; rep. from * to end.

6th row: K.1, *(yarn forward, sl.1, k.1, p.s.s.o.) twice, k.3, (k. 2 tog., yarn forward) twice, k.1; rep. from * to end.

8th row: K.1, *k.1, (yarn forward, sl.1, k.1, p.s.s.o.) twice, k.1, (k. 2 tog., yarn forward) twice, k.2; rep. from * to end.

10th row: K.1, *(yarn forward, sl.1, k.1, p.s.s.o.) twice, yarn forward, sl.1, k. 2 tog., p.s.s.o., yarn forward, (k. 2 tog., yarn forward) twice, k.1; rep. from * to end.

12th row: K.1, *k.3, k. 2 tog., yarn forward, k.1, yarn forward, sl.1, k.1, p.s.s.o., k.4; rep. from * to end.

14th row: K.1, *k.2, k. 2 tog., yarn forward, k.3, yarn forward, sl.1, k.1, p.s.s.o., k.3; rep. from * to end.

16th row: K.1, *k.1, (k. 2 tog., yarn forward) twice, k.1, (yarn forward, sl.1, k.1, p.s.s.o.) twice, k.2; rep. from * to end.

18th row: K.1, * (k. 2 tog., yarn forward) twice, k.3, (yarn forward, sl.1, k.1, p.s.s.o.) twice, k.1; rep. from * to end.

20th row: K. 2 tog., yarn forward, *(k. 2 tog., yarn forward) twice, k.1, (yarn forward, sl.1, k.1, p.s.s.o.) twice, yarn forward, sl.1, k. 2 tog., p.s.s.o., yarn forward; rep. from * ending (k. 2 tog., yarn forward) twice, k.1, (yarn forward, sl.1, k.1, p.s.s.o.) 3 times.
These 20 rows form the pattern.

218 *Open and Closed Diamonds*

No. 219 Open Diamonds 12 sts. plus 1

1st row: (wrong side) P. to end.

2nd row: K.1, *(yarn forward, sl.1, k.1, p.s.s.o.) twice, yarn forward, sl.1, k. 2 tog., p.s.s.o., yarn forward, (k. 2 tog., yarn forward) twice, k.1; rep. from * to end.

3rd row and foll. alt. rows: As 1st row.

4th row: K.1, *k.1, (yarn forward, sl.1, k.1, p.s.s.o.) twice, k.1, (k. 2 tog., yarn forward) twice, k.2; rep. from * to end.

6th row: As 2nd row.

8th row: As 4th row.

10th row: As 2nd row.

12th row: K. 2 tog., yarn forward, *(k. 2 tog., yarn forward) twice, k.1, (yarn forward, sl.1, k.1, p.s.s.o.) twice, yarn forward, sl.1, k. 2 tog., p.s.s.o., yarn forward; rep. from * to end, ending last rep., (k. 2 tog., yarn forward) twice, k.1, (yarn forward, sl.1, k.1, p.s.s.o.) 3 times.

14th row: K.1, (k. 2 tog., yarn forward) twice, k.3, (yarn forward, sl.1, k.1, p.s.s.o.) twice, k.1; rep. from * to end.

16th row: As 12th row.

18th row: As 14th row.

20th row: As 12th row.
These 20 rows form the pattern.

219 *Open Diamonds*

220 Falling Leaf Pattern

221 Midas Lace Pattern

No. 220 Falling Leaf Pattern 11 sts. plus 1

1st row: K. 2 tog.,* k.5, yarn forward, k.1, yarn forward, k.2, sl.1, k. 2 tog., p.s.s.o.; rep. from * ending last rep., sl.1, k.1, p.s.s.o. instead of sl.1, k. 2 tog., p.s.s.o.

2nd row and foll. alt. rows: P. to end.

3rd row: K. 2 tog., *k.4, yarn forward, k.3, yarn forward, k.1, sl.1, k. 2 tog., p.s.s.o.; rep. from * ending last rep., sl.1, k.1, p.s.s.o. instead of sl.1, k. 2 tog., p.s.s.o.

5th row: K. 2 tog., *k.3, yarn forward, k.5, yarn forward, sl.1, k. 2 tog., p.s.s.o.; rep. from * ending last rep., sl.1, k.1, p.s.s.o. instead of sl.1, k. 2 tog., p.s.s.o.

7th row: K. 2 tog., *k.2, yarn forward, k.1, yarn forward, k.5, sl.1, k. 2 tog., p.s.s.o.; rep. from * ending last rep., sl.1, k.1, p.s.s.o., instead of sl.1, k. 2 tog., p.s.s.o.

9th row: K. 2 tog., *k.1, yarn forward, k.3, yarn forward, k.4, sl.1, k. 2 tog., p.s.s.o.; rep. from * ending last rep., sl.1, k.1, p.s.s.o., instead of sl.1, k. 2 tog., p.s.s.o.

11th row: K. 2 tog., *yarn forward, k.5, yarn forward, k.3, sl.1, k. 2 tog., p.s.s.o.; rep. from * ending last rep., sl.1, k.1, p.s.s.o. instead of sl.1, k. 2 tog., p.s.s.o.

12th row: P. to end.

These 12 rows form the pattern.

No. 221 Midas Lace Pattern 16 sts. plus 2

1st row: K.1, *k.5, k. 2 tog., yarn round needle, k.2, yarn round needle, sl.1, k.1, p.s.s.o., k.5; rep. from * to last st., k.1.

2nd row: K.1, *p.4, p. 2 tog. t.b.l., yarn round needle, p.4, yarn round needle, p. 2 tog., p.4; rep. from * to last st., k.1.

3rd row: K.1, *k.3, k. 2 tog., yarn forward, k.6, yarn forward, sl.1, k.1, p.s.s.o., k.3; rep. from * to last st., k.1.

4th row: K.1, *p.2, p. 2 tog. t.b.l., yarn round needle, p.4, yarn round needle, p. 2 tog., p.2, yarn round needle, p. 2 tog., p.2; rep. from * to last st., k.1.

5th row: K.1, *k.1, k. 2 tog., yarn forward, k.5, yarn forward, sl.1, k.1, p.s.s.o., k.3, yarn forward, sl.1, k.1, p.s.s.o., k.1; rep. from * to last st., k.1.

6th row: K.1, *p. 2 tog. t.b.l., yarn round needle, p.6, yarn round needle, p. 2 tog., p.4, yarn round needle, p. 2 tog.; rep. from * to last st., k.1.

7th row: K.1, *sl. 1 purlwise, k.1, yarn forward, sl.1, k.1, p.s.s.o., k.4, yarn forward, sl.1, k.1, p.s.s.o., k.2, k.

2 tog., yarn forward, k.1, sl. 1 purlwise; rep. from * to last st., k.1.

8th row: K.1, p.3, *yarn round needle, p. 2 tog., p.3, yarn round needle, p. 2 tog., p.1, p. 2 tog. t.b.l., yarn round needle, p.2, k. through front strand of second st. on left hand needle having right hand needle behind the left, then k. the first st. in the usual way and slip both loops off needle together, p.2; rep. from * ending last rep., yarn round needle, p.3, k.1.

9th row: K.1, *yarn forward, sl.1, k.1, p.s.s.o., k.2, yarn forward, sl.1, k.1, p.s.s.o., k.4, k. 2 tog., yarn forward, k.4; rep. from * to last st., k.1.

10th row: K.1, *yarn round needle, p. 2 tog., p.3, yarn round needle, p. 2 tog., p.2, p. 2 tog. t.b.l., yarn round needle, p.5; rep. from * to last st., k.1.

11th row: K.1, *yarn forward, sl.1, k.1, p.s.s.o., k.4, yarn forward, sl.1, k.1, p.s.s.o., k. 2 tog., yarn forward, k.6; rep. from * to last st., k.1.

12th row: K.1, *yarn round needle, p. 2 tog., p.2, p. 2 tog. t.b.l., yarn round needle, p.1, sl. 2 purlwise, p.1, yarn round needle, p. 2 tog., p.4; rep. from * to last st., k.1.

13th row: K.1, *yarn forward, sl.1, k.1, p.s.s.o., k.1, k. 2 tog., yarn forward, k.2, k. the second st. on left hand needle, then k. the first st. and slip both loops off needle together, k.2, yarn forward, sl.1, k.1, p.s.s.o., k.3; rep. from * to last st., k.1.

14th row: K.1, *p.2, p. 2 tog. t.b.l., yarn round needle, p.4, yarn round needle, p. 2 tog., p.2, yarn round needle, p. 2 tog., p.2; rep. from * to last st., k.1.

The 5th to 14th rows form the pattern.

No. 222 Renaissance Lace 9 sts. plus 4

1st row: K.1, *k.2, yarn forward, k.1, yarn forward, k.2, k. 2 tog. t.b.l., k. 2 tog.; rep. from * to last 3 sts., k.3.

2nd row and foll. alt. rows: P. to end.

3rd, 5th, 7th and 9th rows: As 1st row.

11th row: K.1, *k.2, k. 2 tog. t.b.l., k. 2 tog., k.2, yarn forward, k.1, yarn forward; rep. from * to last 3 sts., k.3.

13th, 15th, 17th and 19th rows: As 11th row.

20th row: As 2nd row.

These 20 rows form the pattern.

222 Renaissance Lace

223 Beaumont Lace

No. 223 Beaumont Lace 10 sts. plus 1

1st row: K.1, *k. 2 tog., k.2, yarn forward, k.1, yarn forward, k.2, k. 2 tog. t.b.l., k.; rep. from * to end.
2nd row and foll. alt. rows: P. to end.
3rd row: K.1, *k. 2 tog., k.1, yarn forward, k.3, yarn forward, k.1, k. 2 tog. t.b.l., k.1; rep. from * to end.
5th row: K.1, *k. 2 tog., yarn forward, k.5, yarn forward, k. 2 tog. t.b.l., k.1; rep. from * to end.
7th row: K.1, *yarn forward, k.2, k. 2 tog. t.b.l., k.1, k. 2 tog., k.2, yarn forward, k.1; rep. from * to end.
9th row: K.1, *k.1, yarn forward, k.1, k. 2 tog. t.b.l., k.1, k. 2 tog., k.1, yarn forward, k.2; rep. from * to end.
11th row: K.1, *k.2, yarn forward, k. 2 tog. t.b.l., k.1, k. 2 tog., yarn forward, k.3; rep. from * to end.
12th row: As 2nd row.
These 12 rows form the pattern.

224 Petit Choux Pattern

No. 224 Petit Choux Pattern 12 sts. plus 2

1st row: K.1, *sl.1, k.1, p.s.s.o., k.3, yarn round needle, p.2, yarn over needle, k.3, k. 2 tog.; rep. from * to last st., k.1.
2nd row: K.1, *p. 2 tog., p.2, yarn over needle, k.4, yarn round needle, p.2, p. 2 tog. t.b.l.; rep. from * to last st., k.1.
3rd row: K.1, *sl.1, k.1, p.s.s.o., k.1, yarn round needle, p.6, yarn over needle, k.1, k. 2 tog.; rep. from * to last st., k.1.
4th row: K.1, *p. 2 tog., yarn over needle, k.8, yarn round needle, p. 2 tog. t.b.l.; rep. from * to last st., k.1.
5th row: K.1, *p.1, yarn over needle, k.3, k. 2 tog., sl.1, k.1, p.s.s.o., k.3, yarn round needle, p.1; rep. from * to last st., k.1.
6th row: K.1, *k.2, yarn round needle, p.2, p. 2 tog. t.b.l., p. 2 tog., p.2, yarn over needle, k.2; rep. from * to last st., k.1.
7th row: K.1, *p.3, yarn over needle, k.1, k. 2 tog., sl.1, k.1, p.s.s.o., k.1, yarn round needle, p.3; rep. from * to last st., k.1.
8th row: K.1, *k.4, yarn round needle, p. 2 tog. t.b.l., p. 2 tog., yarn over needle, k.4; rep. from * to last st., k.1.
These 8 rows form the pattern.

No. 225 Petit Choux Pattern reversed 12 sts. plus 2
The reverse side of No. 224 is also very attractive and
serves as a useful lightweight all-over pattern in the
same way. It is worked to the same instructions but
using the odd numbered rows as the wrong side.

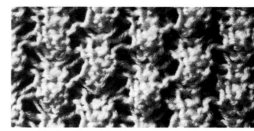

225 Petit Choux Pattern reversed

No. 226 Larch Leaf Pattern 11 sts. plus 2
1st row: K.1, *k. 2 tog., k.3, yarn forward, k.1, yarn
forward, k.3, sl.1, k.1, p.s.s.o.; rep. from * to last st.,
k.1.
2nd row and foll. alt. rows: P. to end.
3rd and 5th rows: As 1st row.
7th row: K.1, *k. 2 tog., k.2, yarn forward, k.3, yarn
forward, k.2, sl.1, k.1, p.s.s.o.; rep. from * to last st.,
k.1.
9th row: K.1, *k. 2 tog., k.1, yarn over needle, k.5, yarn
forward, k.1, sl.1, k.1, p.s.s.o.; rep. from * to last st.,
k.1.
11th and 13th rows: K.1, *k. 2 tog., yarn forward, k.1, k.
2 tog., yarn forward, k.1, yarn forward, sl.1, k.1,
p.s.s.o., k.1, yarn forward, sl.1, k.1, p.s.s.o.; rep. from *
to last st., k.1.
15th row: K.1, *k. 2 tog., k.1, yarn forward, k.5, yarn
forward, k.1, sl.1, k.1, p.s.s.o.; rep. from * to last st.,
k.1.
17th row: K.1, *k. 2 tog., k.2, yarn forward, k.3, yarn
forward, k.2, sl.1, k.1, p.s.s.o.; rep. from * to last st.,
k.1.
18th row: As 2nd row.
These 18 rows form the pattern.

226 Larch Leaf Pattern

No. 227 Dominic's Pattern 8 sts. plus 4
1st row: *P.4, yarn over needle, k.1, p.2, k.1; rep. from *
to last 4 sts., p.4.
2nd row: P.4, *yarn round needle, p.2, k.2, p.2, yarn
round needle, p.4; rep. from * to end.
3rd row: *P.4, yarn over needle, k.3, p.2, k.3, yarn
forward; rep. from * to last 4 sts., p.4.
4th row: P.4, *yarn round needle, p.4, k.2, p.4, yarn
round needle, p.4; rep. from * to end.
5th row: *P.4, k.5, p.2, k.5; rep. from * to last 4 sts.,
p.4.
6th row: P.4, *p.5, k.2, p.9; rep. from * to end.

227 Dominic's Pattern

7th row: *P.4, sl.1, k.1, p.s.s.o., k.3, p.2, k.3, p. 2 tog.; rep. from * to last 4 sts., p.4.

8th row: P.4, *p. 2 tog., p.2, k.2, p.2, p. 2 tog. t.b.l., p.4; rep. from * to end.

9th row: *P.4, sl.1, k.1, p.s.s.o., k.1, p.2, k.1, k. 2 tog.; rep. from * to last 4 sts., p.4.

10th row: P.4, *p. 2 tog., k.2, p. 2 tog. t.b.l., p.4; rep. from * to end.

These 10 rows form the pattern.

FOUR

RAISED SURFACE TEXTURE PATTERNS

There are many patterns that do not fit into any definite category but do not deserve the term 'miscellaneous'. A pattern does not need to be covered with eyelet holes or cables to have a distinctive appeal; indeed, like other artistic ventures, it may be what is left out rather than what is put in that may lift the finished work out of the ordinary.

The patterns in this section are suitable for garments for everyday wear and are simple to substitute for stocking stitch on classical garments. Most of them are well within the scope of the beginner but even the most experienced knitter should also work a practice sample to attain the working tension in the yarn to be used.

An interesting variation in the patterned sweater may be made by working a set number of centimetres (inches) in one pattern, working a break line of, say, two garter stitch ridges then working the same number of centimetres (inches) in a completely contrasting pattern. The two patterns may alternate to the shoulders or a different pattern may be chosen after each break line. A very ambitious knitter could work out a design using two, or even three, patterns concurrently across the rows to form a patchwork effect. These designs look most impressive when worked in one colour only, since the textural difference may be more easily compared when the eye is not distracted by colour.

No. 228 Links Pattern 12 sts. plus 13
1st row: K. to end.
2nd row: P. to end.
3rd row: K.4, *p.5, k.7; rep. from * to last 9 sts., p.5, k.4.

228 Links Pattern

4th row: P.3, *k.7, p.5; rep. from * to last 10 sts., k.7, p.3.

5th row: K.2, *p.9, k.3; rep. from * to last 11 sts., p.9, k.2.

6th row: K.3, *p.7, k.5; rep. from * to last 10 sts., p.7, k.3.

7th row: P.2, *k.9, p.3; rep. from * to last 11 sts., k.9, p.2.

8th to 11th rows: Work from 6th to 3rd rows in backward rotation.

12th row: P. to end.

13th to 20th rows: K. to end.

These 20 rows form the pattern.

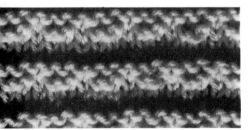

229 Shingle Pattern

230 Trinity Pattern Variation

231 Purl Honeycomb Pattern

No. 229 Shingle Pattern 3 sts. plus 2

1st row: K. to end.

2nd row: As 1st row.

3rd row: K.2, *k. next st. one row below st. on needle letting the st. drop off the left hand needle in the usual way, k.2; rep. from * to end.

4th and 5th rows: K. to end.

6th row: P. to end.

These 6 rows form the pattern.

No. 230 Trinity Pattern Variation 3 sts. plus 2

1st row: K. to end.

2nd row: K. to end.

3rd row: K.1, *(k.1, p.1, k.1) all into next 3 sts. tog. thus making 3 sts. out of 1 st.; rep. from * to last st., k.1.

4th row: P. to end.

These 4 rows form the pattern.

No. 231 Purl Honeycomb Pattern 4 sts. plus 3

1st row: P. to end.

2nd row and foll. alt. rows: K. to end.

3rd row: P.3, *insert point of right hand needle through centre of st. 2 rows below next st. and k.1 gathering the loops together, p.3; rep. from * to end.

5th row: P. to end.

7th row: P.1, *k. a st. through 2 rows below as on 3rd row, p.3; rep. from * ending last rep., p.1 instead of p.3.

8th row: K. to end.

These 8 rows form the pattern.

No. 232 Spot Pattern 4 sts. plus 3
1st row: K. to end.
2nd row: *K.3, (k.1, p.1, k.1) all in next st.; rep. from *
to last 3 sts., k.3.
3rd row: K. to end.
4th row: *K.3, p. 3 tog.; rep. from * to last 3 sts., k.3.
These 4 rows form the pattern.

232 Spot Pattern

No. 233 Cottontail Pattern 5 sts. plus 2
1st row: (wrong side) *K.2, p.3; rep. from * to last 2
sts., k.2.
2nd row: *P.2, k.3 then pass the first 2 of these 3 sts.
over the 3rd, slip remaining st. back on to left hand
needle and k. in front, back and front again of the same
st.; rep. from * to last 2 sts., p.2.
These 2 rows form the pattern.

233 Cottontail Pattern

No. 234 Noisette Pattern 4 sts. plus 1
1st row: P.2, *(k.1, p.1, k.1) all in next st., p.3; rep. from
* ending last rep., p.2 instead of p.3.
2nd row and foll. alt. rows: P. to end.
3rd row: P.2, *k.3, p.3; rep. from * ending last rep., p.2
instead of p.3.
5th row: As 3rd row.
7th row: P.2, *k. 3 tog. t.b.l., p.3; rep. from * ending
last rep., p.2 instead of p.3.
9th and 11th rows: K. to end.
12th row: As 2nd row.
These 12 rows form the pattern.

234 Noisette Pattern

No. 235 Triple Cluster Pattern 14 sts. plus 2
1st row: K.1, *p.2, k. 3 t.b.l., p.4, k. 3 t.b.l., p.2; rep.
from * to last st., k.1.
2nd row: K.1, *k.2, p. 2 t.b.l., k.4, p. 3 t.b.l., k.2; rep.
from * to last st., k.1.
3rd row: K.1, *p.2, k. 3 t.b.l., p.4, yarn over needle, sl.1,
k. 2 tog., p.s.s.o., yarn round needle, p.2; rep. from * to
last st., k.1.
4th row: K.1, *k.2, p.1, p. 1 t.b.l., p.1, k.4, p. 3 t.b.l.,
k.2; rep. from * to last st., k.1.
5th row: As 1st row.
6th row: As 2nd row.
7th row: K.1, *p.2, yarn round needle, sl.1, k. 2 tog.,
p.s.s.o., yarn round needle, p.4, k. 3 t.b.l., p.2; rep.
from * to last st., k.1.

235 Triple Cluster Pattern

8th row: K.1, *k. 2, p. 3 t.b.l., k.4, p.1, p. 1 t.b.l., p.1, k.2; rep. from * to last st., k.1.
These 8 rows form the pattern.

No. 236 Filbert Pattern 6 sts. plus 9

1st row: K.1, k. 2 tog., yarn forward, k.3, *yarn forward, sl.1, k. 2 tog., p.s.s.o., yarn forward, k.3; rep. from * ending last rep., yarn forward, k. 2 tog. t.b.l., k.1.
2nd row: K.2, k. 1 t.b.l., *p.3, k. 1 t.b.l., k.1, k. 1 t.b.l.; rep. from * ending p.3, k. 1 t.b.l., k.2.
3rd row: P.3, *k.3, p.3; rep. from * to end.
4th row: K.3, *p.3, k.3; rep. from * to end.
5th and 6th rows: Rep. 3rd and 4th rows.
7th row: K.3, *yarn forward, sl.1, k. 2 tog., p.s.s.o., yarn forward, k.3; rep. from * to end.
8th row: P.3, *k. 1 t.b.l., k.1, k. 1 t.b.l., p.3; rep. from * to end.
9th row: K.3, *p.3, k.3; rep. from * to end.
10th row: P.3, *k.3, p.3; rep. from * to end.
11th and 12th rows: Rep. 9th and 10th rows.
These 12 rows form the pattern.

236 Filbert Pattern

No. 237 Felindre Pattern 6 sts. plus 3

1st row: K.1, *k.4, p.2; rep. from * to last 2 sts., k.2.
2nd row: P.2, *k.2, p.4; rep. from * to last st., p.1.
3rd and 4th rows: Rep. 1st and 2nd rows once more.
5th row: K.1, *insert right hand needle point between 4th and 5th sts. on left hand needle, yarn round needle and draw loop through to front, then k.1, p.2, k.3; rep. from * to last 2 sts., k.2.
6th row: P.2, *p.3, k.2, p. 2 tog.; rep. from * to last st., p.1.
7th row: K.2, *p.2, k.4; rep. from * to last st., k.1.
8th row: P.1, *p.4, k.2; rep. from * to last 2 sts., p.2.
9th and 10th rows: Rep. 7th and 8th rows once more.
11th row: K.4, rep. from * of 5th row to end, ending last rep., k.2 instead of k.3.
12th row: *P.2, k.2, p. 2 tog., p.1; rep. from * to last 3 sts., p.3.
These 12 rows form the pattern.

237 Felindre Pattern

No. 238   Peal of Bells Pattern 6 sts. plus 5

1st row: *P.2, k.1, p.2, yarn over needle, k.1, yarn round needle; rep. from * to last 5 sts., p.2, k.1, p.2.

2nd row: *K.2, p.1, k.2, p.3; rep. from * to last 5 sts., k.2, p.1, k.2.

3rd row: *P.2, k.1, p.2, k.3; rep. from * to last 5 sts., p.2, k.1, p.2.

4th and 5th rows: Rep. 2nd and 3rd rows once more.

6th row: *K.2, p.1, k.2, p. 3 tog.; rep. from * to last 5 sts., k.2, p.1, k.2.

7th row: *P.2, yarn over needle, k.1, yarn round needle, p.2, k.1; rep. from * omitting k.1 at end of last repeat.

8th row: *K.2, p.3, k.2, p.1; rep. from * to end, omitting p.1 at end of last repeat.

9th row: *P.2, k.3, p.2, k.1; rep. from * to end, omitting k.1 at end of last repeat.

10th and 11th rows: Rep. 8th and 9th rows once more.

12th row: *K.2, p. 3 tog., k.2, p.1; rep. from * to end, omitting p.1 at end of last repeat.

These 12 rows form the pattern.

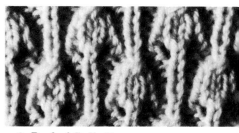

238 Peal of Bells Pattern

No. 239   Embossed Pattern 10 sts. plus 6

Tw. 2 K., twist 2 knit thus: k. in back of second st. on left hand needle, then in first st. and slip both loops off together.

Tw. 2 P., twist 2 purl thus: p. in front of second st. on left hand needle, then in first st. and slip both loops off together.

1st row: K.1, *k.4, p.2, Tw. 2 K., p.2; rep. from * to last 5 sts., k.5.

2nd row: K.1, p.4, *k.2, Tw. 2 P., k.2, p.4; rep. from * to last st., k.1.

3rd to 6th rows: Rep. 1st and 2nd rows twice more.

7th row: K.1, *p.1, Tw. 2 K., p.2, k.4; rep. from * to last 5 sts., p.1, Tw. 2 K., p.1, k.1.

8th row: K.1, p.1, Tw. 2 P., k.1, *k.1, p.4, k.2, Tw. 2 P., k.1; rep. from * to last st., k.1.

9th to 12th rows: Rep. 7th and 8th rows twice more.

These 12 rows form the pattern.

239 Embossed Pattern

240 Mock Cable Pattern

No. 240   Mock Cable Pattern 6 sts.
1st row: *P.1, k.4, p.1; rep. from * to end.
2nd row: *K.1, p.4, k.1; rep. from * to end.
3rd row: As 1st row.
4th row: *K.1, p.1, slip 2, p.1, k.1; rep. from * to end.
5th row: *P.1, k. second st. on left hand needle then k. first st. and slip both loops off together, k. in back of second st. on left hand needle then k. first st. and slip both loops off together, p.1; rep. from * to end.
6th to 9th rows: Rep. 4th and 5th rows twice more.
10th row: As 2nd row.
These 10 rows form the pattern.

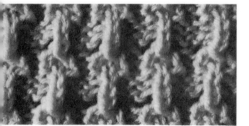

241 Anchor Ridges

No. 241   Anchor Ridges 6 sts. plus 5
1st row: K. to end.
2nd row: P. to end.
3rd and 4th rows: Rep. 1st and 2nd rows.
5th row: P.5, *yarn round needle, k.1, yarn round needle, p.5; rep. from * to end.
6th row: K.5, *p.3, k.5; rep. from * to end.
7th row: P.5, *k.3, p.5; rep. from * to end.
8th row: K.5, *p. 3 tog., k.5; rep. from * to end.
These 8 rows form the pattern.

242 Torch Pattern

No. 242   Torch Pattern 4 sts. plus 9
1st row: (right side) K.4, *p.1, k.3; rep. from * ending last rep., k.4 instead of k.3.
2nd row: K.5, *p.3, k.1; rep. from * to last 4 sts., k.4.
3rd row: K.4, *p.1, yarn over needle, sl.1, k. 2 tog., p.s.s.o., yarn round needle; rep. from * to last 5 sts., p.1, k.4.
4th row: K.6, *p.1, k.3; rep. from * to last 3 sts., k.3.
5th row: K.4, *p.2, k.1, p.1; rep. from * to last 5 sts., p.1, k.4.
6th row: K.6, *p.1, k.3; rep. from * to last 3 sts., k.3.
These 6 rows form the pattern.

243 Candytwist Pattern

No. 243   Candytwist Pattern 4 sts., plus 2
1st row: *P.2, k.2; rep. from * to last 2 sts., p.2.
2nd row: K.2, *p. 2 tog., pick up and k. in front of loop between sts., k.2; rep. from * to end.
3rd row: As 1st row.
4th row: K.2, *pick up and k. in front of loop between sts., p. 2 tog., k.2; rep. from * to end.
These 4 rows form the pattern.

No. 244 Miniature Smock Pattern 4 sts. plus 1

1st row: (wrong side) *P.1, yarn back, sl.3; rep. from * to last st., p.1.
2nd row: *Sl.1, k.3; rep. from * to last st., sl.1.
3rd row: P. to end.
4th row: K.2, *pick up loop made in 1st row and k. it tog. with next st., k.3; rep. from * ending k.2 instead of k.3.
5th row: P.2, *p.1, yarn back, sl.3; rep. from * ending p.3.
6th row: K.2, *sl.1, k.3; rep. from * ending sl.1, k.2.
7th row: P. to end.
8th row: K.4, *pick up loop made in 5th row and k. it tog. with next st., k.3; rep. from * ending k.4 instead of k.3.
These 8 rows form the pattern.

244 Miniature Smock Pattern

No. 245 Tuck Stitch Pattern 4 sts.

1st row: K. to end.
2nd row: (wrong side) P. to end.
3rd row: K.3, *yarn forward, sl.1, k.3, pass the slipped st. over the k.3; rep. from * to last st., k.1.
4th row: K.1, *k.1 winding yarn twice round needle; rep. from * to last st., k.1.
5th row: K. to end dropping extra loops.
6th row: P. to end.
7th row: K.1, *sl.1, k.3, pass the slipped st. over the k.3, yarn forward; rep. from * to last 3 sts., k.3.
8th row: As 4th row.
9th row: As 5th row.
The 2nd to 9th rows form the pattern.

245 Tuck Stitch Pattern

No. 246 Bell Pattern Beginning with 13 sts. plus 3 but decreases to 4 plus 3.
The fullness of this pattern requires a generous number of stitches at the cast on row. Remember that for every 4 sts. needed for your correct tension you will need to cast on an extra 9 sts.
1st row: P.3, *k.10, p.3; rep. from * to end.
2nd row: K.3, *p.10, k.3; rep. from * to end.
3rd row: P.3, *k. 2 tog., k.6, k. 2 tog., p.3; rep. from * to end.
4th row: K.3, *p.8, k.3; rep. from * to end.
5th row: P.3, *k. 2 tog., k.4, k. 2 tog., p.3; rep. from * to end.
6th row: K.3, *p.6, k.3; rep. from * to end.

246 Bell Pattern

7th row: P.3, *k. 2 tog., k.2, k. 2 tog., p.3; rep. from * to end.

8th row: K.3, *p.4, k.3; rep. from * to end.

9th row: P.3, *(k. 2 tog.) twice, p.3; rep. from * to end.

10th row: K.3, *p. 2, k.3; rep. from * to end.

11th row: P.3, *k. 2 tog., p.3; rep. from * to end.

12th row: K.3, *p.1, k.3; rep. from * to end.

13th row: *P.2, p. 2 tog.; rep. from * to last 3 sts., p.3.

14th row: K. to end.

This completes the bell shapes.

15th row: K.3, *cast on 10 sts., k.3; rep. from * to end.

The 2nd to 15th rows will continue this pattern.

247 Punnet Weave

No. 247 Punnet Weave 6 sts. plus 4

1st row: K. to end.

2nd row: P. to end.

3rd row: K. to end.

4th row: K.4, *p.2, k.4; rep. from * to end.

5th to 10th rows: Rep. 3rd and 4th rows 3 times.

11th row: K. to end.

12th row: P. to end.

13th row: K. to end.

14th row: K.1, p.2, *k.4, p.2; rep. from * to last st., k.1.

15th to 20th rows: Rep. 13th and 14th rows 3 times.

These 20 rows form the pattern.

248 Mosaic Pattern

No. 248 Mosaic Pattern 20 sts.

1st row: *P.2, k.2, p.2, k.2, p.2, k.10; rep. from * to end.

2nd row and foll. alt. rows: K. the k. sts. and p. the p. sts. as they present themselves.

3rd row: *P.2, k.2, p.2, k.2, p.12; rep. from * to end.

5th row: As 1st row.

7th row: As 3rd row.

9th row: As 1st row.

11th row: *k.10, p.2, k.2, p.2, k.2, p.2; rep. from * to end.

13th row: *P.12, k.2, p.2, k.2, p.2; rep. from * to end.

15th row: As 11th row.

17th row: As 13th row.

19th row: As 11th row.

20th row: As 2nd row.

These 20 rows form the pattern.

No. 249   Lattice Squares 8 sts.

1st row: K. to end.

2nd row: P.7, *k.2, p.6; rep. from * to last st., p.1.

3rd row to 8th rows: Rep. 1st and 2nd rows 3 times more.

9th row: K.6, *sl. 1 knitwise, k.2, sl. 1 knitwise, k.4; rep. from * to last 2 sts., k.2.

10th row: K.6, *yarn forward, sl. 1 purlwise, yarn back, k.2, yarn forward, sl. 1 purlwise, yarn back, k.4; rep. from * to last 2 sts., k.2.

11th row: As 9th row.

12th row: As 10th row.

13th row: K.6, *sl. next 3 sts. to back on cable needle, k.1, then place the sl. st. from cable needle back on to left hand needle, k. next 2 sts. from cable needle, k.5; rep. from * to last 2 sts., k.2.

14th row: As 2nd row.

These 14 rows form the pattern.

249 *Lattice Squares*

No. 250   Ridged Chevrons 16 sts. plus 2

1st row: K.1, *k. 2 tog., k.5, k. twice in each of next 2 sts., k.5, k. 2 tog.; rep. from * to last st., k.1.

2nd row: P. to end.

3rd to 8th rows: Rep. 1st and 2nd rows 3 times more.

9th row: As 1st row.

10th row: K. to end.

These 10 rows form the pattern.

250 *Ridged Chevrons*

No. 251   Close Chevron Pattern 14 sts. plus 1

1st row: K.1, *inc. 1 by picking up loop between sts. and knitting in back of it, k.5, sl.1, k. 2 tog., p.s.s.o., k.5, inc. 1 between sts. as before, k.1; rep. from * to end.

2nd row: P.1, *inc. 1 by picking up loop between sts. and purling in back of it, p.5, p. 3 tog., p.5, inc. 1 between sts. as before, p.1; rep. from * to end.

These 2 rows form the pattern.

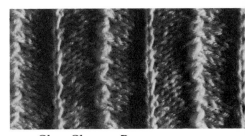

251 *Close Chevron Pattern*

No. 252   Clematis Pattern 6 sts. plus 1

1st row: P.1, *k. 2 tog., yarn forward, k.1, yarn forward, sl.1, k.1, p.s.s.o., p.1; rep. from * to end.

2nd row: K.1, *p.5, k.1; rep. from * to end.

3rd row: P.1, *k.5, p.1; rep. from * to end.

4th row: As 2nd row.

5th row: K.1, *yarn forward, sl.1, k.1, p.s.s.o., p.1, k. 2 tog., yarn forward, k.1; rep. from * to end.

6th row: P.1, *p.2, k.1, p.3; rep. from * to end.

252 *Clematis Pattern*

7th row: K.1, *k.2, p.1, k.3; rep. from * to end.
8th row: As 6th row.
These 8 rows form the pattern.

No. 253 Raised Medallions 8 sts. plus 2

1st row: K.1, p.3, *k.2, p.6; rep. from * ending last rep., p.3, k.1 instead of p.6.
2nd row: (wrong side) K.4, p.2, *k.6, p.2; rep. from * ending last rep., k.4.
3rd and 4th rows: Rep. 1st and 2nd rows.
5th row: K.1, p.2, *k. 2 tog., yarn forward, sl.1, k.1, p.s.s.o., p.4; rep. from * ending last rep., p.2, k.1 instead of p.4.
6th row: K.3, *p.1, k. in front and back of next st., p.1, k.4; rep. from * ending last rep., k.3 instead of k.4.
7th row: K.1, p.1, *k. 2 tog., yarn forward, k.2, yarn forward, sl.1, k.1, p.s.s.o., p.2; rep. from * to end, ending p.1, k.1 instead of p.2.
8th row: K.2, *p.6, k.2; rep. from * to end.
9th row: K.1, *(k. 2 tog., yarn forward) twice, sl.1, k.1, p.s.s.o., yarn forward, sl.1, k.1, p.s.s.o.; rep. from * to last st., k.1.
10th row: K.1, p.3, *k. in front and back of next st., p.6; rep. from * ending last rep., p.3, k.1 instead of p.6.
11th row: K.1, *(yarn forward, sl.1, k.1, p.s.s.o.) twice, k. 2 tog., yarn forward, k. 2 tog.; rep. from * to last st., yarn forward, k.1.
12th row: K.1, k. 1 t.b.l., p.6, *k. in front and back of next st., p.6; rep. from * to last 2 sts., k. 1 t.b.l., k.1.
13th row: K.1, p.1, *yarn forward, sl.1, k. 2 tog., p.s.s.o., yarn forward, k. 3 tog., yarn round needle, p.2; rep. from * ending p.1, k.1 instead of p.2.
14th row: K.2, *k. 1 t.b.l., p.1, k. in front and back of next st., p.1, k. 1 t.b.l., k.2; rep. from * to end.
15th row: K.1, p.2, *yarn forward, sl.1, k.1, p.s.s.o., k. 2 tog., yarn round needle, p.4; rep. from * ending last rep., p.2, k.1, instead of p.4.
16th row: K.3, *k. 1 t.b.l., p.2, k. 1 t.b.l., k.4; rep. from * ending last rep., k.3 instead of k.4.
The 3rd to 16th rows form the pattern.

253 Raised Medallions

No. 254 Coronet Pattern 13 sts. plus 2

1st row: (right side) P. to end.

2nd row: K. to end.

3rd row: K.1, p.6, *(p.1, k.1, p.1, k.1, p.1, k.1) all in next st., p.12; rep. from * ending last rep., p.6, k.1, instead of p.12.

4th row: K.7, *p.6, k.12; rep. from * ending last rep., k.7 instead of k.12.

5th row: K.1, p.6, *k.6, p.12; rep. from * ending last rep., p.6, k.1 instead of p.12.

6th row: As 4th row.

7th row: K.1, (p. 2 tog.) twice, p.2, *k.2, yarn forward, k.2, yarn forward, k.2, p.2, (p. 2 tog.) 4 times, p.2; rep. from * ending last rep., (p. 2 tog.) twice, k.1.

8th row: K.5, *p.8, k.8; rep. from * ending last rep., k.5 instead of k.8.

9th row: K.1, (p. 2 tog.) twice, *(k. 2 tog., yarn forward, k.1, yarn forward) twice, k. 2 tog., (p. 2 tog.) 4 times; rep. from * ending last rep., (p. 2 tog.) twice, k.1.

10th row: K.3, *p.9, k.4; rep. from * ending last rep., k.3 instead of k.4.

These 10 rows form the pattern.

254 Coronet Pattern

No. 255 Embossed Leaves 7 sts. plus 6

1st row: P.6, *yarn forward, k.1, yarn round needle, p.6; rep. from * to end.

2nd row: K.6, *p.3, k.6; rep. from * to end.

3rd row: P.6, *k.1, yarn forward, k.1, yarn forward, k.1, p.6; rep. from * to end.

4th row: K.6, *p.5, k.6; rep. from * to end.

5th row: P.6, *k.2, yarn forward, k.1, yarn forward, k.2, p.6; rep. from * to end.

6th row: K.6, *p.7, k.6; rep. from * to end.

7th row: P.6, *k.3, yarn forward, k.1, yarn forward, k.3, p.6; rep. from * to end.

8th row: K.6, *p.9, k.6; rep. from * to end.

9th row: P.6, *sl.1, k.1, p.s.s.o., k.5, k. 2 tog., p.6; rep. from * to end.

10th row: As 6th row.

11th row: P.6, *sl.1, k.1, p.s.s.o., k.3, k. 2 tog., p.6; rep. from * to end.

12th row: As 4th row.

13th row: P.6, *sl.1, k.1, p.s.s.o., k.1, k. 2 tog., p.6; rep. from * to end.

14th row: As 2nd row.

15th row: P.6, *sl.1, k. 2 tog., p.s.s.o., p.6; rep. from * to end.

255 Embossed Leaves

16th row: K. to end.
17th row: P. to end.
18th and 19th rows: Rep. 16th and 17th rows.
20th row: P. to end.
These 20 rows form the pattern.

256 Waves and Shells Pattern

No. 256 Waves and Shells Pattern 14 sts. plus 3
1st row: K.1, p. 2 tog., *p.3, k.2, yarn forward, k.1, yarn forward, k.2, p.3, p. 3 tog.; rep. from * ending last rep., p. 2 tog., k.1. instead of p. 3 tog.
2nd row: K. the k. sts. and p. the p. sts. as they present themselves.
3rd row: K.1, p. 2 tog., *p.2, k.2, yarn forward, k.3, yarn forward, k.2, p.2, p. 3 tog.; rep. from * ending last rep., p. 2 tog., k.1 instead of p. 3 tog.
4th row: As 2nd row.
5th row: K.1, p. 2 tog., *p.1, k.2, yarn forward, k.5, yarn forward, k.2, p.1, p. 3 tog.; rep. from * ending last rep., p. 2 tog., k.1 instead of p. 3 tog.
6th row: As 2nd row.
7th row: K.1, p. 2 tog., *k.2, yarn forward, k.7, yarn forward, k.2, p. 3 tog.; rep. from * ending last rep., p. 2 tog., k.1, instead of p. 3 tog.
8th row: P. to end.
9th row: K.2, *yarn forward, k.2, p.3, p. 3 tog., p.3, k.2, yarn forward, k.1; rep. from * ending last rep., k.2 instead of k.1.
10th row: As 2nd row.
11th row: K.3, *yarn forward, k.2, p.2, p. 3 tog., p.2, k.2, yarn forward, k.3; rep. from * to end.
12th row: As 10th row.
13th row: K.4, *yarn forward, k.2, p.1, p. 3 tog., p.1, k.2, yarn forward, k.5; rep. from * ending last rep., k.4 instead of k.5.
14th row: As 10th row.
15th row: K.5, *yarn forward, k.2, p. 3 tog., k.2, yarn forward, k.7; rep. from * ending k.5 instead of k.7.
16th row: P. to end.
These 16 rows form the pattern.

No. 257 Bobble and Cross Stitch Pattern 12 sts. plus 1

Cr. 2, cross 2 sts. thus: miss next st. on left hand needle, k. in front of second st., k. the missed st. and slip both loops off together.

M.B., make bobble thus: (k.1, p.1, k.1, p.1, k.1) all in next st., then pass the first 4 of these sts. over the 5th.

1st row: P.1, *Cr. 2, p.3, M.B., p.3, Cr. 2, p.1; rep. from * to end.

2nd row and foll. alt. rows: K.1, *p.2, k.7, p.2, k.1; rep. from * to end.

3rd row: P.1, *Cr. 2, p.2, M.B., p.1, M.B., p.2, Cr.2, p.1; rep. from * to end.

5th row: P.1, *Cr. 2, p.1, (M.B., p.1) 3 times, Cr. 2, p.1; rep., from * to end.

7th row: As 3rd row.

9th row: As 1st row.

10th row: As 2nd row.

The 3rd to 10th rows form the pattern.

257 Bobble and Cross Stitch Pattern

No. 258 Bobble and Diagonal Pattern 8 sts. plus 7

M.B., make bobble thus: On first bobble row, (k.1, p.1, k.1, p.1, k.1) all in next st.; on following row, slip the next 4 sts. purlwise, k.1, then slip the 4 sl. sts. over the k.1.

1st row: (right side) *K.7, p.1; rep. from * to last 7 sts., k.7.

2nd row and foll. alt. rows: P. to end.

3rd row: *P.1, k.7; rep. from * to last 7 sts., p.1, k.6.

5th row: K.1, *p.1, k.7; rep. from * to last 6 sts., p.1, k.5.

7th row: K.2, *p.1, k.3, M.B., k.3; rep. from * to last 5 sts., p.1, k.4.

9th row: K.3, *p.1, k.2, complete M.B., k.4; rep. from * to last 4 sts., p.1, k.3.

11th row: K.4, *p.1, k.7; rep. from * to last 3 sts., p.1, k.2.

13th row: K.5, *p.1, k.7; rep. from * to last 2 sts., p.1, k.1.

15th row: K.6, *p.1, k.3, M.B., k.3; rep. from * to last st., p.1.

17th row: K.7, *p.1, k.2; complete M.B., k.4; rep. from * to end.

The 2nd to 17th rows form the pattern.

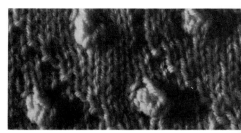

258 Bobble and Diagonal Pattern

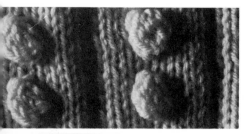

259 Bobble Strip Pattern

No. 259 Bobble Strip Pattern 10 sts. plus 2
M.B., make bobble thus: k. in front, back, front, back,
front of next st., k. the following st., turn and p.5, turn
and k.5, turn and p.5, turn and slip the 2nd, 3rd and
4th and 5th sts. over 1st st., k. in back of bobble st.
1st row: P.2, *k.8, p.2; rep. from * to end.
2nd row: K.2, *p.8, k.2; rep. from * to end.
3rd and 4th rows: Rep. 1st and 2nd rows.
5th row: P.2, *k.3, M.B., k.3, p.2; rep. from * to end.
6th row: As 2nd row.
7th to 10th rows: As 1st to 4th rows.
The 5th to 10th rows form the pattern.

260 Bobble Rib Pattern

No. 260 Bobble Rib Pattern 6 sts. plus 3
M.B., make bobble thus: k. in front, back, front, back of
next st., turn, p.4, turn, k.4, turn, (p. 2 tog.) twice, turn,
slip second st. over the first then slip bobble st. back on
to right hand needle.
1st row: (right side) K.3, *p.3, k.3; rep. from * to end.
2nd row: P.3, *k.3, p.3; rep. from * to end.
3rd row: K.3, *p.1, M.B., p.1, k.3; rep. from * to end.
4th row: As 2nd row.
5th and 6th rows: As 1st and 2nd rows.
These 6 rows form the pattern.

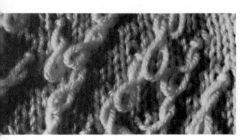

261 Simple Loop Pattern

No. 261 Simple Loop Pattern 4 sts. plus 3
Loop 1, k. next st. winding yarn over needle and first
finger of left hand once then over needle again, then
place the two loops back on left hand needle and k.
them together with st. through back of loops.
1st row: (right side) K. to end.
2nd row: P. to end.
3rd row: K. to end.
4th row: P.1, *loop 1, p.3; rep. from * to last 2 sts., loop
1, p.1.
5th to 7th rows: As 1st to 3rd rows.
8th row: P.3, *loop 1, p.3; rep. from * to end.
These 8 rows form the pattern.

RIBBED TEXTURES
Because of their elasticity, ribbed patterns are most
commonly used in holding and shaping a garment, for
example at the waist, cuffs and neckbands. However,
ribbed patterns need not be confined solely to shaping:
there are many elaborate pattern stitches that look
exactly right for sweaters, and experimentation with

various yarns may alter the appearance of the ribbed pattern again.

Most ribby patterns, by virtue of their stretch quality, tend to cling and this should be borne in mind when using them. Unless a close fit is desirable, allow for more stitches than usual when casting on. A tension sample in the chosen pattern should be measured flat, or, at the most, very slightly stretched.

No. 262   Single Rib Even number of sts.
1st row: K.2, *p.1, k.1; rep. from * to end.
This row forms single rib.

Single Rib Odd number of sts.
1st row: K.2, *p.1, k.1; rep. from * to last st., k.1.
2nd row: K.1, *p.1, k.1; rep. from * to end.
These 2 rows form the pattern.

262 *Single Rib*

No. 263   Double or k.2, p.2 rib 4 sts.
1st row: K.1, *p.2, k.2; rep. from * to last 3 sts., p.2, k.1.
2nd row: K.1, *k.2, p.2; rep. from * to last 3 sts., k.3.
These 2 rows form the pattern.

263 *Double or k.2, p.2 rib*

No. 264   Mistake Rib 4 sts. plus 1
1st row: *P.2, k.2; rep. from * to last st., k.1.
2nd row: *K.2, p.2; rep. from * to last st., p.1.
These 2 rows form the pattern.

264 *Mistake Rib*

No. 265   Ridge Rib 3 sts. plus 1
1st row: *K.2, p.1; rep. from * to last st., k.1.
2nd row: P.1, *k.2, p.1; rep. from * to end.
These 2 rows form the pattern.

265 *Ridge Rib*

266 Ladder Rib

No. 266   Ladder Rib 6 sts. plus 1
1st row: (right side) P.2, *k.1, p.1, k.1, p.3; rep. from *
ending last rep., p.2 instead of p.3.
2nd row: K.2, *p.3, k.3; rep. from * to end, ending last
rep., k.2 instead of k.3.
These 2 rows form the pattern.

267 Slip Stitch Rib

No. 267   Slip Stitch Rib 5 sts. plus 6
1st row: (right side) P.2, k.2, *p.3, k.2; rep. from * to
last 2 sts., p.2.
2nd row: K.2, p.2, *k.1, sl.1, k.1, p.2; rep. from * to last
2 sts., k.2.
These 2 rows form the pattern.

268 Fisherman's Rib

No. 268   Fisherman's Rib Even number of sts.
Note that this pattern stitch, although ribby, has a
tendency to sideways stretch in wear.
1st row: (wrong side) *K.1, p.1; rep. from * to end.
2nd row: Sl. 1 knitwise, *k. through loop below next st.
on left hand needle slipping both loops off needle
together, k.1; rep. from * to last st., k.1.
The 2nd row forms the pattern.

269 Brioche Rib

No. 269   Brioche Rib 3 sts. plus 6
1st row: Sl.1, k.3; *insert needle point in row below next
st. and k. with loop above, slipping both loops off
together, k.2; rep. from * to last 2 sts., k.2.
2nd row: Sl.1, k. to end.
These 2 rows form the pattern.

270 Panelled Rib

No. 270   Panelled Rib 12 sts. plus 3
1st row: K.3, *p.3, k.3; rep. from * to end.
2nd row: P.3, *k.3, p.3; rep. from * to end.
3rd to 12th rows: Rep. 1st and 2nd rows 5 times more.
13th row: K.3, *p.9, k.3; rep. from * to end.
14th row: P.3, *k.9, p.3; rep. from * to end.
15th row: As 13th row.
16th row: As 14th row.
These 16 rows form the pattern.

No. 271 Long Slip Rib 8 sts. plus 4

Avoid pulling yarn tightly behind slipped stitches.

1st row: P.4, *k.4 winding yarn 3 times round needle for each st., p.4; rep. from * to end.

2nd row: K.4, *yarn forward, sl. 4 dropping extra loops, k.4; rep. from * to end.

3rd row: P.4, *yarn back, sl. 4 purlwise, yarn forward, p.4; rep. from * to end.

4th row: K.4, *yarn forward, sl. 4 purlwise, yarn back, k.4; rep. from * to end.

These 4 rows form the pattern.

271 Long Slip Rib

No. 272 Wavy Rib Pattern 3 sts. plus 2

1st row: *P.2, k.1; rep. from * to last 2 sts., p.2.

2nd row: *K.2, p.1; rep. from * to last 2 sts., k.2.

3rd and 4th rows: Rep. 1st and 2nd rows.

5th row: P.1, *p.1, sl. next st. to front on cable needle, p.1 from main needle then k.1 from cable needle – called C.1F.; rep. from * to last st., p.1.

6th row: K.1, *p.1, k.2; rep. from * to last st., p.1.

7th row: K.1, p.1, *p.1, C.1F.; rep. from * to end.

8th row: *P.1, k.2; rep. from * to last st., k.1.

9th row: P.1, *k.1, p.2; rep. from * to last st., k.1.

10th row: As 8th row.

11th row: As 9th row.

12th row: As 8th row.

13th row: *Sl. next st. to back on cable needle, k.1 from main needle then p.1 from cable needle – called C.1B., p.1; rep. from * to last 2 sts., C.1B.

14th row: K.1, p.1, *k.2, p.1; rep. from * to end.

15th row: K.1, p.1, *C.1B., p.1; rep. from * to end.

16th row: *K.2, p.1; rep. from * to last 2 sts., k.2.

These 16 rows form the pattern.

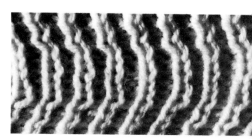

272 Wavy Rib Pattern

No. 273 Multi Twist Rib 10 sts. plus 4

Tw. 2, twist 2 thus: k. next 2 sts. tog. leaving loops on left hand needle, k. first st. again and slip both loops off needle together.

1st row: P.4, *(Tw. 2) 3 times, p.4; rep. from * to end.

2nd row: K.4, *p.6, k.4; rep. from * to end.

These 2 rows form the pattern.

273 Multi Twist Rib

274 Single Twist Rib

No. 274 Single Twist Rib 3 sts. plus 1

Tw. 2, twist 2 thus: k. next 2 sts. tog. leaving loops on left hand needle, k. first st. again and slip both loops off needle together.

1st row: (wrong side) K.1, *p.2, k.1; rep. from * to end.

2nd row: P.1, *Tw. 2, p.1; rep. from * to end.

These 2 rows form the pattern.

275 Rolled Rib

No. 275 Rolled Rib 3 sts. plus 1

1st row: P.1, *yarn back, sl.1, yarn over needle, k.1 and pass the slipped st. over the k. and made sts., p.1; rep. from * to end.

2nd row: K.1, *p.2, k.1; rep. from * to end.

These 2 rows form the pattern.

276 Small Mock Cable Rib

No. 276 Small Mock Cable Rib 4 sts. plus 2

1st row: (wrong side) *K.2, p.2; rep. from * to last 2 sts., k.2.

2nd row: *P.2, k.2; rep. from * to last 2 sts., p.2.

3rd row: As 1st row.

4th row: *P.2, miss next st. on left hand needle, k. the second st. then k. the missed st. and slip both loops off together; rep. from * to last 2 sts., p.2.

These 4 rows form the pattern.

No. 277 Zigzag Rib 4 sts. plus 5

1st row: K.2, *p.1, k. in front of third st. on left hand needle, then in first and second and slip three loops off together; rep. from * to last 3 sts., p.1, k.2.

2nd row: P.2, *k.1, p.3; rep. from * to last 3 sts., k.1, p.2.

3rd row: K.2, *p.1, sl. next st. to front on cable needle, k.2, then k.1 from cable needle; rep. from * to last 3 sts., p.1, k.2.

4th row: As 2nd row.

These 4 rows form the pattern.

277 Zigzag Rib

No. 278   Claw Rib 6 sts.

1st row: P.1, *k.4, p.2; rep. from * to end, ending p.1 instead of p.2.

2nd row: K.1, *p.4, k.2; rep. from * ending k.1 instead of k.2.

3rd row: P.1, *k. in front of second loop on left hand needle then k. first st. and slip both loops off together, k. in back of second st. on left hand needle behind first st., then k. first st. and slip both loops off together, p.2; rep. from * to end, ending p.1 instead of p.2.

4th row: As 2nd row.

These 4 rows form the pattern.

278   Claw Rib

No. 279   Laburnum Pattern Rib 5 sts. plus 2

1st row: (right side) P.2, *k.3, p.2; rep. from * to end.

2nd row: K.2, *p.3, k.2; rep. from * to end.

3rd row: P.2, *keeping yarn forward, slip 1 purlwise, yarn back, k. 2 tog., p.s.s.o., yarn round needle twice, p.2; rep. from * to end.

4th row: K.2, *p. in back of first made st. then in front of second made st., p.1, k.2; rep. from * to end.

These 4 rows form the pattern.

279   Laburnum Pattern Rib

No. 280   Arrowhead Rib 6 sts. plus 5

1st row: P.1, *k.3, p.3; rep. from * ending last rep., p.1 instead of p.3.

2nd row: K.1, *p.3, k.3; rep. from * ending last rep., k.1 instead of k.3.

3rd row: P.1, *yarn forward, k. 3 tog., yarn round needle, p.3; rep. from * ending last rep., p.1 instead of p.3.

4th row: As 2nd row.

These 4 rows form the pattern.

280   Arrowhead Rib

No. 281   Eyelet Rib 5 sts. plus 2

1st row: (right side) P.2, *k.3, p.2; rep. from * to end.

2nd row: K.2, *p.3, k.2; rep. from * to end.

3rd row: P.2, *sl.1, k. 2 tog., p.s.s.o., p.2; rep. from * to end.

4th row: K.2, *(p.1, k.1, p.1) all in next st., k.2; rep. from * to end.

These 4 rows form the pattern.

281   Eyelet Rib

282 Plaited Rib

No. 282 Plaited Rib 7 sts. plus 4

Tw. 2, twist 2 thus: k. in front of second st. on left hand needle, then k. in front of first st. and slip both loops off together.

1st row: (wrong side) K.4, *p.3, k.4; rep. from * to end.
2nd row: P.4, *Tw. 2, k.1, p.4; rep. from * to end.
3rd row: As 1st row.
4th row: P.4, *k.1, Tw. 2, p.4; rep. from * to end.
These 4 rows form the pattern.

283 Twisted Eyelet Rib

No. 283 Twisted Eyelet Rib 5 sts. plus 2

1st row: (right side) P.2, *k.3, p.2; rep. from * to end.
2nd row: K.2, *p.3, k.2; rep. from * to end.
3rd row: P.2, *sl. 1 purlwise, k.2, p.s.s.o., then k.2, p.2; rep. from * to end.
4th row: K.2, *p.1, yarn round needle, p.1, k.2; rep. from * to end.
These 4 rows form the pattern.

284 Narrow Lace Rib

No. 284 Narrow Lace Rib 5 sts. plus 2

1st row: (right side) P.2, *k.1, yarn forward, sl. 1 purlwise, k.1, p.s.s.o., p.2; rep. from * to end.
2nd row: K.2, *p.3, k.2; rep. from * to end.
3rd row: P.2, *k. 2 tog., yarn forward, k.1, p.2; rep. from * to end.
4th row: As 2nd row.
These 4 rows form the pattern.

285 Openwork Rib

No. 285 Openwork Rib 6 sts. plus 3

1st row: (right side) *P.3, yarn over needle, sl.1, k. 2 tog., p.s.s.o., yarn over needle; rep. from * to last 3 sts. p.3.
2nd row: *K.3, p.3; rep. from * to last 3 sts., k.3.
These 2 rows form the pattern.

286 Lacy Rib

No. 286 Lacy Rib 4 sts. plus 2

1st row: P.2, *yarn over needle, k. 2 tog. t.b.l., p.2; rep. from * to end.
2nd row: K.2, *p.2, k.2; rep. from * to end.
3rd row: P.2, *k. 2 tog., yarn round needle, p.2; rep. from * to end.
4th row: As 2nd row.
These 4 rows form the pattern.

No. 287 Fuschia Rib Pattern 6 sts.

1st row: (right side) *P.2, k.2, yarn round needle, p.2; rep. from * to end.
2nd row: *K.2, p.3, k.2; rep. from * to end.
3rd row: *P.2, k.3, yarn round needle, p.2; rep. from * to end.
4th row: *K.2, p.4, k.2; rep. from * to end.
5th row: *P.2, k.4, yarn round needle, p.2; rep. from * to end.
6th row: *K.2, p.5, k.2; rep. from * to end.
7th row: *P.2, k.3, k. 2 tog., p.2; rep. from * to end.
8th row: As 4th row.
9th row: *P.2, k.2, k. 2 tog., p.2; rep. from * to end.
10th row: As 2nd row.
11th row: *P.2, k.1, k. 2 tog., p.2; rep. from * to end.
12th row: *K.2, p.2, k.2; rep. from * to end.
These 12 rows form the pattern.

287 Fuschia Rib Pattern

No. 288 Pleated Triangle Rib 10 sts.

1st row: *P.2, k.8; rep. from * to end.
2nd row: *P.7, k.3; rep. from * to end.
3rd row: *P.4, k.6; rep. from * to end.
4th row: *P.5, k.5; rep. from * to end.
5th row: *P.6, k.4; rep. from * to end.
6th row: *P.3, k.7; rep. from * to end.
7th row: *P.8, k.2; rep. from * to end.
8th row: As 6th row.
9th row: As 5th row.
10th row: As 4th row.
11th row: As 3rd row.
12th row: As 2nd row.
These 12 rows form the pattern.

288 Pleated Triangle Rib

FIVE CABLE AND CROSSOVER PATTERNS

The patterns in this range were, until recently, used almost exclusively for fishing sweaters, sailing wear, cricket and other sportswear. With the growing popularity of hand knitting, designers have drawn on all sources of patterns and, by using different yarns, have given the traditional cable panels a very fashionable quality. These decorative panels have a unique position in the knitting world: they present a challenge that most knitters find hard to resist. Those wanting a fashionable garment may be attracted by cable stitches worked in a luxury yarn; those who love knitting for its own sake will undertake a complicated design in one of the original 'bainin' yarns. It is not unusual to find a newcomer to the craft who has learned the basic stitches in order to move on as soon as possible to the widely loved Aran knitting.

Cable patterns, basically, consist of groups of stitches crossing and twisting by altering the order in which they are worked. This rearrangement is generally made by slipping a given number of stitches on to a cable needle (a small double pointed needle), working the next stitch or stitches from the main needle then returning the stitches from the cable needle back to the main needle to be worked. The cable needle stitches may be left at the back or front of the main work as instructed. The simplest of the cable patterns produces a rope-like effect, since the two halves of the working stitches are twisted around each other at regular intervals.

When designing in the cable type patterns, it must be remembered that the twisting of the stitches draws the fabric together. Tension samples are essential for this type of knitting and, where more than one pattern is to be used across the work, each panel must be separately measured. Many Aran patterned garments have moss stitch variations at the body side edges and the underarm of the sleeve: these serve to set off the elaborate centre panels and can also compensate for any adjustment in the overall measurements.

Only a very few of the existing cable and crossover patterns have accepted authenticity. Since they have received such acclaim recently, it is natural that many new developments have taken place and even in these very intricate stitches innovations happen all the time. Perhaps, simply by altering your cable needle from front to back, you will invent the next one.

No. 289 Honeycomb Twist Pattern 8 sts. plus 8
This pattern is reversible. Although the stitches are cabled, they should not be confused with the following pattern and the term twist has been substituted.
Tw. 2 F., twist 2 front thus: Slip next 2 sts. to front on cable needle, p.2 from main needle, k.2 from cable needle.
Tw. 2 B., twist 2 back thus: Slip next 2 sts. to back on cable needle, k. 2 sts. from main needle, p.2 from cable needle.

289 Honeycomb Twist Pattern

1st row: K.2, *p.4, k.4; rep. from * to last 6 sts., p.4, k.2.
2nd row: P.2, *k.4, p.4; rep. from * to last 6 sts., k.4, p.2.
3rd row: *Tw. 2 F., Tw. 2 B.; rep. from * to end.
4th row: As 1st row.
5th row: As 2nd row.
6th row: As 1st row.
7th row: *Tw. 2 B., Tw. 2 F.; rep. from * to end.
8th row: As 2nd row.
These 8 rows form the pattern.

No. 290 Honeycomb Cable Pattern 8 sts. plus 2
C. 4 B., cable 4 back thus: slip next 2 sts. to back on cable needle, k.2 from main needle, k.2 from cable needle.
C. 4 F., cable 4 front thus: slip next 2 sts. to front on cable needle, k.2 from main needle, k.2 from cable needle.

290 Honeycomb Cable Pattern

1st row: K. to end.
2nd row and foll. alt. rows: P. to end.
3rd row: K.1, *C. 4 B., C. 4 F.; rep. from * to last st., k.1.

5th row: K. to end.
7th row: K.1, *C. 4 F., C. 4 B.; rep. from * to last st., k.1.
8th row: P. to end.
These 8 rows form the pattern.

No. 291 Shadow Cable Pattern 8 sts. plus 2
Special abbreviations as No. 290
1st row: (wrong side) P. to end.
2nd row: K. to end.
3rd row and foll. alt. rows: As 1st row.
4th row: K.1, *C. 4 B., k.4; rep. from * to last st., k.1.
6th row: K. to end.
8th row: K.1, *k.4, C. 4 F.; rep. from * to last st., k.1.
These 8 rows form the pattern.

291 Shadow Cable Pattern

No. 292 Woven Basket Pattern 6 sts. plus 2
B.Cr., back cross thus: slip next st. to back on cable needle, k.2 from main needle then p.1 from cable needle.
F.Cr., front cross thus: slip next 2 sts. to front on cable needle, p.1 from main needle, k.2 from cable needle.
1st row: (wrong side) K.2, *p.4, k.2; rep. from * to end.
2nd row: P.2, *slip next 2 sts. to back on cable needle, k.2 from main needle, k.2 from cable needle, p.2; rep. from * to end.
3rd row and foll. alt. rows: K. the k. sts. and p. the p. sts. as they present themselves.
4th row: P.1, *B.Cr., F.Cr.; rep. from * to last st., p.1.
6th row: P.1, k.2, p.2, *slip next 2 sts. to front on cable needle, k.2 from main needle, k.2 from cable needle, p.2; rep. from * ending k.2, p.1.
8th row: P.1, *F.Cr., B.Cr.; rep. from * to last st., p.1.
These 8 rows form the pattern.

292 Woven Basket Pattern

No. 293 Heavy Trellis Cable Pattern 8 sts. plus 4
Cr. 4 F., cross 4 front thus: slip next 2 sts. to front on cable needle, k.2 from main needle, then k.2 from cable needle.
Cr. 4 B., cross 4 back thus: slip next 2 sts. to back on cable needle, k.2 from main needle, k.2 from cable needle.
Cr. 3 R., cross 3 right thus: slip next st. to back on cable needle, k.2 from main needle, p.1 from cable needle.
Cr. 3 L., cross 3 left thus: slip next 2 sts. to front on cable needle, p.1 from main needle, k.2 from cable needle.

293 Heavy Trellis Cable Pattern

1st row: (right side) P.4, *Cr. 4 F., p.4; rep. from * to end.

2nd row: K.4, *p.4, k.4; rep. from * to end.

3rd row: P.3, *Cr. 3 R., Cr. 3 L., p.2; rep. from * ending last rep., p.3.

4th row: K.3, *p.2, k.2; rep. from * to last st., k.1.

5th row: P.2, *Cr. 3 R., p.2, Cr. 3 L.; rep. from * to last 2 sts., p.2.

6th row: K.2, p.2, *k.4, p.4; rep. from * to last 8 sts., k.4, p.2, k.2.

7th row: P.2, k.2, *p.4, Cr. 4 B.; rep. from * to last 8 sts., p.4, k.2, p.2.

8th row: K.2, p.2, *k.4, p.4; rep. from * to last 8 sts., k.4, p.2, k.2.

9th row: P.2, *Cr. 3 L., p.2, Cr. 3 R.; rep. from * to last 2 sts., p.2.

10th row: K.3, *p.2, k.2; rep. from * to last st., k.1.

11th row: P.3, *Cr. 3 L., Cr. 3 R., p.2; rep. from * to last st., p.1.

12th row: K.4, *p.4, k.4; rep. from * to end.

These 12 rows form the pattern.

No. 294 Miniature Trellis Pattern 4 sts.

C. 4 F., cable 4 front thus: slip next 2 sts. to front on cable needle, k.2 from main needle, k.2 from cable needle.

C. 4 B., cable 4 back thus: slip next 2 sts. to back on cable needle, k.2 from main needle, k.2 from cable needle.

1st row: K.1, *C. 4 F.; rep. from * to last 3 sts., k.3.

2nd row: P. to end.

3rd row: K.3, *C. 4 B.; rep. from * to last st., k.1.

4th row: P. to end.

These 4 rows form the pattern.

294 Miniature Trellis Pattern

No. 295 Smocking Pattern 8 sts. plus 2

1st row: (right side) P.2, *k.2, p.2; rep. from * to end.

2nd row: K.2, *p.2, k.2; rep. from * to end.

3rd row: P.2, *slip next 6 sts. on to cable needle, wind yarn clockwise 4 times round these sts., then k.2, p.2, k.2 these sts., p.2; rep. from * to end.

4th row: As 2nd row.

5th and 6th rows: As 1st and 2nd rows.

7th row: P.2, k.2, p.2, *cable 6 sts. as 3rd row, p.2; rep. from * to last 4 sts., k.2, p.2.

8th row: As 2nd row.

These 8 rows form the pattern.

295 Smocking Pattern

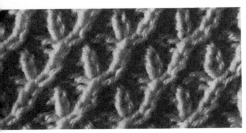

296 Travelling Rib Pattern

No. 296   Travelling Rib Pattern 6 sts. plus 4
Cr. 4, cross 4 thus: slip next 3 sts. to back on cable
needle, k.1, then with yarn in front, slip the 2 purl sts.
from cable needle back on to left hand needle and purl
them, then k. remaining st. from cable needle.
1st row: (wrong side) P.1, *k.2, p.1; rep. from * to end.
2nd row: K.1, *p.2, k.1; rep. from * to end.
3rd row: As 1st row.
4th row: *Cr. 4, p.2; rep. from * to last 4 sts., Cr. 4.
5th, 6th and 7th rows: Rep. 1st, 2nd and 3rd rows.
8th row: K.1, p.2, *Cr. 4, p.2; rep. from * to last st., k.1.
These 8 rows form the pattern.

297 Cross Cable Pattern

No. 297   Cross Cable Pattern 4 sts. plus 2.
This pattern has a tendency to bias. Only yarn that can
be pressed should be used, check the yarn ball band for
pressing directions.
C. 4 B., cable 4 back thus: slip next 2 sts. to back on
cable needle, k.2 from main needle, k.2 from cable
needle.
1st row: (right side) K. to end.
2nd row: P. to end.
3rd row: K.1, *C. 4 B.; rep. from * to last st., k.1.
4th row: P. to end.
These 4 rows form the pattern.

298 Zigzag Cable All-over Pattern

No. 298   Zigzag Cable All-over Pattern 4 sts. plus 3
1st row: K.1, *p.2, p.1 winding yarn twice round needle,
p.1; rep. from * to last 2 sts., p.1, k.1.
2nd row: K.1, *k.2, sl. 1 purlwise dropping extra loop,
k.1; rep. from * to last 2 sts., k.2.
3rd row: K.1, *p.2, keeping yarn forward, sl.1, p.1; rep.
from * to last 2 sts., p.1, k.1.
4th row: K.1, *k. 3rd st. on left hand needle, then 1st st.
then 2nd st. and sl. all 3 loops off together, k.1; rep.
from * to last 2 sts., k.2.
5th, 6th and 7th rows: As 1st, 2nd and 3rd rows.
8th row: K.2, *k.1, sl. next st. to front on cable needle,
k.2 from main needle then k.1 from cable needle; rep.
from * to last st., k.1.
These 8 rows form the pattern.

No. 299 Crossover Diamond Pattern 6 sts. plus 2

1st row: K.1, sl.1, *k.4, sl.2; rep. from * ending last rep., sl.1, k.1.

2nd row: P.1, sl.1, *p.4, sl.2; rep. from * ending last rep., sl.1, p.1.

3rd row: K.1, *sl. next st. to front on cable needle, k.2, from main needle, k.1 from cable needle, k. in front of 3rd st. on left hand needle then k. 1st and 2nd sts. and slip all 3 loops off together; rep. from * to last st., k.1.

4th row: P.3, *p. 2nd st. on left hand needle, then 1st. and sl. both loops off together, p.4; rep. from * to end ending last rep., p.3 instead of p.4.

5th row: K.3, *sl.2, k.4; rep. from * ending last rep., k.3 instead of k.4.

6th row: P.3, *sl.2, p.4; rep. from * ending last rep., p.3 instead of p.4.

7th row: K.1, *k. in front of 3rd st. on left hand needle, then k. 1st and 2nd sts. and sl. all 3 loops off together, sl. next st. to front on cable needle, k.2 from main needle, k.1 from cable needle; rep. from * to last st., k.1.

8th row: P.6, *p. 2nd st. on left hand needle, then 1 st. and sl. both loops off together, p.4; rep. from * to last 2 sts., p.2.

These 8 rows form the pattern.

299 Crossover Diamond Pattern

No. 300 Single Lattice Pattern 8 sts.

B.Cr., back cross thus: slip next st. to back on cable needle, k.1 from main needle then k.1 from cable needle.

F.Cr., front cross thus: slip next st. to front on cable needle, k.1 from main needle, k.1 from cable needle.

B.Cr.P., back cross purl thus: as B.Cr. but p.1 from cable needle.

F.Cr.P., front cross purl, thus: as F.Cr. but p.1 from main needle then k.1 from cable needle.

1st row: (right side) P.3, B.Cr., *p.6, B.Cr.; rep. from * to last 3 sts., p.3.

2nd row and foll. alt. rows: K. the k. sts. and p. the p. sts. as they present themselves.

3rd row: P.2, *B.Cr.P., F.Cr.P., p.4; rep. from * ending last rep. p.2 instead of p.4.

5th row: P.1, *B.Cr.P., p.2, F.Cr.P., p.2; rep. from * ending last rep., p.1 instead of p.2.

7th row: *B.Cr.P., p.4, F.Cr.P.; rep. from * to end.

9th row: K.1, *p.6, F.Cr.; rep. from * ending p.6, k.1.

11th row: *F.Cr.P., p.4, B.Cr.P.; rep. from * to end.

300 Single Lattice Pattern

13th row: P.1, *F.Cr.P., p.2, B.Cr.P., p.2; rep. from *
ending last rep., p.1 instead of p.2.
15th row: P.2, *F.Cr.P., B.Cr.P., p.4; rep. from *
ending last rep. p.2 instead of p.4.
16th row: As 2nd row.
These 16 rows form the pattern.

No. 301 Cable Checks 12 sts. plus 6

1st row: (right side) P.6, *k.6, p.6; rep. from * to end.
2nd row: K.6, *p.6, k.6; rep. from * to end.
3rd and 4th rows: Rep. 1st and 2nd rows.
5th row: P.6, *sl. next 3 sts. to back on cable needle, k.3
from main needle, k.3 from cable needle, p.6; rep. from
* to end.
6th row: K.6, *p.6, k.6; rep. from * to end.
7th row: P.6, *k.6, p.6; rep. from * to end.
8th row: K.6, *p.6, k.6; rep. from * to end.
9th row: K.6, *p.6, k.6; rep. from * to end.
10th row: P.6, *k.6, p.6; rep. from * to end.
11th and 12th rows: As 9th and 10th rows.
13th row: *Sl. next 3 sts. to back on cable needle, k.3
from main needle, k.3 from cable needle, p.6; rep. from
* to last 6 sts., sl. next 3 sts. to back on cable needle, k.3
from main needle, k.3 from cable needle.
14th row: P.6, *k.6, p.6; rep. from * to end.
15th row: K.6, *p.6, k.6; rep. from * to end.
16th row: As 14th row.
These 16 rows form the pattern.

301 Cable Checks

No. 302 Rib and Twist Cable 8 sts. plus 3

A very adaptable pattern, useful as an all-over fabric on
sweaters and, as it was probably originally intended, for
use as a fancy welt on traditional Aran sweaters.
1st row: (right side) *K.3, p.1, k. 1 t.b.l., p.1, k. 1 t.b.l.,
p.1; rep. from * to last 3 sts., k.3.
2nd row: P.3, *k.1, p. 1 t.b.l., k.1, p. 1 t.b.l., k.1, p.3;
rep. from * to end.
3rd to 6th rows: Rep. 1st and 2nd rows twice more.
7th row: K.3, *p.1, sl. next 2 sts. to front on cable
needle, k. 1 t.b.l. from main needle, p. 1 t.b.l. in second
st. on cable needle then k. 1 t.b.l. in first st. on cable
needle and sl. both loops off cable needle together, p.1,
k.3; rep. from * to end.
8th row: As 2nd row.
These 8 rows form the pattern.

302 Rib and Twist Cable

No. 303 Cable Smocking 10 sts. plus 8

Cr. 4, cross 4 thus: sl. next st. to front on cable needle, then k. in front of third st. on left hand needle then into first and second sts. on left hand needle, slip all three sts. off needle, k.1 from cable needle.

1st row: K. to end.

2nd row: P. to end.

3rd row: As 1st row.

4th row: P.2, *sl. 1 purlwise, p.2, sl. 1 purlwise, p.6; rep. from * to last 6 sts., sl. 1 purlwise, p.2, sl. 1 purlwise, p.2.

5th row: K.2, *Cr. 4, k.6; rep. from * to last 6 sts., Cr. 4, k.2.

6th row: P. to end.

7th row: K. to end.

8th row: P.7, *sl.1, p.2, sl.1, p.6; rep. from * to last st., p.1.

9th row: K.7, *Cr. 4, k.6; rep. from * to last st., k.1.

10th row: P. to end.

The 3rd to 10th rows form the pattern.

303 Cable Smocking

No. 304 Eight Stitch Cable Back 12 sts. plus 4

This type of cable is the most commonly used. It is found in all varieties of garments from socks, sportswear and school wear to high fashion.

C. 8 B., cable 8 back thus: slip next 4 sts. to back on cable needle, k.4 from main needle, k.4 from cable needle.

1st row: (right side) P.4, *k.8, p.4; rep. from * to end.

2nd row: K.4, *p.8, k.4; rep. from * to end.

3rd to 6th rows: Rep. 1st and 2nd rows twice more.

7th row: P.4, *C. 8 B., p.4; rep. from * to end.

8th row: As 2nd row.

9th to 12th rows: Rep. 1st and 2nd rows twice more.

These 12 rows form the pattern.

304 Eight Stitch Cable Back

No. 305 Eight Stitch Cable Front 12 sts. plus 4

This is similar to No. 304, but the cable needle is held to the front of the work thus twisting the stitches in the opposite direction. This is most useful when the cables form an outline to, say, a central pattern. It is usual to work each cable in corresponding sequence.

C. 8 F., cable 8 front thus: slip next 4 sts. to front on cable needle, k.4 from main needle, k.4 from cable needle.

1st row: (right side) P.4, *k.8, p.4; rep. from * to end.

2nd row: K.4, *p.8, k.4; rep. from * to end.

305 Eight Stitch Cable Front

3rd to 6th rows: Rep. 1st and 2nd rows twice more.
7th row: P.4, *C. 8 F., p.4; rep. from * to end.
8th row: As 2nd row.
9th to 12th rows: Rep. 1st and 2nd rows twice more.
These 12 rows form the pattern.

No. 306 Horseshoe Cable Pattern 17 sts. plus 18
C. 12, cable 12 thus: slip next 3 sts. to back on cable
needle, k.3 from main needle, k.3 from cable needle, slip
next 3 sts. to front on cable needle, k.3 from main
needle, k.3 from cable needle.
1st row: (wrong side) K.3, *p.12, k.5; rep. from * ending
p.3 instead of p.5.
2nd row: K.1, p.2, *C. 12, p.2, k.1, p.2; rep. from *
ending last rep., p.2, k.1.
3rd row: As 1st row.
4th row: K.1, p.2, *k.12, p.2, k.1, p.2; rep. from *
ending last rep., p.2, k.1.
5th to 8th rows: Rep. 3rd and 4th rows twice more.
These 8 rows form the pattern.

306 Horseshoe Cable Pattern

No. 307 Ring Cable Pattern 10 sts. plus 2
C. 4 F.P., cable 4 front purl thus: slip next 2 sts. to
front on cable needle, p.2 from main needle, k.2 from
cable needle.
C. 4 B.P., cable 4 back purl thus: slip next 2 sts. to back
on cable needle, k.2 from main needle, p.2 from cable
needle.
C. 4 B., cable 4 back thus: slip next 2 sts. to back on
cable needle, k.2 from main needle, k.2 from cable
needle.
C. 4 F., cable 4 front thus: slip next 2 sts. to front on
cable needle, k.2 from main needle, k.2 from cable
needle.
1st row: P.2, *k.8, p.2; rep. from * to end.
2nd row: K.2, *p.8, k.2; rep. from * to end.
3rd row: P.2, *C. 4 F.P., C. 4 B.P., p.2; rep. from * to
end.
4th and 6th rows: K.2, *k.2, p.4, k.4; rep. from * to end.
5th row: P.2, *p.2, k.4, p.4; rep. from * to end.
7th row: P.2, *C. 4 B., C. 4 F., p.2; rep. from * to end.
8th row: As 2nd row.
These 8 rows form the pattern.

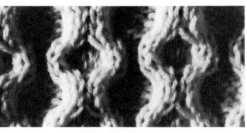

307 Ring Cable Pattern

No. 308　Antler Cable Pattern 12 sts. plus 2

C. 4 F., cable 4 front thus: slip next 2 sts. to front on cable needle, k.2 from main needle, k.2 from cable needle.

C. 4 B., cable 4 back thus: slip next 2 sts. to back on cable needle, k.2 from main needle, k.2 from cable needle.

1st row: K. to end.

2nd row: K.2, *p.10, k.2; rep. from * to end.

3rd row: (right side) K.2, *C. 4 B., k.2, C. 4 F., k.2; rep. from * to end.

4th row: K.2, *p.10, k.2; rep. from * to end.

5th row: K. to end.

6th to 13th rows: Rep. 4th and 5th rows 4 times.

14th row: As 2nd row.

The 3rd to 14th rows form the pattern.

308　Antler Cable Pattern

No. 309　Snake Cable Pattern 11 sts. plus 2

C. 4 F., cable 4 front thus: slip next 2 sts. to front on cable needle, k.2 from main needle, k.2 from cable needle.

C. 4 B., cable 4 back thus: slip next 2 sts. to back on cable needle, k.2 from main needle, k.2 from cable needle.

1st row: (right side) P.2, *k. 4 t.b.l., p.1, k. 4 t.b.l., p.2; rep. from * to end.

2nd row: K.2, *p.4, k.1, p.4, k.2; rep. from * to end.

3rd row: P.2, *C. 4 F., p.1, C. 4 B., p.2; rep. from * to end.

4th row: As 2nd row.

5th row: As 1st row.

6th row: As 2nd row.

7th row: P.2, *C. 4 B., p.1, C. 4 F., p.2; rep. from * to end.

8th row: As 2nd row.

These 8 rows form the pattern.

309　Snake Cable Pattern

No. 310　Twist Rib Cable 9 sts. plus 2

1st row: P.2, *(k. 1 t.b.l., p.1) 4 times, p.1; rep. from * to end.

2nd row: K.2, *(p.1, k.1) 4 times, k.1; rep. from * to end.

3rd to 6th rows: Rep. 1st and 2nd rows twice more.

7th row: P.2, *sl. next 4 sts. to front on cable needle, (k. 1 t.b.l., p.1) twice from main needle, then (k. 1 t.b.l., p.1) twice from cable needle, p.1; rep. from * to end.

8th row: As 2nd row.

310　Twist Rib Cable

9th to 12th rows: Rep. 1st and 2nd rows twice more.
These 12 rows form the pattern.

No. 311 Rib and Cable Cross 10 sts.
1st row: *P.2, k.6, p.2; rep. from * to end.
2nd row: *K.2, p.6, k.2; rep. from * to end.
3rd to 6th rows: Rep. 1st and 2nd rows twice more.
7th row: *P.2, sl. next 3 sts. to back on cable needle, k.3 from main needle, k.3 from cable needle, p.2; rep. from * to end.
8th, 10th and 12th rows: As 2nd row.
9th and 11th rows: As 1st row.
13th, 15th, 17th and 19th rows: *P.4, k.2, p.4; rep. from * to end.
14th, 16th, 18th and 20th rows: *K.4, p.2, k.4; rep. from * to end.
These 20 rows form the pattern.

311 Rib and Cable Cross

No. 312 Figure Eight Cable Pattern 12 sts.
B.Cr., back cross thus: slip next st. to back on cable needle, k.2 from main needle, p.1 from cable needle.
F.Cr., front cross thus: slip next 2 sts. to front on cable needle, p.1 from main needle, k.2 from cable needle.
C. 4 B., cable 4 back thus: slip next 2 sts. to back on cable needle, k.2 from main needle, k.2 from cable needle.
1st row: (wrong side) *K.5, p.2, k.5; rep. from * to end.
2nd row: *P.4, k.4, p.4; rep. from * to end.
3rd row and foll. alt. rows: K. the k. sts. and p. the p. sts. as they present themselves.
4th row: *P.3, B.Cr., F.Cr., p.3; rep. from * to end.
6th row: *P.2, B.Cr., p.2, F.Cr., p.2; rep. from * to end.
8th row: *P.2, F.Cr., p.2, B.Cr., p.2; rep. from * to end.
10th row: *P.3, F.Cr., B.Cr., p.3; rep. from * to end.
12th row: *P.4, C. 4 B., p.4; rep. from * to end.
14th row: As 4th row.
16th row: As 6th row.
18th row: As 8th row.
20th row: As 10th row.
21st row: *K.4, p.4, k.4; rep. from * to end.
22nd, 24th and 26th rows: *P.5, k.2, p.5; rep. from * to end.
23rd, 25th and 27th rows: *K.5, p.2, k.5; rep. from * to end.
28th row: *P.5, k.2, p.5; rep. from * to end.
These 28 rows form the pattern.

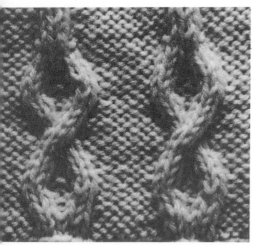

312 Figure Eight Cable Pattern

No. 313   Chain Link Knotted Cable Pattern   10 sts.

1st row: (right side) *(p.2, k.2) twice, p.2; rep. from * to end.

2nd row: *(K.2, p.2) twice, k.2; rep. from * to end.

3rd row: *P.2, sl. next 4 sts. to front on cable needle, k.2 from main needle, then sl. the p. 2 sts. from cable needle back on to left hand needle, pass the cable needle with remaining 2 sts. to back of work, p.2 from left hand needle, k.2 from cable needle, p.2; rep. from * to end.

4th, 6th and 8th rows: As 2nd row.

5th, 7th and 9th rows: As 1st row.

10th row: As 2nd row.

These 10 rows form the pattern.

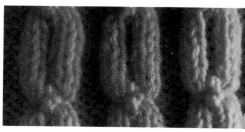

313 Chain Link Knotted Cable Pattern

No. 314   Aran Twist Stitch Rib Diamond   13 sts.

B.Cr., back cross thus: slip next st. to back on cable needle, k. 1 t.b.l. from main needle, p.1 from cable needle.

F.Cr., front cross thus: slip next st. to front on cable needle, p.1 from main needle, k. 1 t.b.l. from cable needle.

1st row: (right side) *P.5, sl. next 2 sts. to front on cable needle, k. 1 t.b.l. from main needle, p.1 then k. 1 t.b.l. both from cable needle, p.5; rep. from * to end.

2nd row: *K.5, p.3, k.5; rep. from * to end.

3rd row: *P.4, B.Cr., k. 1 t.b.l., F.Cr., p.4; rep. from * to end.

4th row and foll. alt. rows: K. the k. sts. and p. the p. sts. as they present themselves.

5th row: *P.3, B.Cr. *knitting* both sts. t.b.l., p.1, k. 1 t.b.l., p.1, F.Cr. *knitting* both sts. t.b.l., p.3; rep. from * to end.

7th row: *P.2, B.Cr., (k. 1 t.b.l., p.1) twice, k. 1 t.b.l., F.Cr., p.2; rep. from * to end.

9th row: *P.2, F.Cr., (k. 1 t.b.l., p.1) twice, k. 1 t.b.l., B.Cr., p.2; rep. from * to end.

11th row: *P.3, F.Cr., p.1, k. 1 t.b.l., p.1, B.Cr., p.3; rep. from * to end.

13th row: *P.4, F.Cr., p.1, B.Cr., p.4; rep. from * to end.

14th row: *K.5, p.1, k.1, p.1, k.5; rep. from * to end.

These 14 rows form the pattern.

314 Aran Twist Stitch Rib Diamond

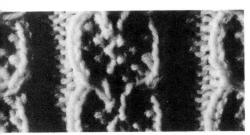

315 Wishbone Cable Pattern

No. 315 Wishbone Cable Pattern 12 sts.

1st row: (right side) *P.2, sl. next 3 sts. to back on cable needle, k.1 from main needle then p.1, k.1, p.1 from cable needle, sl. next st. to front on cable needle, k.1, p.1, k.1 from main needle, then k.1 from cable needle, p.2; rep. from * to end.

2nd, 4th and 6th rows: *K.2, (p.1, k.1) 3 times, p.2, k.2; rep. from * to end.

3rd and 5th rows: *P.2, (k.1, p.1) 3 times, k.2, p.2; rep. from * to end.

7th row: *P.2, k.1, p.1, k.3, p.1, k.2, p.2; rep. from * to end.

8th row: *K.2, p.1, k.1, p.3, k.1, p.2, k.2; rep. from * to end.

These 8 rows form the pattern.

316 Lobster Claw Cable

No. 316 Lobster Claw Cable 12 sts.

1st row: (wrong side) K. to end.

2nd row: *P.2, k.1, p.6, k.1, p.2; rep. from * to end.

3rd, 5th and 7th rows: *K.2, p.2, k.4, p.2, k.2; rep. from * to end.

4th and 6th rows: *P.2, k.2, p.4, k.2, p.2; rep. from * to end.

8th row: *P.2, sl. next 2 sts. to front on cable needle, p.2, yarn forward, k. 2 tog. t.b.l. from cable needle, sl. next 2 sts. to back on cable needle, k. 2 tog., yarn round needle, p.2 from cable needle, p.2; rep. from * to end.

These 8 rows form the pattern.

317 Single Cable Twists

No. 317 Single Cable Twists 12 sts. plus 7

1st row: (wrong side) K. to end.

2nd row: P.1, *k.1, p.3, k.1, p.7; rep. from * ending last rep., p.1 instead of p.7.

3rd row: K.1, *p.1, k.3, p.1, k.7; rep. from * ending last rep., k.1 instead of k.7.

4th and 5th rows: Rep. 2nd and 3rd rows.

6th row: P.1, *sl. next 4 sts. to back on cable needle, k.1 from main needle, then sl. the 3 purl sts. back on to left hand needle and p. them, then k. the last st. from cable needle, p.7; rep, from * ending last rep., p.1 instead of p.7.

7th row: As 3rd row.

8th and 9th rows: As 2nd and 3rd rows.

10th row: As 6th row.

11th row: As 3rd row.

12th and 13th rows: As 2nd and 3rd rows.

14th row: P. to end.

15th row: K. to end.
16th row: P.7, *k.1, p.3, k.1, p.7; rep. from * to end.
17th row: K.7, *p.1, k.3, p.1, k.7; rep. from * to end.
18th and 19th rows: Rep. 16th and 17th rows.
20th row: P.7, *sl. next 4 sts. to back on cable needle, k.1 from main needle, then sl. the 3 purl sts. back on to left hand needle and p. them then k. the last st. from cable needle, p.7; rep. from * to end.
21st row: As 17th row.
22nd and 23rd rows: As 16th and 17th rows.
24th row: As 20th row.
25th row: As 17th row.
26th and 27th rows: As 16th and 17th rows.
28th row: P. to end.
These 28 rows form the pattern.

No. 318 Fancy Plait Cable 32 sts.

This pattern is set out as a centre panel between edge stitches. It is readily adaptable for use as an all-over fabric.

C. 4 F., cable 4 front thus: slip next 2 sts. to front on cable needle, k.2 from main needle, k.2 from cable needle.

C. 4 B., cable 4 back thus: slip next 2 sts. to back on cable needle, k.2 from main needle, k.2 from cable needle.

1st row: K.3, *p.2, C. 4 F., k.2, p.2*, k.1, yarn forward, k. 3 tog. t.b.l., yarn forward, k.2, rep. from * to *, k.3.
2nd row: K.1, p.2, k.2, (p.6, k.2) 3 times, p.2, k.1.
3rd row: K.3, *p.2, k.2, C. 4 B., p.2*, k.2, yarn forward, k. 3 tog., yarn forward, k.1, rep. from * to *, k.3.
4th row: As 2nd row.
5th to 12th rows: Rep. 1st to 4th rows twice.
13th row: K.3, *p.2, k.1, yarn forward, k. 3 tog. t.b.l., yarn forward, k.2, p.2*, C. 4 F., k.2, rep. from * to *, k.3.
14th row: As 2nd row.
15th row: K.3, *p.2, k.2, yarn forward, k. 3 tog., yarn forward, k.1, p.2*, k.2, C. 4 B., rep. from * to *, k.3.
16th row: As 2nd row.
17th to 24th rows: Rep. 13th to 16th rows twice.
These 24 rows form the pattern.

318 Fancy Plait Cable

319 Chevron Cable and Twist Stitch

No. 319 Chevron Cable and Twist Stitch 26 sts.
R.Tw., right twist thus: k. second st. on left hand needle, k. first st. and slip both loops off together.
L.Tw., left twist thus: k. t.b.l. second st. on left hand needle, k. first st. and slip both loops off together.
C. 4 F., cable 4 front thus: slip next 2 sts. to front on cable needle, k.2 from main needle, k.2 from cable needle.
B.Cr., back cross thus: slip next st. to back on cable needle, k.2 from main needle, p.1 from cable needle.
F.Cr., front cross thus: slip next 2 sts. to front on cable needle, p.1 from main needle, then k.2 from cable needle.
1st row: (right side) K. 1 t.b.l., p.1, R.Tw., L.Tw., p.1, (p.4, C. 4 F., p.4,) p.1, R.Tw., L.Tw., p.1, k. 1 t.b.l.
2nd row: P.1, k.1, p.4, k.1, (k.4, p.4, k.4,) k.1, p.4, k.1, p.1.
3rd row: K. 1 t.b.l., p.1, R.Tw., L.Tw., p.1, (p.3, B.Cr., F.Cr., p.3,) p.1, R.Tw., L.Tw., p.1, k. 1 t.b.l.
4th row and foll. alt. rows: K. the k. sts. and p. the p. sts. as they present themselves.
5th row: K. 1 t.b.l., p.1, R.Tw., L.Tw., p.1, (p.2, B.Cr., p.2, F.Cr., p.2,) p.1, R.Tw., L.Tw., p.1, k. 1 t.b.l.
7th row: K. 1 t.b.l., p.1, R.Tw., L.Tw., p.1, (p.1, B.Cr., p.4, F.Cr., p.1,) p.1, R.Tw., L.Tw., p.1, k. 1 t.b.l.
9th row: K. 1 t.b.l., p.1, R.Tw., L.Tw., p.1, (B.Cr., p.1, C. 4 F., p.1, F.Cr.,) p.1, R.Tw., L.Tw., p.1, k. 1 t.b.l.
10th row: As 4th row.
The 3rd to 10th rows form the pattern. For the chevron pattern only, work the bracketed portion on each row.

No. 320 Diamond and Step Cable Pattern 22 sts.
C. 6 F., cable 6 front thus: slip next 3 sts. to front on cable needle, k.3 from main needle, k.3 from cable needle.
C. 3 B., cable 3 back thus: slip next 3 sts. to back on cable needle, k.3 from main needle, k.3 from cable needle.
C. 6 B.P., cable 6 back purl thus: slip next 3 sts. to back on cable needle, k.3 from main needle, p.3 from cable needle.
C. 6 F.P., cable 6 front purl thus: slip next 3 sts. to front on cable needle, p.3 from main needle, k.3 from cable needle.
1st row: P.8, k.6, p.8.
2nd row and foll. alt. rows: K. the k. sts. and p. the p. sts. as they present themselves.
3rd row: As 1st row.

320 Diamond and Step Cable Pattern

5th row: P.5, k.3, C. 6 F., k.3, p.5.
7th row: P.5, k.12, p.5.
9th row: As 7th row.
11th row: P.2, k.3, C. 6 B.P., C. 6 F.P., k.3, p.2.
13th row: P.2, k.6, p.6, k.6, p.2.
15th row: As 13th row.
17th row: P.2, C. 6 B.P., p.6, C. 6 F.P., p.2.
19th row: P.2, k.3, p.12, k.3, p.2.
21st row: As 19th row.
23rd row: P.2, C. 6 F., p.6, C. 6 B., p.2.
25th and 27th rows: As 13th row.
29th row: P.5, C. 6 F., C. 6 B., p.5.
31st and 33rd rows: As 7th row.
35th row: P. 8, C. 6 F., p.8.
36th row: K.8, p.6, k.8.
These 36 rows form the pattern.

No. 321   Bobble Fan Pattern 15 sts.

M.B., make bobble thus: (k.1, yarn forward, k.1, yarn
forward, k.1) all in next st., turn and p.5, turn and k.5,
turn and p. 2 tog., p.1, p. 2 tog., turn and sl.1, k. 2 tog.,
p.s.s.o. – bobble made.
F.Cr., front cross thus: slip next st. to front on cable
needle, p.1 from main needle, k.1 from cable needle.
B.Cr., back cross thus: slip next st. to back on cable
needle, k.1 from main needle, p.1 from cable needle.

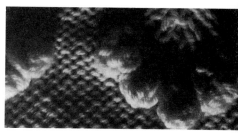

321 Bobble Fan Pattern

1st row: (right side) P. to end.
2nd row: K. to end.
3rd row: P.7, M.B., p.7.
4th row: K.7, p. 1 t.b.l., k.7.
5th row: P.4, M.B., p.2, k. 1 t.b.l., p.2, M.B., p.4.
6th row: K.4, p. 1 t.b.l., k.2, p.1, k.2, p. 1 t.b.l., k.4.
7th row: P.2, M.B., p.1, F.Cr., p.1, k. 1 t.b.l., p.1,
B.Cr., p.1, M.B., p.2.
8th row: K.2, p. 1 t.b.l., k.2, (p.1, k.1) 3 times, k.1, p. 1
t.b.l., k.2.
9th row: P.2, F.Cr., p.1, F.Cr., k. 1 t.b.l., B.Cr., p.1,
B.C.r., p.2.
10th row: K.3, B.Cr., k.1, p.3, k.1, F.Cr., k.3.
11th row: P.4, F.Cr., pick up loop between sts. and p. in
back of it, sl.1, k. 2 tog., p.s.s.o., pick up loop between
sts. and p. in back of it, B.Cr., p.4.
12th row: K.5, B.Cr., p.1, F.Cr., k.5.
13th row: P.5, p. in front and back of next st., sl.1, k. 2
tog., p.s.s.o., p. in front and back of next st., p.5.
14th row: K.7, p.1, k.7.
15th and 16th rows: As 1st and 2nd rows.
These 16 rows form the pattern.

322 Gull Stitch

323 Aran Triangles

No. 322 Gull Stitch 8 sts. plus 2
1st row: *P.2, k.2, yarn back, sl. 2 purlwise, k.2; rep.
from * to last 2 sts., p.2.
2nd row: *K.2, p.2, yarn forward, sl. 2 purlwise, p.2;
rep. from * to last 2 sts., k.2.
3rd row: *P.2, sl. next 2 sts. to back on cable needle, k.1
from main needle, k.2 from cable needle, sl. next st. to
front on cable needle, k.2 from main needle, k.1 from
cable needle; rep. from * to last 2 sts., p.2.
4th row: P. to end.
These 4 rows form the pattern.

No. 323 Aran Triangles 14 sts. plus 5
Tw. 3, twist 3 thus: k. third st. on left hand needle,
from front, then work the second st. then the first st.
and slip all three loops off together.
Cr. 1 B., cross 1 back thus: slip next st. to back on cable
needle, k. 1 t.b.l., then k. 1 t.b.l. from cable needle.
Cr. 1 F., cross 1 front thus: slip next st. to front on
cable needle, k. 1 t.b.l., then k. 1 t.b.l. from cable
needle.
1st row: K.1, *Tw. 3, p.5, k.1 t.b.l., p.5; rep. from * to
last 4 sts., Tw. 3, k.1.
2nd row: K.1, *p.3, k.5, p. 1 t.b.l., k.5; rep. from * to
last 4 sts., p.3, k.1.
3rd row: K.1, *k.3, p.4, k. 3 t.b.l., p.4; rep. from * to
last 4 sts., k.4.
4th row: K.1, *p.3, k.4, p. 3 t.b.l., k.4; rep. from * to
last 4 sts., p.3, k.1.
5th row: K.1, *Tw. 3, p.3, Cr. 1 B., k. 1 t.b.l., Cr. 1 F.,
p.3; rep. from * to last 4 sts., Tw. 3, k.1.
6th row: K.1, *p.3, k.3, p. 5 t.b.l., k.3; rep. from * to
last 4 sts., p.3, k.1.
7th row: K.1, *k.3, p.2, Cr. 1 B., k. 3 t.b.l., Cr. 1 F.,
p.2; rep. from * to last 4 sts., k.4.
8th row: K.1, *p.3, k.2, p. 7 t.b.l., k.2; rep. from * to
last 4 sts., p.3, k.1.
9th row: K.1, *Tw. 3, p.1, Cr. 1 B., k. 5 t.b.l., Cr. 1 F.,
p.1; rep. from * to last 4 sts., Tw. 3, k.1.
10th row: K.1, *p.3, k.1, p. 9 t.b.l., k.1; rep. from * to
last 4 sts., p.3, k.1.
11th row: K.1, *k.3, p.5, k. 1 t.b.l., p.5; rep. from * to
last 4 sts., k.4.
12th row: K.1, *p.3, k.5, p. 1 t.b.l., k.5; rep. from * to
last 4 sts., p.3, k.1.
These 12 rows form the pattern.

No. 324 Braided Cable Pattern 16 sts.

A single repeat of this pattern makes an excellent centre panel for an Aran sweater. It also forms a fascinating all-over pattern when repeated across the row.

F.Cr., front cross thus: slip next 2 sts. to front on cable needle, p.1 from main needle, k.2 from cable needle.
B.Cr., back cross thus: slip next st. to back on cable needle, k.2, k.2 from main needle, p.1 from cable needle.

1st row: K.2, p.4, k.4, p.4, k.2.
2nd row and foll. alt. rows: K. the k. sts. and p. the p. sts. as they present themselves.
3rd row: K.2, p.4, sl. next 2 sts. to back on cable needle, k.2 from main needle, k.2 from cable needle, p.4, k.2.
5th row: F.Cr., p.2, B.Cr., F.Cr., p.2, B.Cr.
7th row: P.1, F.Cr., B.Cr., p.2, F.Cr., B.Cr., p.1.
9th row: P.2, C. 4 back as 3rd row, p.4, C. 4 back as 3rd row, p.2.
11th row: P.2, k.4, p.4, k.4, p.2.
13th row: As 9th row.
15th row: P.1, B.Cr., F.Cr., p.2, B.Cr., F.Cr., p.1.
17th row: B.Cr., p.2, F.Cr., B.Cr., p.2, F.Cr.
19th row: As 3rd row.
20th row: As 2nd row.
These 20 rows form the pattern.

324 Braided Cable Pattern

No. 325 Tree of Life 11 sts. plus 2

A traditional Aran pattern that can be used as an all-over pattern or as one of a number of panels on a typical Aran sweater.

1st row: P.2, *k. 1 t.b.l., p.2, k. 3 t.b.l., p.2, k. 1 t.b.l., p.2; rep. from * to end.
2nd row: K.2, *k.3, p. 3 t.b.l., k.5; rep. from * to end.
3rd row: P.2, *p.2, sl. next st. to back on cable needle, k. 1 t.b.l., then p.1 from cable needle, k. 1 t.b.l., sl. next st. to front on cable needle, p.1, then k.1 from cable needle, p.4; rep. from * to end.
4th row: K.2, *k.2, p. 1 t.b.l., k.1, p. 1 t.b.l., k.1, p. 1 t.b.l., k.4; rep. from * to end.
5th row: P.2, *p.1, sl. next st. to back on cable needle, k. 1 t.b.l., then p.1 from cable needle, p.1, k. 1 t.b.l., p.1, sl. next st. to front on cable needle, p.1, then k. 1 t.b.l. from cable needle, p.3; rep. from * to end.
6th row: K.2, *k.1, p. 1 t.b.l., k.2, p. 1 t.b.l., k.2, p. 1 t.b.l., k.3; rep. from * to end.
7th row: P.2, *sl. next st. to back on cable needle, k. 1

325 Tree of Life

t.b.l., then p.1 from cable needle, p.1, k. 3 t.b.l., p.1, sl. next st. to front on cable needle, p.1, k. 1 t.b.l. from cable needle, p.2; rep. from * to end.

8th row: K.2, *k.3, p. 3 t.b.l., k.5; rep. from * to end.

9th row: P.2, *p.2, sl. next st. to back on cable needle, k. 1 t.b.l., p.1 from cable needle, k. 1 t.b.l., sl. next st. to front on cable needle, p.1, then k.1 from cable needle, p.4; rep. from * to end.

10th row: K.2, *k.2, p. 1 t.b.l., k.1, p. 1 t.b.l., k.1, p. 1 t.b.l., k.4; rep. from * to end.

The 5th to 10th rows form the pattern.

326 *Zigzag and Irish Moss*

No. 326   Zigzag and Irish Moss 7 sts.

F.Cr., front cross thus: slip next 2 sts. to front on cable needle, p.1 from main needle, k.2 from cable needle. B.Cr., back cross thus: sl. next st. to back on cable needle, k.2 from main needle, p.1 from cable needle.

1st row: F.Cr., p.4.

2nd row and foll. alt. rows: (wrong side) K. the k. sts. and p. the p. sts. as they present themselves.

3rd row: K.1, F.Cr., p.3.

5th row: P.1, k.1, F.Cr., p.2.

7th row: K.1, p.1, k.1, F.Cr., p.1.

9th row: (P.1, k.1) twice, F.Cr.

11th row: (K.1, p.1) twice, B.Cr.

13th row: P.1, k.1, p.1, B.Cr., p.1.

15th row: K.1, p.1, B.Cr., p.2.

17th row: P.1, B.Cr., p.3.

19th row: B.Cr., p.4.

20th row: As 2nd row.

These 20 rows form the pattern.

327 *Mock Cable Panels*

No. 327   Mock Cable Panels 18 sts.

Tw. 2, twist 2 thus: k. 2 tog. but leave loops on needle, k. in front of first of these loops then slip both loops off together.

1st row: P.2, k.2, Tw. 2, p.2, k.1, yarn forward, k.1, p.2, k.2, Tw. 2, p.2.

2nd row: K.2, p.4, k.2, p.3, k.2, p.4, k.2.

3rd row: P.2, k.1, Tw. 2, k.1, p.2, k.3, p.2, k.1, Tw. 2, k.1, p.2.

4th row: As 2nd row.

5th row: P.2, Tw. 2, k.2, p.2, yarn back, sl.1, k.2, pass the sl. st. over the k.2, p.2, Tw. 2, k.2, p.2.

6th row: K.2, p.4, k.2, p.2, k.2, p.4, k.2.

These 6 rows form the pattern.

No. 328   Zigzag and Bobble Pattern 14 sts.

F.Cr., front cross thus: slip next 2 sts. to front on cable needle, p.1 from main needle, k.2 from cable needle. B.Cr., back cross thus: slip next st. to back on cable needle, k.2 from main needle, p.1 from cable needle.

1st row: (right side) P.3, k.2, p.9.

2nd row and foll. alt. rows: K. the k. sts. and p. the p. sts. as they present themselves.

3rd row: P.3, F.Cr., p.8.

5th row: P.4, F.Cr., p.7.

7th row: P.5, F.Cr., p.6.

9th row: P.6, F.Cr., p.5.

11th row: P.7, F.Cr., p.4.

13th row: P.5, p.1 leaving loop on left hand needle, k. in front and back of same loop 4 times more then drop loop (thus making 5 sts. out of 1 st.), p.2, F.Cr., p.3.

14th row: K.3, p.2, k.3, p.5, k.5.

15th row: P.5, sl. next 5 sts. on to right hand needle, yarn round needle then slip, one at a time, each of these 5 sts. over the yarn round needle, p.2, B.Cr., p.3.

17th row: P.7, B.Cr., p.4.

19th row: P.6, B.Cr., p.5.

21st row: P.5, B.Cr., p.6.

23rd row: P.4, B.Cr., p.7.

25th row: P.3, B.Cr., p.2, make 5 sts. out of next st. as 13th row, p.5.

26th row: K.5, p.5, k.3, p.2, k.3.

27th row: P.3, F.Cr., p.2, work 5 sts. tog. as 15th row, p.5.

28th row: As 2nd row.

The 5th to 28th rows form the pattern.

328 Zigzag and Bobble Panel

No. 329   Aran Braid and Diamond 16 sts.

C. 4 B., cable 4 back thus: slip next 2 sts. to back on cable needle, k.2, then k.2 from cable needle.

C. 4 F., cable 4 front thus: slip next 2 sts. to front on cable needle, k.2 from main needle, k.2 from cable needle.

C. 3 B., cable 3 back thus: slip next st. to back on cable needle, k.2, then p.1 from cable needle.

C. 3 F., cable 3 front thus: slip next 2 sts. to front on cable needle, p.1 from main needle, k.2 from cable needle.

1st row: (wrong side) K.5, p.6, k.5.

2nd, 6th and 10th rows: P.5, k.2, C. 4 B., p.5.

3rd row and foll. alt. rows: K. the k. sts. and p. the p. sts. as they present themselves.

329 Aran Braid and Diamond

4th, 8th and 12th rows: P.5, C. 4 F., k.2, p.5.
14th row: P.4, C. 3 B., k.2, C. 3 F., p.4.
16th row: P.3, C. 3 B., p.1, k.2, p.1, C. 3 F., p.3.
18th row: P.2, C. 3 B., p.2, k.2, p.2, C. 3 F., p.2.
20th row: P.2, C. 3 F., p.2, k.2, p.2, C. 3 B., p.2.
22nd row: P.3, C. 3 F., p.1, k.2, p.1, C. 3 B., p.3.
24th row: P.4, C. 3 F., k.2, C. 3 B., p.4.
These 24 rows form the pattern.

No. 330   Branch Cable Pattern 18 sts.
Cr. 6 R., cross 6 right thus: slip next 4 sts. to back on
cable needle, k.2, then p.2, k.2 from cable needle.
Cr. 6 L., cross 6 left thus: slip next 2 sts. to front on
cable needle, k.2, p.2, then k.2 from cable needle.
1st row: K.1, p.2, k.2, p.2, k.4, p.2, k.2, p.2, k.1.
2nd row: P.1, k.2, p.2, k.2, p.4, k.2, p.2, k.2, p.1.
3rd to 6th rows: Rep. 1st and 2nd rows twice more.
7th row: K.1, p.2, Cr. 6 R., Cr. 6 L., p.2, k.1.
8th row: As 2nd row.
9th to 11th rows: Rep. 1st and 2nd rows, then 1st row
once more.
12th row: P.1, k.16, p.1.
13th row: K. to end.
14th and 15th rows: As 12th and 13th rows.
16th row: As 12th row.
These 16 rows form the pattern.

330 Branch Cable Pattern

No. 331   Snake Diamonds 18 sts. plus 1
K.f.b., knit front and back thus: k. in front and back of
next st., making 2 sts. out of 1 st.
P.f.b., purl front and back thus: p. in front and back of
next st., making 2 sts. out of 1 st.
1st row: P.1, *k.3, p.11, k.3, p.1; rep. from * to end.
2nd row: K.1, *p.3, k.11, p.3, k.1; rep. from * to end.
3rd row: *P.f.b., k.3, p. 2 tog., p.7, p. 2 tog. t.b.l., k.2,
K.f.b.; rep. from * to last st., p.1.
4th row: K.2, *p.3, k.9, p.3, k.3; rep. from * ending last
rep., k.2 instead of k.3.
5th row: *P.1, P.f.b., k.3, p. 2 tog., p.5, p. 2 tog. t.b.l.,
k.2, K.f.b., p.1; rep. from * to last st., p.1.
6th row: K.3, *p.3, k.7, p.3, k.5; rep. from * ending last
rep., k.3 instead of k.5.
7th row: *P.2, P.f.b., k.3, p. 2 tog., p.3, p. 2 tog. t.b.l.,
k.2, K.f.b., p.2; rep. from * to last st., p.1.
8th row: K.4, *p.3, k.5, p.3, k.7; rep. from * ending last
rep., k.4 instead of k.7.
9th row: *P.3, P.f.b., k.3, p. 2 tog., p.1, p. 2 tog. t.b.l.,

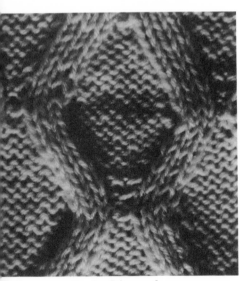

331 Snake Diamonds

k.2, K.f.b., p.3; rep. from * to last st., p.1.

10th row: K.5, *p.3, k.3, p.3, k.9; rep. from * to end, ending k.5 instead of k.9.

11th row: *P.4, P.f.b., k.3, p. 3 tog., k.2, K.f.b., p.4; rep. from * to last st., p.1.

12th row: K.6, *p.3, k.1, p.3, k.11; rep. from * ending last rep., k.6 instead of k.11.

13th row: *P.4, p. 2 tog. t.b.l., k.2, K.f.b., P.f.b., k.3, p. 2 tog., p.3; rep. from * to last st., p.1.

14th row: K.5, *p.3, k.3, p.3, k.9; rep. from * ending last rep., k.5 instead of k.9.

15th row: *P.3, p. 2 tog. t.b.l., k.2, K.f.b., p.2, P.f.b., k.3, p. 2 tog., p.2; rep. from * to last st., p.1.

16th row: K.4, *p.3, k.5, p.3, k.7; rep. from * to end, ending last rep., k.4 instead of k.7.

17th row: P.2, *p. 2 tog. t.b.l., k.2, K.f.b., p.4, P.f.b., k.3, p. 2 tog., p.3; rep. from * ending last rep., p.2 instead of p.3.

18th row: K.3, *p.3, k.7, p.3, k.5; rep. from * ending last rep., k.3 instead of k.5.

19th row: *P.1, p. 2 tog. t.b.l., k.2, K.f.b., p.6, P.f.b., k.3, p. 2 tog.; rep. from * to last st., p.1.

20th row: K.2, *p.3, k.9, p.3, k.3; rep. from * ending last rep., k.2 instead of k.3.

21st row: P. 2 tog. t.b.l., *k.2, K.f.b., p.8, P.f.b., k.3, p. 3 tog.; rep. from * ending last rep., p. 2 tog. instead of p. 3 tog.

22nd row: As 2nd row.

The 3rd to 22nd rows form the pattern.

No. 332 Cloque Pattern

This is the reverse of No. 331. Neither of them is a true cable pattern but has the characteristic raised look to the stitches that earns them a place in this section. The cloque pattern has an embossed diamond effect which is as useful on garments as on rugs cushions and blankets. Work the pattern as No. 331, having the even numbered rows as the right side of the work.

332 Cloque Pattern

333 Cable and Flags

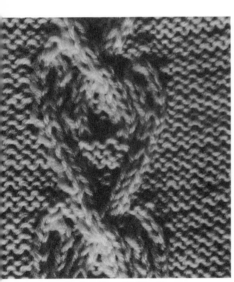

334 Valentine Cable Pattern

No. 333 Cable and Flags 34 sts.

C. 12, cable 12 thus: slip next 6 sts. to front on cable needle, k.6 from main needle, k.6 from cable needle.

1st row: P.2, k.2, p.1, k.24, p.1, k.2, p.2.
2nd row: K.2, p.2, k.2, p.22, k.2, p.2, k.2.
3rd row: P.2, k.2, p.3, k.20, p.3, k.2, p.2.
4th row: K.2, p.2, k.4, p.18, k.4, p.2, k.2.
5th row: P.2, k.2, p.5, k.2, C. 12, k.2, p.5, k.2, p.2.
6th row: K.2, p.2, k.6, p.14, k.6, p.2, k.2.
7th row: P.2, k.2, p.5, k.16, p.5, k.2, p.2.
8th row: As 4th row.
9th row: As 3rd row.
10th row: As 2nd row.
These 10 rows form the pattern.

No. 334 Valentine Cable Pattern 18 sts.

C. 4 F., cable 4 front thus: slip next 2 sts. to front on cable needle, k.2 from main needle, k.2 from cable needle.

B.Cr., back cross thus: slip next st. to back on cable needle, k.2 from main needle, p.1 from cable needle.

F.Cr., front cross thus: slip next 2 sts. to front on cable needle, p.1 from main needle, k.2 from cable needle.

1st row: (right side) P.7, C. 4 F., p.7.
2nd row: K.7, p.4, k.7.
3rd row: P.6, B.Cr., F.Cr., p.6.
4th row: K.6, p.2, k.2, p.2, k.6.
5th row: P.5, B.Cr., p.2, F.Cr., p.5.
6th row: K.5, p.2, k.4, p.2, k.5.
7th row: P.4, B.Cr., p.4, F.Cr., p.4.
8th row: K.4, p.2, k.6, p.2, k.4.
9th row: P.3, (B.Cr.) twice, (F.Cr.) twice, p.3.
10th row: K.3, (p.2, k.1, p.2, k.2) twice, ending second rep., k.3 instead of k.2.
11th row: P.2, (B.Cr.) twice, p.2, (F.Cr.) twice, p.2.
12th row: K.2, p.2, k.1, p.2, k.4, p.2, k.1, p.2, k.2.
13th row: P.2, k.1, sl. next st. to front on cable needle, p.1, then k.1 from cable needle, F.Cr., p.2, B.Cr., sl. next st. to back on cable needle, k.1, then p.1 from cable needle, k.1, p.2.
14th row: K.2, p.1, k.1, p.1, k.1, p.2, k.2, p.2, k.1, p.1, k.1, p.1, k.2.
15th row: P.2, k.1, p.1, cross 1 front as 13th row, F.Cr., B.Cr., cross 1 back as 13th row, p.1, k.1, p.2.
16th row: K.2, p.1, k.2, p.1, k.1, p.4, k.1, p.1, k.2, p.1, k.2.
17th row: P.2, cross 1 front as 13th row, cross 1 back as

13th row, p.1, C. 4 F., p.1, cross 1 front as 13th row, cross 1 back as 13th row, p.2.

18th row: K.3, sl. next st. to back on cable needle, k.1, then k.1 from cable needle, k.2, p.4, k.2, sl. next st. to front on cable needle, k.1, then k.1 from cable needle, k.3.

The 3rd to 18th rows form the pattern.

No. 335   Bobble Flower and Cable Pattern 37 sts.

Tw. 2 F., twist 2 front thus: slip next st. to front on cable needle, p.1, then k. 1 t.b.l. from cable needle.

Tw. 2 B., twist 2 back thus: slip next st. to back on cable needle, k. 1 t.b.l. from main needle, p.1 from cable needle.

M.B., make bobble thus: (k.1, p.1, k.1, p.1) all in next st., turn and k.4, turn and p.4, slip 2nd, 3rd and 4th sts. over the 1st st. – bobble made.

C. 9, cable 9 thus: slip next 3 sts. to back on cable needle, k.3 from main needle, bring cable needle between the two needles to front, k.3 from main needle, k.3 from cable needle.

335 Bobble Flower and Cable Pattern

1st row: P.2, k.9, p.6, k. 3 t.b.l., p.6, k.9, p.2.

2nd row: K.2, p.9, k.6, p. 3 t.b.l., k.6, p.9, k.2.

3rd row: P.2, k.9, p.5, Tw. 2 B., k. 1 t.b.l., Tw. 2 F., p.5, k.9, p.2.

4th row: K.2, p.9, k.5, (p. 1 t.b.l., k.1) twice, p. 1 t.b.l., k.5, p.9, k.2.

5th row: P.2, k.9, p.4, Tw. 2 B., p.1, k. 1 t.b.l., p.1, Tw. 2 F., p.4, k.9, p.2.

6th row: K.2, p.9, k.4, (p. 1 t.b.l., k.2) twice, p. 1 t.b.l., k.4, p.9, k.2.

7th row: P.2, k.9, p.3, Tw. 2 B., p.2, k. 1 t.b.l., p.2, Tw. 2 F., p.3, k.9, p.2.

8th row: K.2, p.9, k.3, (p. 1 t.b.l., k.3) 3 times, p.9, k.2.

9th row: P.2, k.9, p.2, Tw. 2 B., p.3, k. 1 t.b.l., p.3, Tw. 2 F., p.2, k. 9, p.2.

10th row: K.2, p.9, k.2, (p. 1 t.b.l., k.4) twice, p. 1 t.b.l., k.2, p.9, k.2.

11th row: P.2, C. 9, p.2, M.B., p.4, k. 1 t.b.l., p.4, M.B., p.2, C. 9, p.2.

12th row: K.2, p.9, k.7, p. 1 t.b.l., k.7, p.9, k.2.

These 12 rows form the pattern.

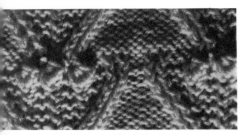

336 Chevron Bobble Pattern

No. 336 Chevron Bobble Pattern 21 sts.

C. 4 B., cable 4 back thus: slip next st. to back on cable needle, k. 1 t.b.l., p.1, k. 1 t.b.l. all from main needle, k.1 from cable needle.

C. 4 F., cable 4 front thus: slip next 3 sts. to front on cable needle, k.1 from main needle, k. 1 t.b.l., p.1, k. 1 t.b.l. all from cable needle.

M.B., make bobble thus: (k.1, yarn forward, k.1, yarn forward, k.1) all in next st., turn and p.5, turn and k.3, k. 2 tog., then pass the k. 3 sts. over the k. 2 tog. – bobble made.

1st row: (wrong side) K.7, p.1, k.1, p.3, k.1, p.1, k.7.
2nd row: P.6, C. 4 B., k. 1 t.b.l., C. 4 F., p.6.
3rd row: K.6, (p.1, k.1) 4 times, p.1, k.6.
4th row: P.5, C. 4 B., k.1, k. 1 t.b.l., k.1, C. 4 F., p.5.
5th row: K.5, p.1, k.1, (p.1, k.2) twice, p.1, k.1, p.1, k.5.
6th row: P.4, C. 4 B., k.2, k. 1 t.b.l., k.2, C. 4 F., p.4.
7th row: K.4, p.1, k.1, p.2, k.2, p.1, k.2, p.2, k.1, p.1, k.4.
8th row: P.3, C. 4 B., (k. 1 t.b.l., k.2) twice, k. 1 t.b.l., C. 4 F., p.3.
9th row: K.3, (p.1, k.1) twice, (p.1, k.2) twice, (p.1, k.1) twice, p.1, k.3.
10th row: P.2, C. 4 B., k.1, (k. 1 t.b.l., k.2) twice, k. 1 t.b.l., k.1, C. 4 F., p.2.
11th row: K.2, p.1, k.1, (p.1, k.2) 4 times, p.1, k.1, p.1, k.2.
12th row: P.1, C. 4 B., (k.2, k. 1 t.b.l.) 3 times, k.2, C. 4 F., p.1.
13th row: (K.1, p.1) twice, k.3, (p.1, k.2) twice, p.1, k.3, (p.1, k.1) twice.
14th row: (P.1, k. 1 t.b.l.) twice, k.3, (M.B., k.2) twice, M.B., k.3, (k. 1 t.b.l., p.1) twice.
15th row: (K.1, p.1) twice, k.3, (p. 1 t.b.l., k.2) twice, p. 1 t.b.l., k.3, (p.1, k.1) twice.
16th row: (P.1, k. 1 t.b.l.) twice, p.3, k. 1 t.b.l., p.1, k. 3 t.b.l., p.1, k. 1 t.b.l., p.3, (k. 1 t.b.l., p.1) twice.
These 16 rows form the pattern.

337 Fan Rib and Bobble Pattern

No. 337 Fan Rib and Bobble Pattern 19 sts.

M.B., make bobble thus: (p.1, k.1, p.1, k.1, p.1) all in next st., turn and k.5, turn and p.5, slip the 2nd, 3rd, 4th and 5th sts. over the 1st st. – bobble made.

B.Cr., back cross thus: slip next st. to back on cable needle, k.2 from main needle, p.1 from cable needle.

F.Cr., front cross thus: slip next 2 sts. to front on cable needle, p.1 from main needle, k.2 from cable needle.

1st row: (wrong side) K.2, p.2, (k.1, p. 1 t.b.l.) 5 times, k.1, p.2, k.2.

2nd row: P.7, k.2, M.B., k.2, p.7.

3rd row: K.7, p.2, k. 1 t.b.l., p.2, k.7.

4th row: P.6, B.Cr., k. 1 t.b.l., F.Cr., p.6.

5th row: K.6, p.2, k.1, p. 1 t.b.l., k.1, p.2, k.6.

6th row: P.5, B.Cr. *but* k. 1 t.b.l. from cable, p.1, k. 1 t.b.l., p.1, F.Cr. *but* k. 1 t.b.l. from main needle, p.5.

7th row: K.5, p.2, (p.1 t.b.l., k.1) twice, p.1 t.b.l., p.2, k.5.

8th row: P.4, B.Cr., (k. 1 t.b.l., p.1) twice, k. 1 t.b.l., F.Cr., p.4.

9th row: K.4, p.2, (k.1, p. 1 t.b.l.) 3 times, k.1, p.2, k.4.

10th row: P.3, B.Cr. as 6th row, (p.1, k. 1 t.b.l.) 3 times, p.1, F.Cr. as 6th row, p.3.

11th row: K.3, p.2, (p. 1 t.b.l., k.1) 4 times, p. 1 t.b.l., p.2, k.3.

12th row: P.2, B.Cr., (k. 1 t.b.l., p.1) 4 times, k. 1 t.b.l., F.Cr., p.2.

These 12 rows form the pattern.

No. 338 Bobble Bunches Pattern 15 sts.

Cr. 2 B.K., cross 2 back knit thus: slip next st. to back on cable needle, k.1 from main needle, k.1 from cable needle.

Cr. 2 F.K., cross 2 front knit thus: slip next st. to front on cable needle, k.1 from main needle, k.1 from cable needle.

Cr. 2 B.P., cross 2 back purl thus: slip next st. to back on cable needle, k.1 from main needle then p.1 from cable needle.

338 Bobble Bunches Pattern

Cr. 2 F.P., cross 2 front purl thus: slip next st. to front on cable needle, p.1 from main needle, k.1 from cable needle.

M.B., make bobble thus: (k.1, p.1) twice in next st., turn and p.4, turn and k.4, turn and (p. 2 tog.) twice, turn and k. 2 tog. – bobble made.

1st row: (wrong side) K.8, p.2, k.5.

2nd row: P.4, Cr. 2 B.K., Cr. 2 F.K., p.7.

3rd row: K.6, Cr. 2 F.P., p.2, Cr. 2 B.P., k.3.

4th row: P.2, Cr. 2 B.P., Cr. 2 B.K., Cr. 2 F.K., Cr. 2 F.P., p.5.

5th row: K.4, Cr. 2 F.P., k.1, p.4, k.1, Cr. 2 B.P., k.1.

6th row: Cr. 2 B.P., p.1, Cr. 2 B.P., k.2, Cr. 2 F.P., p.1, Cr. 2 F.P., p.3.

7th row: K.3, p.1, k.2, p.1, k.1, p.2, k.1, p.1, k.2, p.1.

8th row: M.B., p.1, Cr. 2 B.P., p.1, k.2, p.1, Cr. 2 F.P., p.1, M.B., p.3.

9th row: K.5, p.1, k.2, p.2, k.2, p.1, k.2.

10th row: P.2, M.B., p.2, k.2, p.2, M.B., p.5.

These 10 rows form the pattern.

339 Aran Moss and Bobble Pattern

No. 339 Aran Moss and Bobble Pattern 15 sts.
M.B., make bobble thus: (k.1, p.1, k.1, p.1, k.1, p.1, k.1) all in next st., slip 2nd, 3rd, 4th, 5th, 6th and 7th sts. on right hand needle over 1st st. – bobble made.
B.Cr., back cross thus: slip next st. to back on cable needle, k.2 from main needle, p.1 from cable needle.
F.Cr., front cross thus: slip next 2 sts. to front on cable needle, p.1 from main needle, k.2 from cable needle.
1st row: (right side) P.5, k.2, M.B., k.2, p.5.
2nd row: K.5, p.5, k.5.
3rd row: P.5, M.B., p.3, M.B., p.5.
4th row: As 2nd row.
5th row: As 1st row.
6th row: As 2nd row.
7th row: P.4, B.Cr., p.1, F.Cr., p.4.
8th row: K.4, p.2, k.1, p.1, k.1, p.2, k.4.
9th row: P.3, B.Cr., k.1, p.1, k.1, F.Cr., p.3.
10th row: K.3, p.3, k.1, p.1, k.1, p.3, k.3.
11th row: P.2, B.Cr., (p.1, k.1) twice, p.1, F.Cr., p.2.
12th row: K.2, p.2, (k.1, p.1) 3 times, k.1, p.2, k.2.
13th row: P.2, k.3, (p.1, k.1) twice, p.1, k.3, p.2.
14th row: As 12th row.
15th row: P.2, F.Cr., (p.1, k.1) twice, p.1, B.Cr., p.2.
16th row: As 10th row.
17th row: P.3, F.Cr., k.1, p.1, k.1, B.Cr., p.3.
18th row: As 8th row.
19th row: P.4, F.Cr., p.1, B.Cr., p.4.
20th row: As 2nd row.
These 20 rows form the pattern.

No. 340 Triple Cable Pattern 26 sts.
C. 4 B., cable 4 back thus: slip next 2 sts. to back on cable needle, k.2 from main needle, k.2 from cable needle.
C. 4 F., cable 4 front thus: slip next 2 sts. to front on cable needle, k.2 from main needle, k.2 from cable needle.
C. 4 B.P., cable 4 back purl thus: slip next 2 sts. to back on cable needle, k.2 from main needle, p.2 from cable needle.
C. 4 F.P., cable 4 front purl thus: slip next 2 sts. to front on cable needle, p.2 from main needle, k.2 from cable needle.
B.Cr., back cross thus: slip next st. to back on cable needle, k.2 from main needle, p.1 from cable needle.
F.Cr., front cross thus: slip next 2 sts. to front on cable needle, p.1 from main needle, k.2 from cable needle.

340 Triple Cable Pattern

1st row: (wrong side) K.11, p.4, k.11.
2nd row: P.11, C. 4 B., p.11.
3rd row: As 1st row.
4th row: P.9, C. 4 B., C. 4 F., p.9.
5th row and foll. alt. rows: K. the k. sts. and p. the p.
sts. as they present themselves.
6th row: P.7, C. 4 B.P., C. 4 F., C. 4 F.P., p.7.
8th row: P.5, C. 4 B.P., p.2, k.4, p.2, C. 4 F.P., p.5.
10th row: P.4, B.Cr., p.4, C. 4 F., p.4, F.Cr., p.4.
12th row: P.3, B.Cr., p.3, C. 4 B., C. 4 F., p.3, F.Cr.,
p.3.
14th row: P.2, B.Cr., p.2, C. 4 B.P., k.4, C. 4 F.P., p.2,
F.Cr., p.2.
16th row: P.2, k.2, p.1, C. 4 B.P., p.2, C. 4 B., p.2, C. 4
F.P., p.1, k.2, p.2.
18th row: P.2, k.2, p.1, k.2, p.4, k.4, p.4, k.2, p.1, k.2,
p.2.
20th row: P.2, k.2, p.1, C. 4 F.P., p.2, C. 4 B., p.2, C. 4
B.P., p.1, k.2, p.2.
22nd row: P.2, F.Cr., p.2, C. 4 F.P., k.4, C. 4 B.P., p.2,
B.Cr., p.2.
24th row: P.3, F.Cr., p.3, C. 4 F.P., C. 4 B.P., p.3,
B.Cr., p.3.
26th row: P.4, F.Cr., p.4, C. 4 F., p.4, B.Cr., p.4.
28th row: P.5, C. 4 B.P., p.2, k.4, p.2, C. 4 B.P., p.5.
30th row: P.7, C. 4 F.P., C. 4 F., C. 4 B.P., p.7.
32nd row: P.9, C. 4 F.P., C. 4 B.P., p.9.
These 32 rows form the pattern.

No. 341   Trellis with Moss Stitch 28 sts.

B.Cr., back cross thus: slip next st. to back on cable
needle, k. 2 t.b.l. from main needle, p.1 from cable
needle.
F.Cr., front cross thus: slip next 2 sts. to front on cable
needle, k.1 from main needle, k. 2 t.b.l. from cable
needle.
F.Cr.P., front cross purl thus: slip next 2 sts. to front on
cable needle, p.1 from main needle, k. 2 t.b.l. from cable
needle.
1st row: (right side) P.5, slip next 2 sts. to front on cable
needle, k. 2 t.b.l. from main needle, k. 2 t.b.l. from
cable needle, p.10, cable 4 front t.b.l. as before, p.5.
2nd row and foll. alt. rows: K. the k. sts. and p. the p.
sts. as they present themselves.
3rd row: P.4, B.Cr., F.Cr., p.8, B.Cr., F.Cr., p.4.
5th row: P.3, (B.Cr., k.1, p.1, F.Cr.), p.6, rep. bracketed
portion once more, p.3.

341 Trellis with Moss Stitch

7th row: P.2, B.Cr., (k.1, p.1) twice, F.Cr., p.4, B.Cr., (k.1, p.1) twice, F.Cr., p.2.
9th row: P.1, B.Cr., (k.1, p.1) 3 times, F.Cr., p.2, B.Cr., (k.1, p.1) 3 times, F.Cr., p.1.
11th row: *B.Cr., (k.1, p.1) 4 times, F.Cr.; rep. from * once more.
13th row: K. 2 t.b.l., (k.1, p.1) 5 times, C. 4 front t.b.l. as 1st row, (k.1, p.1) 5 times, k. 2 t.b.l.
15th row: *F.Cr.P., (k.1, p.1) 4 times, B.Cr.; rep. from * once more.
17th row: P.1, F.Cr.P., (k.1, p.1) 3 times, B.Cr., p.2, F.Cr.P., (k.1, p.1) 3 times, B.Cr., p.1.
19th row: P.2, F.Cr.P., (k.1, p.1) twice, B.Cr., p.4, F.Cr.P., (k.1, p.1) twice, B.Cr., p.2.
21st row: P.3, F.Cr.P., k.1, p.1, B.Cr., p.6, F.Cr.P., k.1, p.1, B.Cr., p.3.
23rd row: P.4, F.Cr.P., B.Cr., p.8, F.Cr.P., B.Cr., p.4.
24th row: As 2nd row.
These 24 rows form the pattern.

342 Cable, Diamonds and Plaits

No. 342   Cable, Diamonds and Plaits 36 sts.
C. 4 F., cable 4 front thus: slip next 2 sts. to front on cable needle, k.2 from main needle, k.2 from cable needle.
C. 4 B., cable 4 back thus: slip next 2 sts. to back on cable needle, k.2 from main needle, k.2 from cable needle.
C. 2 F., cable 2 front thus: slip next st. to front on cable needle, p.1 from main needle, k. 1 t.b.l. from cable needle.
C. 2 B., cable 2 back thus: slip next st. to back on cable needle, k. 1 t.b.l. from main needle, p.1 from cable needle.
Tw. 2, twist 2 thus: k. second st. on left hand needle, then k. first st. and slip both loops off together.
Cr. 2 F.K., cross 2 front knit thus: slip next st. to front on cable needle, k.1 from main needle, then k. 1 t.b.l. from cable needle.
Cr. 2 B.K., cross 2 back knit thus: slip next st. to back on cable needle, k. 1 t.b.l. from main needle, k. 1 from cable needle.
1st row: K.4, p.1, (k. 1 t.b.l., p.1) 6 times, k. 2 t.b.l., (p.1, k. 1 t.b.l.) 6 times, p.1, k.4.
2nd row: P.4, k.1, (p. 1 t.b.l., k.1) 6 times, p. 2 t.b.l., (k.1, p. 1 t.b.l.) 6 times, k.1, p.4.
3rd row: C. 4 F., (p.1, k. 1 t.b.l.) 4 times, (C. 2 B.) 3 times, (C. 2 F.) 3 times, (k. 1 t.b.l., p.1) 4 times, C. 4 B.

4th row: P.4, k.1, (p. 1 t.b.l., k.1) 3 times, p. 2 t.b.l., (k.1, p. 1 t.b.l.) twice, k.2, (p. 1 t.b.l., k.1) twice, p. 2 t.b.l., (k.1, p. 1 t.b.l.) 3 times, k.1, p.4.

5th row: K.4, p.1, (k. 1 t.b.l., p.1) 3 times, (C. 2 B.) 3 times, Tw. 2, (C. 2 F.) 3 times, (p.1, k. 1 t.b.l.) 3 times, p.1, k.4.

6th row: P.4, k.1, (p. 1 t.b.l., k.1) 6 times, p.2, (k.1, p. 1 t.b.l.) 6 times, k.1, p.4.

7th row: C. 4 F., (p.1, k. 1 t.b.l.) 3 times, (C. 2 B.) 3 times, p.1, Tw. 2, p.1, (C. 2 F.) 3 times, (k. 1 t.b.l., p.1) 3 times, C. 4 B.

8th row: P.4, (k.1, p. 1 t.b.l.) 3 times, (p. 1 t.b.l., k.1) 3 times, k.1, p.2, k.1, (k.1, p. 1 t.b.l.) 3 times, (p. 1 t.b.l., k.1) 3 times, p.4.

9th row: K.4, (p.1, k. 1 t.b.l.) twice, p.1, (C. 2 B.) 3 times, p.2, Tw. 2, p.2, (C. 2 F.) 3 times, (p.1, k. 1 t.b.l.) twice, p.1, k.4.

10th row: P.4, (k.1, p. 1 t.b.l.) 5 times, k.3, p.2, k.3, (p. 1 t.b.l., k.1) 5 times, p.4.

11th row: C. 4 F., (p.1, k. 1 t.b.l.) twice, (C. 2 B.) 3 times, p.3, Tw. 2, p.3, (C. 2 F.) 3 times, (k. 1 t.b.l., p.1) twice, C. 4 B.

12th row: P.4, (k.1, p. 1 t.b.l.) twice, (p. 1 t.b.l., k.1) 3 times, k.3, p.2, k.3, (k.1, p. 1 t.b.l.) 3 times, (p. 1 t.b.l., k.1) twice, p.4.

13th row: K.4, p.1, k. 1 t.b.l., p.1, (C. 2 B.) 3 times, p.4, Tw. 2, p.4, (C. 2 F.) 3 times, p.1, k. 1 t.b.l., p.1, k.4.

14th row: P.4, (k.1, p. 1 t.b.l.) 4 times, k.5, p.2, k.5, (p. 1 t.b.l., k.1) 4 times, p.4.

15th row: C. 4 F., p.1, k. 1 t.b.l., (C. 2 B.) 3 times, p.5, Tw. 2, p.5, (C. 2 F.) 3 times, k. 1 t.b.l., p.1, C. 4 B.

16th row: P.4, k.1, p. 2 t.b.l., (k.1, p. 1 t.b.l.) twice, k.6, p.2, k.6, (p. 1 t.b.l., k.1) twice, p. 2 t.b.l., k.1, p.4.

17th row: K.4, p.1, k. 1 t.b.l., (C. 2 F.) 3 times, p.5, Tw. 2, p.5, (C. 2 B.) 3 times, k. 1 t.b.l., p.1, k.4.

18th row: P.4, k.1, (p. 1 t.b.l., k.1) 4 times, k.4, p.2, k.5, (p. 1 t.b.l., k.1) 4 times, p.4.

19th row: C. 4 F., p.1, k. 1 t.b.l., p.1, C. 2 F.K., (C. 2 F.) twice, p.4, Tw. 2, p.4, (C. 2 B.) twice, C. 2 B.K., p.1, k. 1 t.b.l., p.1, C. 4 B.

20th row: P.4, (k.1, p. 1 t.b.l.) twice, (p. 1 t.b.l., k.1) 3 times, k.3, p.2, k.3, (k.1, p. 1 t.b.l.) 3 times, (p. 1 t.b.l., k.1) twice, p.4.

21st row: K.4, (p.1, k. 1 t.b.l.) twice, (C. 2 F.) 3 times, p.3, Tw. 2, p.3, (C. 2 B.) 3 times, (k. 1 t.b.l., p.1.) twice, k.4.

22nd row: P.4, (k.1, p. 1 t.b.l.) 5 times, k.3, p.2, k.3,

(p. 1 t.b.l., k.1) 5 times, p.4.

23rd row: C. 4 F., (p.1, k. 1 t.b.l.) twice, p.1, C. 2 F.K., (C. 2 F.) twice, p.2, Tw. 2, p.2, (C. 2 B.) twice, C. 2 B.K., (p.1, k. 1 t.b.l.) twice, p.1, C. 4 B.

24th row: P.4, k.1, (p. 1 t.b.l., k.1) twice, p. 2 t.b.l., (k.1, p. 1 t.b.l.) twice, k.2, p.2, k.2, (p. 1 t.b.l., k.1) twice, p. 2 t.b.l., (k.1, p. 1 t.b.l.) twice, k.1, p.4.

25th row: K.4, p.1, (k. 1 t.b.l., p.1) twice, k. 1 t.b.l., (C. 2 F.) 3 times, p.1, Tw. 2, p.1, (C. 2 B.) 3 times, (k. 1 t.b.l., p.1.) 3 times, k.4.

26th row: P.4, (k.1, p. 1 t.b.l.) 6 times, k.1, p.2, k.1, (p. 1 t.b.l., k.1) 6 times, p.4.

27th row: C. 4 F., p.1, (k. 1 t.b.l., p.1) 3 times, C. 2 F.K., (C. 2 F.) twice, Tw. 2, (C. 2 B.) twice, C. 2 B.K., (p.1, k. 1 t.b.l.) 3 times, p,1, C. 4 B.

28th row: P.4, (k.1, p. 1 t.b.l.) 4 times, (p. 1 t.b.l., k.1) twice, p. 1 t.b.l., p.2, p. 1 t.b.l., (k.1, p. 1 t.b.l.) twice, (p. 1 t.b.l., k.1) 4 times, p.4.

29th row: K.4, (p.1, k. 1 t.b.l.) 4 times, (C. 2 F.) 3 times, (C. 2 B.) 3 times, (k. 1 t.b.l., p.1) 4 times, k.4.
The 2nd to 19th rows form the pattern.

343 Diamonds within Diamonds

No. 343 Diamonds within Diamonds 18 sts.

1st row: K. 1 t.b.l., p.5, k. 1 t.b.l., p.1, (k. 1 t.b.l.) twice, p.1, k. 1 t.b.l., p.5, k. 1 t.b.l.

2nd row: P. 1 t.b.l., k.5, p. 1 t.b.l., k.1, (p. 1 t.b.l.) twice, k.1, p. 1 t.b.l., k.5, p. 1 t.b.l.

3rd row: K. 1 t.b.l., p.4, (sl. next st. to back on cable needle, k. 1 t.b.l. from main needle, p.1 from cable needle) twice, (sl. next st. to front on cable needle, p.1 from main needle, k. 1 t.b.l. from cable needle) twice, p.4, k. 1 t.b.l.

4th row: P. 1 t.b.l., k.4, p. 1 t.b.l., k.1, p. 1 t.b.l., k.2, p. 1 t.b.l., k.1, p. 1 t.b.l., k.4, p. 1 t.b.l.

5th row: K. 1 t.b.l., p.3, (sl. next st. to back on cable needle, k. 1 t.b.l. from main needle, p.1 from cable needle) twice, p.2, (sl. next st. to front on cable needle, p.1 from main needle, k. 1 t.b.l. from cable needle) twice, p.3, k. 1 t.b.l.

6th row: P. 1 t.b.l., k.3, p. 1 t.b.l., k.1, p. 1 t.b.l., k.4, p. 1 t.b.l., k.1, p. 1 t.b.l., k.3, p. 1 t.b.l.

7th row: K. 1 t.b.l., p.2, (sl. next st. to back on cable needle, k. 1 t.b.l. from main needle, p.1 from cable needle) twice *but k.1 from cable needle on second repeat*, p.4, (sl. next st. to front on cable needle, k. 1 t.b.l. from main needle, k. 1 t.b.l. from cable needle) twice, *but p.1 from main needle on second repeat*, p.2, k. 1 t.b.l.

8th row: P. 1 t.b.l., k.2, p. 1 t.b.l., k.1, (p. 1 t.b.l.) twice, k.4, (p. 1 t.b.l.) twice, k.1, p. 1 t.b.l., k.2, p. 1 t.b.l.

9th row: K. 1 t.b.l., p.1, (sl. next st. to back on cable needle k. 1 t.b.l., p.1 from cable needle) twice, sl. next st. to front on cable needle, p.1 from main needle, k. 1 t.b.l. from cable needle, p.2, sl. next st. to back on cable needle, k. 1 t.b.l. from main needle, p. 1 from cable needle, (sl. next st. to front on cable needle, p.1 from main needle, k. 1 t.b.l. from cable needle) twice, p.1, k. 1 t.b.l.

10th row: (P. 1 t.b.l., k.1) twice, p. 1 t.b.l., (k.2, p. 1 t.b.l.) 3 times, (k.1, p. 1 t.b.l.) twice.

11th row: K. 1 t.b.l., (sl. next st. to back on cable needle, k. 1 t.b.l., then p.1 from cable needle) twice, p.2, sl. next st. to front on cable needle, p.1, then k. 1 t.b.l. from cable needle, sl. next st. to back on cable needle k. 1 t.b.l., then p.1 from cable needle, p.2, (sl. next st. to front on cable needle, p.1, then k. 1 t.b.l. from cable needle) twice, k. 1 t.b.l.

12th row: (P. 1 t.b.l.) twice, k.1, p. 1 t.b.l., k.4, sl. next st. to front on cable needle, p. 1 t.b.l., p.1 from cable needle, k.4, p. 1 t.b.l., k.1, (p. 1 t.b.l.) twice.

13th row: K. 1 t.b.l., (sl. next st. to front on cable needle, p.1, then k. 1 t.b.l. from cable needle) twice, p.2, sl. next st. to back on cable needle, k. 1 t.b.l., then p.1 from cable needle, sl. next st. to front on cable needle, p.1, then k. 1 t.b.l. from cable needle, p.2, (sl. next st. to back on cable needle, k. 1 t.b.l., then p.1 from cable needle) twice, k. 1 t.b.l.

14th row: (P. 1 t.b.l., k.1) twice, p. 1 t.b.l., (k.2, p. 1 t.b.l.) 3 times, (k.1, p. 1 t.b.l.) twice.

15th row: K. 1 t.b.l., p.1, (sl. next st. to front on cable needle, p.1, then k. 1 t.b.l. from cable needle) twice, sl. next st. to back on cable needle, k. 1 t.b.l., then p.1 from cable needle, p.2, sl. next st. to front on cable needle, p.1, then k. 1 t.b.l. from cable needle, (sl. next st. to back on cable needle, k. 1 t.b.l. then p.1 from cable needle) twice, p.1, k. 1 t.b.l.

16th row: As 8th row.

17th row: K. 1 t.b.l., p.2, (sl. next st. to front on cable needle, p.1, then k. 1 t.b.l. from cable needle) twice, p.4, (sl. next st. to back on cable needle, k. 1 t.b.l., then p.1 from cable needle) twice, p.2, k. 1 t.b.l.

18th row: As 6th row.

19th row: K. 1 t.b.l., p.3, (sl. next st. to front on cable needle, p.1, then k. 1 t.b.l. from cable needle) twice, p.2, (sl. next st. to back on cable needle, k. 1 t.b.l., then p.1 from cable needle) twice, p.3, k. 1 t.b.l.

20th row: As 4th row.

21st row: K. 1 t.b.l., p.4, (sl. next st. to front on cable needle, p.1, then k. 1 t.b.l. from cable needle) twice, (sl. next st. to back on cable needle, k. 1 t.b.l., then p.1 from cable needle) twice, p.4, k. 1 t.b.l.

22nd row: P. 1 t.b.l., k.5, p. 1 t.b.l., k.1, sl. next st. to front on cable needle, p. 1 t.b.l., p.1 from cable needle, k.1, p. 1 t.b.l., k.5, p. 1 t.b.l.

The 3rd to 22nd rows form the pattern.

No. 344   Multi Cable Pattern 49 sts.

This elaborate pattern of cables within cables makes an ideal centre panel for an Aran patterned garment. Although it requires some concentration it is not exceptionally difficult to work.

C. 4 F., cable 4 front thus: slip next 2 sts. to front on cable needle, k.2 from main needle, k.2 from cable needle.

C. 4 B., cable 4 back thus: slip next 2 sts. to back on cable needle, k.2 from main needle, k.2 from cable needle.

Inc. loop p., pick up loop between sts. and p. in back of it.

1st row: (right side) (p.2, k.4) 4 times, p.1, (k.4, p.2) 4 times.

2nd row: (K.2, p.4) 4 times, k.1, (p.4, k.2) 4 times.

3rd row: (P.2, C. 4 F., p.2, k.4) twice, p.1, (k.4, p.2, C. 4 B., p.2) twice.

4th, 6th and 8th rows: As 2nd row.

5th row: As 1st row.

7th row: P.2, C. 4 F., p.2, k.4, p.2, C. 4 F., p.2, sl. next 5 sts. to front on cable needle, k.4, then sl. the p. st. back on to left hand needle and p. it, then k.4 from cable needle, p.2, C. 4 B., p.2, k.4, p.2, C. 4 B., p.2.

9th row: P.2, k.4, p.2, *inc. loop p., (k.4, p.2) twice, k.4, inc. loop p.*, p.1, rep. from * to *, p.2, k.4, p.2.

10th row: K.2, p.4, *k.3, p.4, (k.2, p.4) twice; rep. from * once more, k.3, p.4, k.2.

11th row: P.2, C. 4 F., p.3, inc. loop p., k.4, p. 2 tog., C. 4 F., p. 2 tog., k.4, inc. loop p., p.3, inc. loop p., k.4, p. 2 tog., C. 4 B., p. 2 tog., k.4, inc. loop p., p.3, C. 4 B., p.2.

12th row: K.2, p.4, k.4, *(p.4, k.1) twice, p.4*, k.5 rep. from * to *, k.4, p.4, k.2.

13th row: P.2, k.4, p.4, *inc. loop p., k.3, sl.1, k.1, p.s.s.o., k.4, k. 2 tog., k.3, inc. loop p., p.5, rep. from * to *, p.4, k.4, p.2.

344 Multi Cable Pattern

14th row: K.2, p.4, k.5, p.12, k.7, p.12, k.5, p.4, k.2.
15th row: P.2, C. 4 F., p.5, inc. loop p., k.4, C. 4 F., k.4, inc. loop p., p.7, inc. loop p., k.4, C. 4 B., k.4, inc. loop p., p.5, C. 4 B., p.2.
16th row: K.2, p.4, k.6, p.12, k.9, p.12, k.6, p.4, k.2.
17th row: P.2, k.4, p.6, sl. next 8 sts. to back on cable needle, k.4 from main needle, then sl. the last 4 sts. from cable needle back on to left hand needle and k. them, then k.4 from cable needle (thus crossing the 8 sts.), p.9, sl. next 8 sts. to front on cable needle, k.4 from main needle, sl. the last 4 sts. from cable needle back on to left hand needle and k. them, then k.4 from cable needle, p.6, k.4, p.2.
18th, 20th, 22nd and 24th rows: Repeat 16th, 14th, 12th and 10th rows in that order.
19th row: P.2, C. 4 F., p.4, p. 2 tog., k.4, C. 4 F., k.4, p. 2 tog., p.5, p. 2 tog., k.4, C. 4 B., k.4, p. 2 tog., p.4, C. 4 B., p.2.
21st row: P.2, k.4, p.3, *p. 2 tog., (k.4, inc. loop p.) twice, k.4, p. 2 tog., p.3; rep. from * to last 6 sts., k.4, p.2.
23rd row: P.2, C. 4 F., p.2, p. 2 tog., k.4, inc. loop p., p.1, C. 4 F., p.1, inc. loop p., k.4, p. 2 tog., p.1, p. 2 tog., k.4, inc. loop p., p.1, C. 4 B., p.1, inc. loop p., k.4, p. 2 tog., p.2, C. 4 B., p.2.
25th row: P.2, k.4, p.1, p. 2 tog., *(k.4, p.2) twice, k.4*, p. 3 tog., rep. from * to *, p. 2 tog., p.1, k.4, p.2.
26th row: As 2nd row.
27th row: As 7th row.
28th row: As 2nd row.
These 28 rows form the pattern.

SIX INTRODUCING COLOUR

Working rows of pattern in contrasting colours is probably the simplest method of introducing this different concept of knitted fabric. It can range from straightforward striped garter and stocking stitches to multi-coloured and devious stitch arrangements.

While some of the patterns in this section do involve carrying the colours not in use loosely along the back of the work, they should not be confused with Fair Isle or true jacquard knitting. The jacquard technique is quite separate and since it does not use intrinsic stitch arrangement (being more a system of building up a picture or decoration on stocking stitch), it is not dealt with here.

When working in two or several colours, a little more planning is necessary. First, consider the colours. Will they look as attractive when knitted together as they do in the skeins? Remember that the twists of the stitches may bring together a joining of colours that was not foreseen, and results that can vary from a disaster to an effective and successful design. The inexperienced knitter may prefer to restrict the colour work to small portions of the garment. For instance, the yoke of a jumper can be enlivened by introducing colour; a man's waistcoat looks good with colour patterned fronts and just one of the colours used for the back, and children's clothes are especially attractive with bright splashes of colour pattern contrast on, say, the sleeves and collar. Small left-over balls of yarn can be used up by working rows of colour into a raised texture pattern stitch against a smooth pattern in the main colour. It is not advisable to use random dyed yarns for patterned work since neither the stitch nor the colour quality is shown to advantage.

Be prepared to work many samples before beginning the intended garment. Keep to a set of colours that will either contrast well, for example, navy blue and pink, brown and cream etc., or tone suitably, such as dark and pale blue, maroon red and pink, etc. Having decided upon the colours, choose the pattern stitch equally carefully. Only trial and error will show just how the knitted fabric will look. Try working the samples in this section but also experiment with other patterns previously worked in only single colour. This could produce surprising and often useful results.

It may not be easy to calculate how much yarn you will require for a colour pattern. Where patterns involving slipped stitches are used, these have a tendency to draw in the over-all measurements. Should slightly thicker knitting needles be used to compensate for this, it could affect the amount of yarn needed. Since it is assumed that the knitter will simply be adapting a commercial pattern in the first instance and introducing colour without altering shape, the proportions are best calculated in the following manner. First, knit a small sample square of pattern in the single colour of the original yarn. Then work a similar square, using the colour or colours in the proportions intended for the finished pattern. Having measured the tension of the colour sample – this will save having to work a tension sample later – unpick both squares and measure with a tape measure how much has been used for each. Where the stitch pattern is an equal number of rows, this may not be necessary as the proportions will obviously be equal, but in other cases it will show the correct ratio of proportional yardage. The size of the sample square is not important but it must contain one or more complete pattern repeats in both width and depth.

These patterns start with the easiest colour pattern of all: striped garter stitch. Colour patterns provide an infinite variety of knitted fabrics – the permutations are endless and could not possibly all be contained here. There are many more just waiting to be discovered, and whilst these have been worked in similar yarn qualities, a whole new range of texture and pattern may emerge if you venture into mixing stitch, colour and yarn quality.

No. 345   Single Ridge Striped Garter Stitch Any number of sts.

1st and 2nd rows: With A., sl. 1 knitwise, k. to end.
3rd and 4th rows: With B., sl. 1 knitwise, k. to end.
These 4 rows form the pattern

345 Single Ridge Striped Garter Stitch

151

346 Single Row Tri-coloured Stocking Stitch Stripes

347 Merged Purl Stripe Pattern

348 Pinstripe Pattern

No. 346   Single Row Tri-coloured Stocking Stitch Stripes Any number of sts.
1st row: With A., k. to end.
2nd row: With B., p. to end.
3rd row: With C., k. to end.
4th row: With A., p. to end.
5th row: With B., k. to end.
6th row: With C., p. to end.
These 6 rows form the pattern.

No. 347   Merged Purl Stripe Pattern Any number of sts.
1st row: (right side) With A., p. to end.
2nd row: With A., k. to end.
3rd row: With B., p. to end.
4th row: With B., k. to end.
These 4 rows form the pattern.

No. 348   Pinstripe Pattern Any number of sts.
Note that double pointed needles are required for this pattern.
1st row: (right side) With A., k. to end.
2nd row: (wrong side) With A., p. to end.
3rd row: With A., k. to end.
4th row: With A., p. to end.
5th row: With B., k. to end and return to beginning of row.
6th row: (right side) With A., k. to end.
7th row: (wrong side) With B., p. to end and return to beginning of row.
8th row: With A., p. to end.
9th row: With A., k. to end.
10th row: With A., p. to end.
11th row: With A., k. to end and return to beginning of row.
12th row: With B., k. to end.
13th row: With A., p. to end and return to beginning of row.
14th row: With B., p. to end.
These 14 rows form the pattern.

No. 349   Ruched Pattern Any number of sts.
1st row: (wrong side) With B., p. to end.
2nd row: With B., k. in front and back of each st. to end.
3rd row: With B., p. to end.
4th row: With B., k. to end.
5th and 6th rows: Rep. 3rd and 4th rows.
7th row: As 3rd row.
8th row: With B., (k. 2 tog.) to end.
Change to needles one size thicker.
9th to 16th rows: With A., beginning p. row, work in
stocking stitch.
These 16 rows form the pattern.

349 *Ruched Pattern*

No. 350   Slip Stitch Stripes 2 sts. plus 1
1st row: With B., *k.1, sl. 1 purlwise; rep. from * to last
st., k.1.
2nd row: With B., p. to end.
3rd row: With B., k. to end.
4th row: As 2nd row.
5th row: With A., sl. 1 purlwise, *k.1, sl. 1 purlwise;
rep. from * to end.
6th to 8th rows: Using A. instead of B., as 2nd to 4th
rows.
9th to 12th rows: Using C., instead of B., as 1st to 4th
rows.
13th to 16th rows: As 5th to 8th rows.
These 16 rows form the pattern.

350 *Slip Stitch Stripes*

No. 351   Moss Stitch Stripes 2 sts. plus 1
1st row: (right side) With A., k. to end.
2nd row: With A., p. to end.
3rd and 4th rows: With A., rep. 1st and 2nd rows.
5th and 6th rows: With B., k.1, *p.1, k.1; rep. from * to
end.
These 6 rows form the pattern.

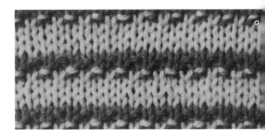

351 *Moss Stitch Stripes*

No. 352   Three Colour Brioche Pattern 4 sts.
plus 1
1st row: (right side) With B., k. to end.
2nd row: With B., *k.1, k. in next st. but into loop of
row below, at the same time slipping st. above off the
needle; rep. from * to last st., k.1.
3rd row: With C., k. to end.
4th row: With C., k.2, *k. in next st. but into loop of
row below at the same time slipping st. above off the
needle, k.1; rep. from * to last st., k.1.

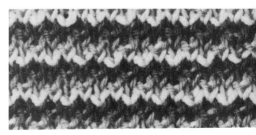

352 *Three Colour Brioche Pattern*

5th row: With A., k. to end.
6th row: With A., as 2nd row.
7th row: With B., k. to end.
8th row: With B., as 4th row.
9th row: As 3rd row.
10th row: With C., as 2nd row.
11th row: As 5th row.
12th row: With A., as 4th row.
These 12 rows form the pattern.

No. 353   Three Colour Brioche Pattern
reversed 4 sts. plus 1
This attractive pattern is formed by working No. 352 in reverse, having the 1st row and following alternate rows as the wrong side of the work.

353 Three Colour Brioche Pattern reversed

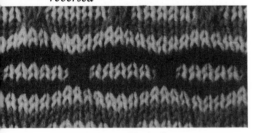

354 Colour Chain Pattern

No. 354   Colour Chain Pattern 8 sts. plus 6
1st row: (right side) With B., k. to end.
2nd row: With B., p. to end.
3rd row: With A., k.6, *with yarn at back, sl. 2 purlwise, k.6; rep. from * to end.
4th row: With A., p.6, *with yarn at front, sl. 2 purlwise, p.6; rep. from * to end.
5th row: With B., as 3rd row.
6th row: With B., p. to end.
7th row: With A., k. to end.
8th row: With A., p. to end.
9th and 10th rows: With C., as 1st and 2nd rows.
11th row: With A., k.2, sl. 2 purlwise as before, *k.6, sl. 2 purlwise as before; rep. from * to last 2 sts., k.2.
12th row: With A., p.2, sl. 2 purlwise as before, *p.6, sl. 2 purlwise; rep. from * to last 2 sts., p.2.
13th row: With C., as 11th row.
14th row: With C., p. to end.
15th and 16th rows: As 7th and 8th rows.
These 16 rows form the pattern.

No. 355   Ripple Colour Pattern 3 sts. plus 2
1st row: With B., k.1, *k.2, sl. 1 purlwise; rep. from * to
last st., k.1.
2nd row: With B., k. to end.
3rd row: With A., k.1, *k.2, sl. 1 purlwise; rep. from *
to last st., k.1.
4th row: With A., k. to end.
These 4 rows form the pattern.

355 Ripple Colour Pattern

No. 356   Fancy Striped Pattern Even number of
sts.
1st row: With A., k. to end.
2nd row: With A., (k. 2 tog.) to end.
3rd row: With A., k. in front and back of each st. to end.
4th row: With A., k.1, p. to last st., k.1.
5th to 8th rows: With B., as 1st to 4th rows.
These 8 rows form the pattern.

356 Fancy Striped Pattern

No. 357   Beechnut Weave 4 sts.
1st and 2nd rows: With A., *k.2, p.2; rep. from * to end.
3rd and 4th rows: With A., *p.2, k.2; rep. from * to end.
5th and 6th rows: With B., *k.2, p.2; rep. from * to end.
7th and 8th rows: With A., *p.2, k.2; rep. from * to end.
9th and 10th rows: With A., *k.2, p.2; rep. from * to end.
11th and 12th rows: With B., *p.2, k.2; rep. from * to
end.
These 12 rows form the pattern.

357 Beechnut Weave

No. 358   Tabard Stripes Even number of sts.
1st row: With B., *k.1, p.1; rep. from * to end.
2nd row: With B., p. to end.
3rd row: With B., *p.1, k.1; rep. from * to end.
4th row: With B., p. to end.
5th to 8th rows: With A., as 1st to 4th rows.
These 8 rows form the pattern.

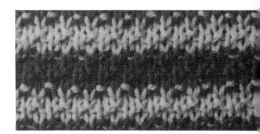

358 Tabard Stripes

No. 359   Crinkle Colour Pattern 4 sts. plus 2
K. lp., knit loop thus: pick up loop between sts. and k.
it.
Work two foundation rows of stocking stitch before
commencing pattern.
1st row: With B., k.4, *K. lp., k.1, K. lp., k.3; rep. from *
ending last rep., k.1 instead of k.3.
2nd row: With B., p.1, *p. 3 tog., p.3; rep. from *
ending last rep., p.4, instead of p.3.

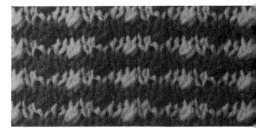

359 Crinkle Colour Pattern

3rd row: With A., k.2, *K. lp, k.1, K. lp., k.3; rep. from *
to end.
4th row: With A., p.3, *p. 3 tog., p.3; rep. from *
ending last rep., p.2 instead of p.3.
These 4 rows form the pattern.

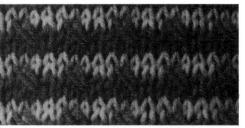

360 Cross Weave Colour

No. 360 Cross Weave Colour 4 sts. plus 1
Y.3 r.n., k.1 winding yarn 3 times round needle.
Sl. lp., slip loop thus: slip loop dropping extra loops to
form a long st.
Tw. 3, twist 3 thus: drop long loop off needle, then,
holding it at front of work, k. next 2 sts. from main
needle, slip the long loop back on to right hand needle
without knitting it.
1st row: With B., k.1, *k.1, Y.3 r.n., k.3; rep. from * to
end.
2nd row: With A., *p.3, Sl. lp.; rep. from * to last st.,
p.1.
3rd row: With A., *k.1, Tw. 3; rep. from * to last st.,
k.1.
4th row: With B., p. to end.
These 4 rows form the pattern.

361 Vertical Pin Stripes

No. 361 Vertical Pin Stripes 2 sts. plus 1
Slip all sts. purlwise on this pattern.
1st row: With B., keeping yarn at back of work, *sl.1,
k.1; rep. from * to last st., sl.1.
2nd row: With B., keeping yarn at front of work, *sl.1,
p.1; rep. from * to last st., sl.1.
3rd row: With A., keeping yarn at back of work, *k.1,
sl.1; rep. from * to last st., k.1.
4th row: With A., keeping yarn at front of work, *p.1,
sl.1; rep. from * to last st., p.1.
These 4 rows form the pattern.

362 Speckled Rib

No. 362 Speckled Rib 3 sts. plus 1
Double pointed knitting needles are required for this
pattern. Slip all slip sts. purlwise.
1st row: (right side) With B., k.1, *yarn back, sl.2, yarn
forward, p.1; rep. from * to last 3 sts., yarn back, sl.2,
k.1.
2nd row: (wrong side) With A., k.1, yarn forward, *p.2,
sl.1; rep. from * to last 3 sts., p.2, k.1.
3rd row: (right side) With A., *sl.1, k.2; rep. from * to
last st., k.1.
4th row: As 2nd row.
5th row: With A., sl.1, k. to end.

6th row: (wrong side) With B., k.1, *yarn forward, sl.2, yarn back, k.1; rep. from * to end and return to beginning of row.

7th row: (wrong side) As 2nd row.

8th row: (right side) As 3rd row.

9th row: (wrong side) As 2nd row.

10th row: (right side) With A., sl.1, k. to end and return to beginning of row.

These 10 rows form the pattern.

No. 363 Two Colour Slip Stitch Rib 4 sts. plus 3

Despite its title this is a slightly raised pattern without the usual elasticity of rib.

Slip all slipped sts. purlwise on this pattern.

1st row: (right side) With B., k.1, *with yarn at back, sl.1, k.3; rep. from * to last 2 sts., sl.1, k.1.

2nd row: With B., p.1, *keeping yarn at front, sl.1, p.3; rep. from * to last 2 sts., sl.1, p.1.

3rd row: With A., k.3, *with yarn at back, sl.1, k.3; rep. from * to end.

4th row: With A., p.3, *with yarn at front, sl.1, p.3; rep. from * to end.

These 4 rows form the pattern.

363 Two Colour Slip Stitch Rib

No. 364 Shadow Check Pattern 6 sts. plus 5

Slip all slipped sts. purlwise on this pattern.

1st row: (wrong side) With A., k. to end.

2nd row: With B., *k.5, sl.1; rep. from * to last 5 sts., k.5.

3rd row: With B., *k.5, yarn forward, sl.1, yarn back; rep. from * to last 5 sts., k.5.

4th row: With A., *k.2, sl.1; rep. from * to last 2 sts., k.2.

5th row: With A., *k.2, yarn forward, sl.1, yarn back; rep. from * to last 2 sts., k.2.

6th row: With A., k.2, *sl.1, k.5; rep. from * to last 3 sts., sl.1, k.2.

These 6 rows form the pattern.

364 Shadow Check Pattern

No. 365 Little Block Checks 4 sts. plus 2

Slip all sts. purlwise on this pattern and take care to carry yarn not in use loosely across the back of the work.

1st row: With A., k. to end.

2nd row: With A., p. to end.

3rd row: With B., *k.2, sl.2; rep. from * to last 2 sts., k.2.

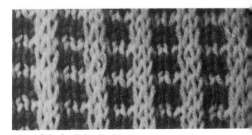

365 Little Block Checks

4th row: With B., *p.2, sl.2; rep. from * to last 2 sts., p.2.
These 4 rows form the pattern.

No. 366   Laddered Checks 10 sts. plus 13
Slip all slipped sts. purlwise on this pattern.
1st row: With A., k. to end.
2nd row: With A., p. to end.
3rd row: With B., k.1, with yarn at back sl.1, k.1, sl.1, *k.5, sl.1, (k.1, sl.1) twice; rep. from * to end, omitting last sl.1.
4th row: With B., (k.1, yarn forward, sl.1, yarn back) twice, *k.5, (yarn forward, sl.1, yarn back, k.1) twice, yarn forward, sl.1, yarn back; rep. from * to last 9 sts., k.5, (yarn forward, sl.1, yarn back, k.1) twice.
5th row: With A., sl.1, k.1, sl.1, *k.7, sl.1, k.1, sl.1; rep. from * to end.
6th row: With A., p. to end.
The 3rd to 6th rows form the pattern.

366 Laddered Checks

No. 367   Slip Stitch Checks 6 sts. plus 4
Slip all slipped sts. purlwise on this pattern.
1st row: With B., (k.5, sl.1) to last 4 sts., k.4.
2nd row: With B., p.4, *sl.1, p.5; rep. from * to end.
3rd row: With A., k.4, *sl.1, k.5; rep. from * to end.
4th row: With A., *p.5, sl.1; rep. from * to last 4 sts., p.4.
These 4 rows form the pattern.

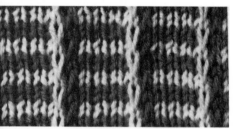

367 Slip Stitch Checks

No. 368   Stocking Stitch over Checks 10 sts. plus 6
The horizontal stripes in the pattern are knitted in. The vertical stripes are worked with a crochet hook, instructions for which follow the pattern. If preferred, the vertical stripes may be embroidered with chain stitch.
1st row: With B., k.2, *p.2, k.8; rep. from * to last 4 sts., p.2, k.2.
2nd row: With B., p.2, *k.2, p.8; rep. from * to last 4 sts., k.2, p.2.
3rd row: With B., as 1st row.
4th row: With A., as 2nd row.
5th row: With A., as 1st row.
6th row: With A., as 2nd row.
7th to 14th rows: Rep. last 2 rows 4 times more.
These 14 rows form the basic pattern.
When all the pieces have been completed, work the vertical stripes thus: beginning at lower edge, using B.

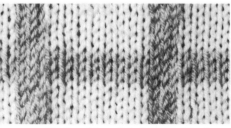

368 Stocking Stitch over Checks

and a crochet hook, with yarn at back of work, insert hook through first st. from front to back, draw loop through, *insert hook into st. in next row above, draw loop through then through loop on hook; rep. from * to top of work. Repeat the stripe up second purl line and work a third line between these two.

No. 369 Block Check Pattern 7 sts. plus 5
1st row: K. 5 A., *2 B., 5 A.; rep. from * to end.
2nd row: P. 5 A., *2 B., 5 A; rep. from * to end.
3rd to 8th rows: Rep. 1st and 2nd rows 3 times more.
9th row: K. 5 B., *2 A., 5 B.; rep. from * to end.
10th row: P. 5 B., *2 A., 5 B.; rep. from * to end.
These 10 rows form the pattern.

369 Block Check Pattern

No. 370 Flannel Check Pattern 4 sts. plus 3
Always slip the long st. knitwise on this pattern to form a twisted bar on the right side of the work.
1st row: (wrong side) With B., *p.3, k.1; rep. from * to last 3 sts., p.3.
2nd row: With B., *k.3, k.1 winding yarn twice round needle; rep. from * to last 3 sts., k.3.
3rd row: With A., *p.3, keeping yarn at front, sl. 1 (see note above) dropping extra loop; rep. from * to last 3 sts., p.3.
4th row: With A., *k.3, sl.1; rep. from * to last 3 sts., k.3.
5th row: With A., *p.3, sl.1; rep. from * to last 3 sts., p.3.
6th row: With A., as 4th row.
These 6 rows form the pattern.

370 Flannel Check Pattern

No. 371 Broken Check Pattern 8 sts. plus 10
Slip all slipped sts. purlwise on this pattern.
Double pointed needles are required for this pattern.
1st row: (right side) With B., k.3, *sl.1, k.2, sl.1, k.4; rep. from * ending last rep., k.3 instead of k.4.
2nd row: With B., p.3, *sl.1, p.2, sl.1, p.4; rep. from * ending last rep., p.3 instead of p.4.
3rd row: With A., k.2, *miss next st., k. into front of sl. st., k. the missed st., then drop loops off left hand needle, k.1, miss next st., k. sl. st., k. missed st., k.3; rep. from * to end.
Return to beginning of row.
4th row: (right side) With B., k.2, *with needle at back of work k. into back of 2nd st. on left hand needle, sl.

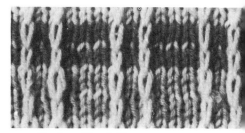

371 Broken Check Pattern

1st st. then drop loops off left hand needle, k.1, k. into back of 2nd st. on left hand needle, sl. 1st st. and drop loops off as before, k.3; rep. from * to end.

5th row: (wrong side) With B., p.3, *sl.1, p.2, sl.1, p.4; rep. from * ending last rep., p.3 instead of p.4. Return to beginning of row.

6th row: (wrong side) With A., p. to end.

7th row: With C., as 1st row.

8th row: With C., as 2nd row.

9th row: With A., as 3rd row.

10th row: With C., as 4th row.

11th row: With C., as 5th row.

12th row: With A., p. to end.

13th row: With A., as 1st row.

14th row: With A., as 2nd row.

15th row: With A., as 3rd row.

16th row: With A., *p.4, sl.1, p.2, sl.1; rep. from * to last 2 sts., p.2.

17th row: With A., as 4th row.

18th row: With A., p. to end.

These 18 rows form the pattern.

372 *Hexagon Pattern*

No. 372 Hexagon Pattern 6 sts. plus 5

1st row: With B., k. to end.

2nd row: As 1st row.

3rd row: With A., k.5, *sl. 1 purlwise, k.5; rep. from * to end.

4th row: With A., p.5, *sl. 1 purlwise, p.5; rep. from * to end.

5th row: As 3rd row.

6th row: As 4th row.

7th and 8th rows: As 1st and 2nd rows.

9th row: With A., k.2, *sl. 1 purlwise, k.5; rep. from * to last 3 sts., sl.1, k.2.

10th row: With A., p.2, *sl. 1 purlwise, p.5; rep. from * to last 3 sts., sl.1, p.2.

11th and 12th rows: As 9th and 10th rows.

These 12 rows form the pattern.

373 *Wave Colour Stripes*

No. 373 Wave Colour Stripes 11 sts.

1st row: (right side) With A., k. to end.

2nd row: With A., k.1, p. to last st., k.1.

3rd row: With A., *(p. 2 tog.) twice, (inc. 1 by picking up loop between sts. and knitting in back of it, k.1) 3 times, inc. 1 as before, (p. 2 tog.) twice; rep. from * to end.

4th row: As 2nd row.

5th to 8th rows: With B., as 1st to 4th rows.

9th to 12th rows: With C., as 1st to 4th rows.
These 12 rows form the pattern.

No. 374   Feathered Stripes 9 sts. plus 1
1st row: With A., k.1, *yarn forward, k.1, sl.1, k.1,
p.s.s.o., k.2, k. 2 tog., k.1, yarn forward, k.1; rep. from *
to end.
2nd row: With A., p. to end.
3rd row: With A., as 1st row.
4th row: With B., p. to end.
5th row: With B., p. to end.
6th row: With B., k. to end.
7th row: With B., as 1st row.
The 2nd to 7th rows form the pattern.

374 Feathered Stripes

No. 375   Striped Scallop Pattern 18 sts. plus 1
1st row: (right side) With B., k. to end.
2nd row: As 1st row.
3rd row: With B., p. to end.
4th row: As 1st row.
5th row: With A., *k.1, (k. 2 tog.) 3 times, yarn forward,
(k.1, yarn forward) 5 times, (k. 2 tog. t.b.l.) 3 times; rep.
from * to last st., k.1.
6th row: With A., p. to end.
7th to 16th rows: Rep. 5th and 6th rows 5 times.
These 16 rows form the pattern.

375 Striped Scallop Pattern

No. 376   Striped Chevrons 16 sts.
1st row: With A., k.1, *k. twice in next st., k.5, sl.1, k. 2
tog., p.s.s.o., k.5, k. twice in next st., k.1; rep. from * to
end.
2nd row: With A., p.1, *p. twice in next st., p.5, p. 3
tog., p.5, p. twice in next st., p.1; rep. from * to end.
3rd and 4th rows: With B., as 1st and 2nd rows.
5th and 6th rows: As 1st and 2nd rows.
7th and 8th rows: With C., as 1st and 2nd rows.
These 8 rows form the pattern.

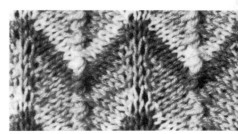

376 Striped Chevrons

No. 377   Mini Check Pattern 4 sts.
Slip all slipped sts. purlwise on this pattern, taking care
not to tighten yarn across back of work.
1st row: (right side) With B., k.3, *sl.2, k.2; rep. from *
to last st., k.1.
2nd row: With B., p.3, *sl.2, p.2; rep. from * to last st.,
p.1.
3rd row: With A., k. to end.
4th row: With C., p.1, *sl.2, p.2; rep. from * to last 3
sts., sl.2, p.1.

377 Mini Check Pattern

5th row: With C., k.1, *sl.2, k.2; rep. from * to last 3 sts., sl.2, k.1.
6th row: With A., p. to end.
These 6 rows form the pattern.

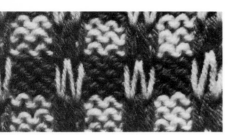

378 Mosaic Squares

No. 378 Mosaic Squares 6 sts.
1st row: With B., *k.2, (yarn round needle, p.1) twice, k.2; rep. from * to end.
2nd row: With A., *k.2, (sl. 1 purlwise dropping off yarn round needle of previous row) twice, k.2; rep. from * to end.
3rd row: With A., *k.2, yarn forward, sl. 2 purlwise, yarn back, k.2; rep. from * to end.
4th row: With A., *k.2, keeping yarn back, sl. 2 purlwise, k.2; rep. from * to end.
5th row: As 3rd row.
6th row: As 4th row.
7th row: With A., *k.2, (yarn round needle, p.1) twice, k.2; rep. from * to end.
8th to 13th rows: With B., rep. 2nd to 7th rows.
The 2nd to 13th rows form the pattern.

379 Piazza Pattern

No. 379 Piazza Pattern 5 sts. plus 3
Slip all slipped sts. purlwise on this pattern.
1st row: With B., k.3, *sl.2, k.3; rep. from * to end.
2nd row: With B., p.3, *(p.1 winding yarn twice round needle) twice, p.3; rep. from * to end.
3rd row: With A., k.3, *sl. 2 dropping extra loops thus making 2 long sts., k.3; rep. from * to end.
4th row: With A., k.3, *yarn forward, sl.2, yarn back, k.3; rep. from * to end.
5th row: With A., k.3, *sl.2, k.3; rep. from * to end.
6th row: With A., p.3, *(p.1 winding yarn twice round needle) twice, p.3; rep. from * to end.
7th row: With B., k.3, *sl. 2 dropping extra loops as before, k.3; rep. from * to end.
8th row: With B., k.3, *yarn forward, sl.2, yarn back, k.3; rep. from * to end.
These 8 rows form the pattern.

No. 380   Bird's Eye Tweed Pattern 2 sts. plus 3
1st row: With B., p. to end.
2nd row: (right side) With B., p. to end.
3rd row: With A., p.1, *keeping yarn forward, sl. 1 purlwise, p.1; rep. from * to last 2 sts., sl. 1 purlwise, p.1.
4th row: With A., p.1, *yarn back, sl. 1 purlwise, yarn forward, p.1; rep. from * to last 2 sts., sl. 1 purlwise, p.1.
5th and 6th rows: With B., p. to end.
7th row: With A., p.1, *p.1, keeping yarn forward, sl. 1 purlwise; rep. from * to last 2 sts., p.2.
8th row: With A., p.1, *p.1, yarn back, sl. 1 purlwise, yarn forward; rep. from * to last 2 sts., p.2.
These 8 rows form the pattern.

380 Bird's Eye Tweed Pattern

No. 381   Bird's Eye Tweed Pattern reversed 2 sts. plus 3
By working the 1st row and following alternate rows of No. 380 as the right side of the work, one finds yet another well-textured all-over pattern.

381 Bird's Eye Tweed Pattern reversed

No. 382   Speckled Moss Tweed 2 sts. plus 1
1st row: With A., k.1, *p.1, k.1; rep. from * to end.
2nd row: With B., as 1st row.
3rd row: With C., as 1st row.
These 3 rows form the pattern with no breaking and joining of colours necessary.

382 Speckled Moss Tweed

No. 383   Brioche Tweed Even number of sts.
1st row: (right side) With B., *k. 1 through next st. in row below, p.1; rep. from * to end.
2nd row: With B., k. to end.
3rd row: With A., *p.1, k. 1 through next st. in row below; rep. from * to end.
4th row: With A., k. to end.
These 4 rows form the pattern.

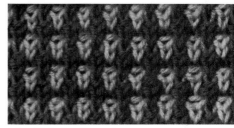

383 Brioche Tweed

384 Donegal Tweed Pattern

No. 384   Donegal Tweed Pattern 4 sts. plus 2
1st row: With A., k.2, *yarn forward sl. 2 sts. purlwise, yarn back sl. the 2 sts. back on to left hand needle, yarn forward, sl. the 2 sts. on to right hand needle again, yarn back, thus making 2 loops round the 2 sl. sts., k.2; rep. from * to end.
2nd row: With A., p. to end.
3rd row: With B., k.4, then rep. from * to 1st row to last 2 sts., k.2.
4th row: With B., p. to end.
These 4 rows form the pattern.

385 Knots Pattern

No. 385   Knots Pattern 2 sts. plus 1
1st row: (right side) With B., *k. in front and back of next st., yarn forward, sl. 1 purlwise, yarn back; rep. from * to last st., k. in front and back of last st.
2nd row: With B., p. 2 tog., *yarn back, sl.1, yarn forward, p. 2 tog.; rep. from * to end.
3rd and 4th rows: With A., k. to end.
These 4 rows form the pattern.

386 Knots Pattern reversed

No. 386   Knots Pattern reversed
The chunky knitted effect of pattern No. 385 is completely contrasted by its reversed side. Either side of this cellular type of fabric is suitable for outdoor wear, rugs, pram covers, etc.

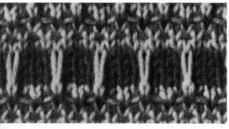

387 Mexican Pattern

No. 387   Mexican Pattern 4 sts. plus 3
Slip all slipped sts. purlwise on this pattern.
1st row: With B., k.1, *yarn forward, sl.1, yarn back, k.1; rep. from * to end.
2nd row: With B., p. to end.
3rd row: With A., yarn forward, sl.1, *yarn back, k.1, yarn forward, sl.1; rep. from * to end.
4th row: With A., p. to end.
5th row: With B., k.1, *sl.1, k.3; rep. from * to last 2 sts., sl.1, k.1.
6th row: With B., p.1, *sl.1, p.3; rep. from * ending last rep., p.1 instead of p.3.
7th and 8th rows: Rep. 5th and 6th rows.
9th and 10th rows: With A., k. 1 row, then p. 1 row.
11th to 14th rows: Rep. 1st to 4th rows.

15th row: With B., k.3, *sl.1, k.3; rep. from * to end.
16th row: With B., p.3, *sl.1, p.3; rep. from * to end.
17th and 18th rows: Rep. 15th and 16th rows.
19th and 20th rows: With A., k. 1 row then p. 1 row.
These 20 rows form the pattern.

No. 388   Two Colour Blocks 4 sts.
1st row: (right side) With B., k.1, *yarn forward, sl.2 purlwise, yarn back, k.2; rep. from * to last 3 sts., yarn forward, sl. 2 purlwise, yarn back, k.1.
2nd row: With B., sl.1, *p.2, yarn back, sl. 2 purlwise, yarn forward; rep. from * to last 3 sts., p.2, sl.1.
3rd row: With A., as 1st row.
4th row: With A., as 2nd row.
These 4 rows form the pattern.

388 Two Colour Blocks

No. 389   Slip Stitch Honeycomb 2 sts. plus 1
Slip all slipped sts. purlwise on this pattern.
1st row: (right side) With A., k. to end.
2nd row: With A., k.1, *sl.1, k.1; rep. from * to end.
3rd row: With B., k. to end.
4th row: With B., sl.1, *k.1, sl.1; rep. from * to end.
These 4 rows form the pattern.

389 Slip Stitch Honeycomb

No. 390   Crossgates Pattern 4 sts.
1st row: (wrong side) With A., *p.1, sl. 1 purlwise, k.2; rep. from * to end.
2nd row: With A., as 1st row.
3rd row: With B., *k.2, p.1, sl. 1 purlwise; rep. from * to end.
4th row: With B., as 3rd row.
5th and 6th rows: With C., as 1st row.
7th and 8th rows: With A., as 3rd row.
9th and 10th rows: With B., as 1st row.
11th and 12th rows: With C., as 3rd row.
These 12 rows form the pattern.

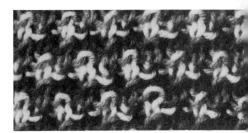

390 Crossgates Pattern

No. 391   Tri-colour Tweed 4 sts. plus 2
1st row: (wrong side) With A., *k.1, p.1; rep. from * to end.
2nd row: With C., *sl. 2 purlwise, k.1, p.1, yarn back; rep. from * to last 2 sts., sl.2.
3rd row: With B., *k.1, p.1, sl. 2 purlwise, yarn back; rep. from * to last 2 sts., k.1, p.1.
4th row: With A., *k.1, p.1; rep. from * to end.
5th row: With C., p. to end.

391 Tri-colour Tweed

165

6th row: With B., *sl.2, k.2; rep. from * to last 2 sts., sl.2.

These 6 rows form the pattern.

No. 392   Linen Weave 2 sts. plus 1
Slip all slipped sts. purlwise for this pattern.
1st row: (right side) With A., k.1, *yarn forward, sl.1, yarn back, k.1; rep. from * to end.
2nd row: With B., p. to end.
3rd row: With C., *yarn forward, sl.1, yarn back, k.1; rep. from * to last st., yarn forward, sl.1.
4th row: With A., p. to end.
5th row: With B., as 1st row.
6th row: With C., p. to end.
7th row: With A., as 3rd row.
8th row: With B., p. to end.
9th row: With C., as 1st row.
10th row: With A., p. to end.
11th row: With B., as 3rd row.
12th row: With C., p. to end.

These 12 rows form the pattern.

392 Linen Weave

No. 393   Worsted Pattern 2 sts. plus 1
1st row: With B., *k.1, keeping yarn back, sl. 1 purlwise; rep. from * to last st., k.1.
2nd row: With B., k. to end.
3rd row: With A., *keeping yarn back, sl. 1 purlwise, k.1; rep. from * to last st., sl. 1 purlwise.
4th row: With A., k. to end.

These 4 rows form the pattern.

393 Worsted Pattern

No. 394   Giant Houndstooth Check 12 sts.
1st row: K. *1 A., 4 B., 7 A.; rep. from * to end.
2nd row: P. *7 A., 3 B., 2 A.; rep. from * to end.
3rd row: K. *1 B., 2 A., 3 B., 6 A.; rep. from * to end.
4th row: P. *6. A., 2 B., 2 A., 2 B.; rep. from * to end.
5th row: K. *3 B., 2 A., 1 B., 6 A.; rep. from * to end.
6th row: P. *9 A., 3 B.; rep. from * to end.
7th row: K. *7 B, 4 A., 1 B.; rep. from * to end.
8th row: P. *1 B., 3 A., 8 B.; rep. from * to end.
9th row: K. *9 B., 3 A.; rep. from * to end.
10th row: P. *2 A., 3 B., 1 A., 6 B.; rep. from * to end.
11th row: K. *6 B., 2 A., 3 B., 1 A.; rep. from * to end.
12th row: P. *3 B., 3 A., 6 B.; rep. from * to end.

These 12 rows form the pattern.

394 Giant Houndstooth Check

No. 395 Diced Stocking Stitch 8 sts. plus 3

1st row: K. to end with A.

2nd row: P. to end with A.

3rd and 4th rows: Rep. 1st and 2nd rows.

5th row: With B., k.3, *drop next st. down 3 rows and k. the st. 3 rows below together with the 3 loops above, k.3; rep. from * to end.

6th and 8th rows: With B., p. to end.

7th row: With B., k. to end.

9th row: With A., k.1, *drop next st. down 3 rows and k. the st. 3 rows below together with the 3 loops above, k.3; rep. from * ending last rep., k.1 instead of k.3.

10th, 11th and 12th rows: With A., as 6th, 7th and 8th rows.

The 5th to 12th rows form the pattern.

395 Diced Stocking Stitch

No. 396 Lozenge Pattern 4 sts.

1st row: K. 2 B., *1 A., 3 B.; rep. from * to last 2 sts., 1 A., 1 B.

2nd row: P. 1 B., *2 A., 2 B.; rep. from * to last 3 sts., 2 A., 1 B.

3rd row: K. *2 A., 2 B.; rep. from * to end.

4th row: P. *3 B., 1 A.; rep. from * to end.

These 4 rows form the pattern.

396 Lozenge Pattern

No. 397 Slip Weave Pattern 4 sts.

1st row: (right side) With B., k.3, *keeping yarn at back, sl. 2 purlwise, k.2; rep. from * to last st., k.1.

2nd row: With B., p.3, *with yarn towards you, sl. 2 purlwise, p.2; rep. from * to last st., p.1.

3rd row: With A., k.3, *miss 1 sl. st., k. in back of second sl. st. then k. in front of missed st. and slip both loops off together, k.2; rep. from * to last st., k.1.

4th row: With A., p. to end.

5th row: With B., k.1, *sl. 2 as 1st row, k.2; rep. from * to end, ending last rep., k.1 instead of k.2.

6th row: With B., p.1, *sl. 2 as 2nd row, p.2; rep. from * to end, ending last rep., p.1 instead of p.2.

7th row: With A., k.1, *cross next 2 sts. as 3rd row, k.2; rep. from * to last 3 sts., cross next 2 sts., k.1.

8th row: With A., p. to end.

These 8 rows form the pattern.

397 Slip Weave Pattern

398 Ridges and Slip Stitch Pattern

No. 398 Ridges and Slip Stitch Pattern 8 sts. plus 6

1st row: With B., k. to end.

2nd row: As 1st row.

3rd row: With A., k.6, *keeping yarn at back, sl. 2 purlwise, k.6; rep. from * to end.

4th row: With A., p.6, *keeping yarn towards you, sl. 2 purlwise, p.6; rep. from * to end.

5th row: With A., k.6, *keeping yarn at back, sl. 1 purlwise, k.1, yarn forward to make a st., then holding yarn over right hand needle, p.s.s.o. the k. st. and the made st., k.6; rep. from * to end.

6th row: With A., p. to end.

7th row: With B., k. to end.

8th row: As 7th row.

9th row: With A., k.2, *keeping yarn at back, sl. 2 purlwise, k.6; rep. from * to last 4 sts., sl. 2 as before, k.2.

10th row: With A., p.2, sl. 2 purlwise, *p.6, sl. 2 purlwise; rep. from * to last 2 sts., p.2.

11th row: With A., k.2, keeping yarn at back, sl. 1 purlwise, k.1, yarn forward to make a st., then holding yarn over right hand needle, p.s.s.o. the k. st. and the made st., *k.6, keeping yarn at back, sl. 1 purlwise, k.1, yarn forward to make a st., holding yarn over right hand needle, p.s.s.o. the k. st. and the made st.; rep. from * to last 2 sts., k.2.

12th row: With A., p. to end.

These 12 rows form the pattern.

No. 399 Castellated Pattern 8 sts. plus 2

Slip all slipped sts. purlwise for this pattern.

1st row: With A., k.1, *with yarn at back, sl.1, k.6, sl.1; rep. from * to last st., k.1.

2nd row: With B., k.1, *with yarn at front, sl.1, p.6, sl.1; rep. from * to last st., k.1.

3rd row: As 1st row.

4th row: As 2nd row.

5th row: With B., k. to end.

6th row: With B., p. to end.

7th row: With C., k.1, *k.3, with yarn at back, sl.2, k.3; rep. from * to last st., k.1.

8th row: With C., k.1, *p.3, with yarn at front, sl.2, p.3; rep. from * to last st., k.1.

9th and 10th rows: As 7th and 8th rows.

11th and 12th rows: With C., as 5th and 6th rows.

13th to 18th rows: With A., as 1st to 6th rows.

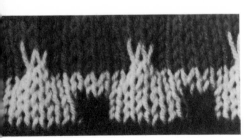

399 Castellated Pattern

19th to 24th rows: With B., as 7th to 12th rows.
25th to 30th rows: With C., as 1st to 6th rows.
31st to 36th rows: With A., as 7th to 12th rows.
These 36 rows form the pattern.

No. 400 Dogtooth Check 4 sts. plus 1
1st row: K. *2 A., 1 B., 1 A.; rep. from * to last st., 1 A.
2nd row: P. *1 A., 3 B.; rep. from * to last st., 1 A.
3rd row: K. *3 B., 1 A.; rep. from * to last st., 1 B.
4th row: As 2nd row.
5th row: K. *1 A., 1 B., 2 A.; rep. from * to last st., 1 A.
6th row: P. 1 A., *1 A., 1 B., 2 A.; rep. from * to end.
7th row: K. *1 A., 3 B.; rep. from * to last st., 1 A.
8th row: P. 1 B., *1 A., 3 B.; rep. from * to end.
9th row: As 7th row.
10th row: P. 1 A., *2 A., 1 B., 1 A.; rep. from * to end.
These 10 rows form the pattern.

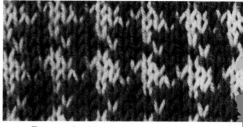

400 *Dogtooth Check*

No. 401 Diced Checks 6 sts. plus 3
The pattern looks the same on both sides but notice that
the colours reverse.
1st row: With B., k.3, *p.3, k.3; rep. from * to end.
2nd row: With B., p.3, *k.3, p.3; rep. from * to end.
3rd row: As 1st row.
4th row: As 2nd row.
5th row: With A., k.1, drop next st. down 4 rows, insert
needle knitwise into dropped st. under 4 loops and k.
the st., *k.1, p.3, k.1, drop next st. down 4 rows, insert
needle knitwise into loop and under 4 loops and k. the
st.; rep. from * to last st., k.1.
6th row: With A., p.3, *k.3, p.3; rep. from * to end.
7th row: With A., k.3, *p.3, k.3; rep. from * to end.
8th row: As 6th row.
9th row: With B., k.3, *p.1, drop next st. down 4 rows,
put needle behind 4 loops and into dropped st. and p.
the st., p.1, k.3; rep. from * to end.
10th row: With B., as 2nd row.
11th row: With B., as 1st row.
12th row: As 10th row.
The 5th to 12th rows form the pattern.

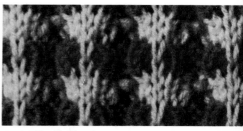

401 *Diced Checks*

402 Slip Stitch Diagonal Pattern

No. 402 Slip Stitch Diagonal Pattern 6 sts. plus 8
1st row: (right side) With A., k.5, *yarn back, sl. 2 purlwise, k.4; rep. from * to last 3 sts., sl. 2 purlwise, k.1.
2nd row: With A., k.1, *yarn forward, sl. 2 purlwise, p.4; rep. from * to last st., k.1.
3rd row: With B., k.3, *sl. 2 purlwise, k.4; rep. from * to last 5 sts., sl.2, k.3.
4th row: With B., k.1, p.2, *sl. 2 purlwise, p.4; rep. from * to last st., k.1.
5th row: With A., k.5, *sl. 2 purlwise, k.4; rep. from * to last 3 sts., sl. 2 purlwise, k.1.
6th row: With A., k.1, *p.4, sl. 2 purlwise; rep. from * to last st., k.1.
7th row: With B., as 1st row.
8th row: With B., as 2nd row.
9th row: With A., as 3rd row.
10th row: With A., as 4th row.
11th row: With B., as 5th row.
12th row: With B., as 6th row.
These 12 rows form the pattern.

403 Crossed Trellis

No. 403 Crossed Trellis 8 sts. plus 2
Tr. 8., trellis 8 sts. thus: slip next 8 sts. on to right hand needle dropping extra loops to form long sts., insert point of left hand needle through 5th, 6th, 7th and 8th sts. and cross them over 1st, 2nd, 3rd and 4th sts. and on to left hand needle, then slip the first four sts. back on to left hand needle and k.8 as now set.
1st, 2nd, 3rd and 4th rows: With A., k. to end.
5th row: With B., k.1, *k.1 winding yarn 4 times round needle; rep. from * to last st., k.1.
6th row: With B., k.1, *Tr. 8; rep. from * to last st., k.1.
These 6 rows form the pattern.

404 Lollipop Pattern

No. 404 Lollipop Pattern 2 sts. plus 1
Foundation row: (wrong side) P.1, *p.1 winding yarn 3 times round needle, p.1; rep. from * to end.
1st row: (right side) With B., (k. in front, back, then front) of next st. – called make 3, *with yarn at back sl. 1 letting extra loops drop, make 3 in next st.; rep. from * to end.
2nd row: With B., p.3, *with yarn at front, sl.1, p.3; rep. from * to end.
3rd row: With B., k.3, *sl.1, k.3; rep. from * to end.
4th row: With B., p. 3 tog., *sl.1, p. 3 tog. winding yarn twice round needle; rep. from * to last 4 sts., sl.1, p. 3 tog.

5th row: With A., k.1, *make 3 in next st., sl. 1 letting extra loops drop; rep. from * to last 2 sts., make 3 in next st., k.1.

6th row: With A., k.1, *p.3, sl.1; rep. from * to last 4 sts., p.3, k.1.

7th row: With A., k.1, *k.3, sl.1; rep. from * to last 4 sts., k.4.

8th row: With A., k.1, *p. 3 tog. winding yarn twice round needle, sl.1; rep. from * to last 4 sts., p. 3 tog. winding yarn twice round needle, k.1.

These 8 rows form the pattern.

No. 405   Two Colour Quilt Pattern 4 sts. plus 5

1st row: (wrong side) With A., sl. 1 knitwise, p. to last st., k.1.

2nd row: With B., k.1, *yarn back, sl. 3 purlwise, yarn forward, p.1; rep. from * to last 4 sts., yarn back, sl.3, k.1.

3rd row: As 2nd row.

4th row: With A., k. to end.

5th row: With A., sl. 1 purlwise, p. to last st., k.1.

6th row: With B., k.1, yarn back, sl. 1 purlwise, *yarn forward, insert needle purlwise in next st., then under B. bar formed in 3rd row and p., yarn back, sl. 3 purlwise; rep. from * to last 3 sts., yarn forward, p.1 with B. bar as before, yarn back, sl.1, k.1.

7th row: With B., k.1, yarn back, sl. 1 purlwise, *yarn forward, p.1, yarn back, sl. 3 purlwise; rep. from * to last 3 sts., yarn forward, p.1, yarn back, sl.1, k.1.

8th row: With A., k. to end.

9th row: With A., sl.1, p. to last st., k.1.

10th row: With B., insert needle under B. bar formed in 7th row, then into 1st st. and k., *yarn back sl. 3 purlwise, yarn forward, p.1 with B. bar; rep. from * to last 4 sts., yarn back, sl.3, k.1 with B. bar.

11th row: With B., k.1, *yarn back, sl. 3 purlwise, yarn forward, p.1; rep. from * to last 4 sts., yarn back, sl.3, k.1.

The 4th to 11th rows form the pattern. Purl the bar from 11th row in 6th row.

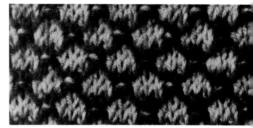

405 Two Colour Quilt Pattern

406 Small Net Pattern

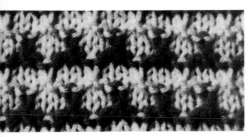

407 Pyramid Checks

No. 406   Small Net Pattern 4 sts. plus 5

Carry contrast yarn very loosely across the front of the work.

1st row: (wrong side) P. 1 A., *with B. to right side of work, sl. next 3 sts. purlwise, with B. to wrong side of work, p. 1 A.; rep. from * to end.

2nd row: With A., k. to end.

3rd row: With A., p. to end.

4th row: K. 2 A., *insert right hand needle under B. loop 3 rows below, then into 1st st. on left hand needle, then using B. k. both loops together, k. 3 A.; rep. from * to last 3 sts., k. loop and st. together, k. 2 A.

5th row: P. 3 A., *rep. from * of 1st row to last 2 sts., p. 2 A.

6th row: With A., k. to end.

7th row: With A., p. to end.

8th row: K. 4 A., rep. from * of 4th row to last st., k. 1 A.

These 8 rows form the pattern.

No. 407   Pyramid Checks 4 sts. plus 3

Slip all slipped stitches purlwise on this pattern.

1st row: With A., k. to end.

2nd row: As 1st row.

3rd row: With A., keeping yarn at back of work, *k.3, sl. 1 purlwise; rep. from * to last 3 sts., k.3.

4th row: With A., *p.3, sl. 1 purlwise; rep. from * to last 3 sts., p.3.

5th row: With B., *k.3, sl. 1 purlwise; rep. from * to last 3 sts., k.3.

6th row: With B., k. to end.

7th row: With A., k.1, *sl. 1 purlwise, k.3; rep. from * to last 2 sts., sl.1, k.1.

8th row: With A., p.1, *sl. 1 purlwise, p.3; rep. from * to last 2 sts., sl.1, p.1.

9th row: With A., k.1, *sl. 1 purlwise, k.3; rep. from * to last 2 sts., sl.1, k.1.

10th row: With A., k. to end.

The 3rd to 10th rows form the pattern.

No. 408 Broken Stripes 4 sts. plus 3

1st row: With A., k. to end.

2nd row: With A., p. to end.

3rd row: With B., *k.3, insert needle in next st. 3 rows below, k. in the usual way, draw loop through and slip it on to the left hand needle, then k. it together with next st. through back of loops; rep. from * to last 3 sts., k.3.

4th row: With B., k. to end.

5th row: With A., k.1, *sl. 1 purlwise, k.3; rep. from * to last 2 sts., sl. 1 purlwise, k.1.

6th row: With A., p.1, *sl. 1 purlwise, p.3; rep. from * to last 2 sts., sl. 1 purlwise, p.1.

7th row: As 5th row.

8th row: With A., p. to end.

These 8 rows form the pattern.

408 *Broken Stripes*

No. 409 Greek Key Pattern 6 sts. plus 2

Slip all slipped stitches purlwise on this pattern.

1st row: (right side) With A., k. to end.

2nd row: As 1st row.

3rd row: With B., k.1, *sl.1, k.5; rep. from * to last st., k.1.

4th row and foll. alt. rows: Keeping yarn towards you slip all slip sts. and k. all k. sts. of previous row.

5th row: With A., k.2, *sl.1, k.3, sl.1, k.1; rep. from * to end.

7th row: With A., k.1, *sl.1, k.3, sl.1, k.1; rep. from * to last st., k.1.

9th row: With A., k.6, *sl.1, k.5; rep. from * to last 2 sts., sl.1, k.1.

11th and 12th rows: With B., as 1st and 2nd rows.

13th row: With A., k.4, *sl.1, k.5; rep. from * to last 4 sts., sl.1, k.3.

15th row: With B., *k.3, sl.1, k.1, sl.1; rep. from * to last 2 sts., k.2.

17th row: With A., k.2, *sl.1, k.1, sl.1, k.3; rep. from * to end.

19th row: With B., k.3, *sl.1, k.5; rep. from * to last 5 sts., sl.1, k.4.

20th row: As 4th row.

These 20 rows form the pattern.

409 *Greek Key Pattern*

SEVEN

BORDERS, INSERTIONS AND TRIMMINGS

Due to the changing fashion attitude to hand knitting, many needle techniques previously thought old fashioned are being given a new lease of life. Only five years ago it would have been unusual to find a commercial knitting pattern with frills, beads or lacy collars to a lady's sweater. However, to be prepared for the vagaries of fashion, no comprehensive guide should be without a few examples of these stitches. It should be remembered that, generally speaking, most garments are attractive enough when worked in some type of pattern, no matter how small or delicate, and adding lace or beads must be done with great care.

When working with beads it is best to buy a small sample packet first and to work a sample square. Not only will this give a notion of how the finished work will look, but from this square the total number of beads needed may be calculated. To do this, work out how many beads are needed for each complete pattern repeat (in rows as well as stitches), then draw a rough diagram of the pattern pieces, writing in the measurements. Calculate according to the tension how many stitches and rows will have to be worked for each pattern piece, marking them into pattern repeats. Multiply the number of repeats by the number of beads used for each repeat on the sample square.

Many patterns will lend themselves to having beads added. The small knitting beads are unlikely to fit yarn thicker than 4 ply, but there are plenty of fascinating beads with larger threading holes suitable for double knitting and similar yarns. Experiment with beading new patterns; it is usually only necessary to slip a stitch while pushing the bead to the right side of the work.

Beginners might like to start by adding beads to the collars and cuffs of an evening jumper before going on to more elaborate items. A bead shop can be enchanting with its wonderful samples, and it is hardly surprising that, in the quieter days of the Victorian era, ladies were happy to fill their leisure time with knitting bead purses or fine lace.

Although the directions for working each bead or sequin stitch is given with the individual pattern, the method of threading the beads and sequins is always the same. First, make sure that your sewing needle will slide through the bead hole. Take a length of sewing thread, fold it in half and thread it doubled through the eye of the sewing needle. Pass the end of the knitting yarn through the loop of the doubled yarn. Slide the bead (or sequin) over the needle, along the doubled thread and down over the yarn. To prevent the yarn coming out of the loop, leave a bead on the yarn before adding the next bead (see diagram).

No. 410   Simple All-over Beading 2 sts. plus 1
B.1, bead 1 thus: yarn forward, sl. 1 purlwise, slide bead to front of sl. st., yarn back.
Work 2 rows stocking stitch before commencing work.
1st row: K.1, *B.1, k.1; rep. from * to end.
2nd row: P. to end.
3rd row: K.1, *k.1, B.1; rep. from * to last 2 sts., k.2.
4th row: P. to end.
These 4 rows form the pattern.

410 Simple All-over Beading

No. 411   Sequins on Lace 4 sts.
To knit a sequin stitch: before inserting needle point, push a sequin up close to back of work, k. next st. then press sequin through to front of work through centre of stitch – called sequin 1.
Work 2 rows stocking stitch before commencing work.
1st row: K.4, *sequin 1, k.3; rep. from * to last 2 sts., k.2.
2nd row and foll. alt. rows: P. to end.
3rd row: K.2, *k.1, yarn forward, sl.1, k. 2 tog. t.b.l., p.s.s.o., yarn forward; rep. from * to last 4 sts., k.4.
5th row: K.2, *sequin 1, k.3; rep. from * to end.
7th row: *K.1, yarn forward, sl.1, k. 2 tog. t.b.l., p.s.s.o., yarn forward; rep. from * to last 2 sts., k.2.
8th row: P. to end.
These 8 rows form the pattern.

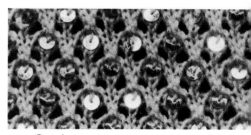

411 Sequins on Lace

412 All-over Sequins

No. 412 All-over Sequins 2 sts. plus 1

Fairly large sequins will be needed to obtain the overlapping scales effect. To knit sequin, push sequin up close to the previous stitch on the wrong side of the work, and push through the centre of the stitch to the right side after working.

Work 2 rows stocking stitch before commencing sequin knitting.

1st row: K.1, *k. next st. with sequin, k. 1 t.b.l.; rep. from * to end.

2nd row: P. to end.

3rd row: K.1, *k. 1 t.b.l., k. next st. with sequin; rep. from * to end.

4th row: P. to end.

These 4 rows form the pattern.

413 Sequinned Squares

No. 413 Sequinned Squares 24 sts. plus 2

Thread corresponding sequins on to contrasting coloured yarns. The size of squares may be varied, 12 sts. are given for this version. Use a separate small ball of each colour for each square, twisting the yarns when changing colour to avoid making a hole in the work.

To knit a sequin, push sequin up to work, k.1 then push sequin through centre of stitch to front – called sequin 1.

1st row: With B., k.1, *(sequin 1, k. 1 t.b.l.) 6 times, with A., (sequin 1, k. 1 t.b.l.) 6 times; rep. from * to last st., with A., k.1.

2nd row: P. 1 A., *12 A., 12 B.; rep. from * to last st., 1 B.

3rd row: With B., k.1, *(k. 1 t.b.l., sequin 1) 6 times, with A., (k. 1 t.b.l., sequin 1) 6 times; rep. from * to last st., with A., k.1.

4th row: As 2nd row.

5th to 12th rows: Rep. 1st to 4th rows twice more.

13th to 24th rows: As 1st to 12th rows, working A. instead of B. and B. instead of A.

These 24 rows form the pattern.

414 Faggoting Pattern with Sequins

No. 414 Faggoting Pattern with Sequins 6 sts. plus 8

Extra large sequins are used for this pattern; the hole is to one side, not centralised, but threaded in the usual way. The pattern could be worked in one colour but for this sample the sequins were threaded on to a contrast colour.

To prevent work spreading, use needles one size finer for the faggoting (eyelet) rows.

1st row: With A., k.1, (yarn forward, k. 2 tog.) to last st., k.1.

2nd row: With A., p. to end.

3rd row: With A., k.1, *k. 2 tog., yarn forward; rep. from * to last st., k.1.

4th row: As 2nd row.

5th to 8th rows: Rep. 1st to 4th rows once more.

9th row: With B., *k.1, p.1; rep. from * to end.

10th row: With B., *p.1, k.1; rep. from * to end.

11th to 13th rows: Rep. 9th and 10th rows then 9th row again.

14th row: Moss st. 3, *push sequin up close to back of work, sl.1 holding sequin, moss st. 5; rep. from * to last 5 sts., sl.1 holding sequin, moss st. 4.

These 14 rows form the pattern.

No. 415 Beads and Pattern 8 sts. plus 9

Thread beads in the usual manner but note that the working is different from other patterns. Wooden beads were used for this sample but other beads, e.g. pearl or faceted, may be substituted successfully.

1st row: K.3, *p.3, k.5; rep. from * ending last rep., k.3 instead of k.5.

2nd row: P.2, *k.5, p.3; rep. from * ending last rep., p.2 instead of p.3.

3rd row: K.1, *p.2, k.3, p.2, k.1; rep. from * to end.

4th row: K.2, *p.5, k.3; rep. from * ending last rep., k.2 instead of k.3.

5th row: P.1, *k.3, p.1; rep. from * to end.

6th row: K.2, *p.2, yarn back, push bead up to work and k. next st. t.b.l., p.2, k.3; rep. from * ending last rep., k.2 instead of k.3.

7th row: As 3rd row.

8th row: As 2nd row.

9th row: As 1st row.

10th row: As 4th row.

11th row: P.3, *k.3, p.5; rep. from * ending last rep., p.3 instead of p.5.

12th row: P.2, *k.2, p.1, k.2, p.3; rep. from * ending last rep., p.2 instead of p.3.

13th row: K.3, *p.3, k.5; rep. from * ending last rep., k.3 instead of k.5.

14th row: K.1, *p.3, k.1; rep. from * to end.

15th row: K.3, *p.3, k.2, yarn forward, push bead up to work and p. next st. t.b.l., k.2; rep. from * to last 6 sts., p.3, k.3.

16th row: As 12th row.

415 Beads and Pattern

17th row: As 11th row.
18th row: As 4th row.
These 18 rows form the pattern.

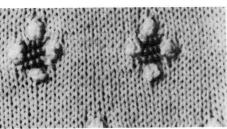

416 Bobble and Beads Pattern

No. 416 Bobble and Beads Pattern 14 sts. plus 1
B.3, work 3 beads thus: slip next st. purlwise, move
three beads to front of work.
M.B., make bobble thus: (k.1, p.1, k.1, p.1) all in next
st., turn and k.4, turn and k. 4 together.
1st row: K.1, *k.13, M.B.; rep. from * to last 14 sts.,
k.14.
2nd row and foll. alt. rows: P. to end.
3rd row: K.13, *p.1, B.3, p.1, k.11; rep. from * to last 2
sts., k.2.
5th row: K.12, *M.B., p.1, B.3, p.1, M.B., k.9; rep.
from * to last 3 sts., k.3.
7th row: As 3rd row.
9th row: As 1st row.
10th to 16th rows: Beg. p. row, in stocking stitch.
17th row: K.7, M.B., *k.13, M.B.; rep. from * to last 7
sts., k.7.
19th row: K.6, *p.1, B.3, p.1, k.11; rep. from * to last 9
sts., p.1, B.3, p.1, k.6.
21st row: K.5, *M.B., p.1, B.3, p.1, M.B., k.9; rep. from
* to last 10 sts., M.B., p.1, B.3, p.1, M.B., k.5.
23rd row: As 19th row.
25th row: As 17th row.
26th row to 32nd rows: Beg. p. row in stocking stitch.
These 32 rows form the pattern.

417 Beaded Diamonds

No. 417 Beaded Diamonds 12 sts. plus 7
B.1, bead 1 thus: bring yarn to front of work, slide bead
up close to front of work, slip 1 purlwise, yarn to back
leaving bead at front of slipped stitch.
1st row: K.6, *k. 2 tog., yarn forward, k.3, yarn forward,
sl.1, k.1, p.s.s.o., k.5; rep. from * to last st., k.1.
2nd row and foll. alt. rows: P. to end.
3rd row: K.5, *k. 2 tog., yarn forward, k.2, B.1, k.2,
yarn forward, sl.1, k.1, p.s.s.o., k.3; rep. from * to last 2
sts., k.2.
5th row: K.4, *k. 2 tog., yarn forward, k.7, yarn
forward, sl.1, k.1, p.s.s.o., k.1; rep. from * to last 3 sts.,
k.3.
7th row: K.3, k. 2 tog., yarn forward, *k.2, B.1, k.3, B.1,
k.2, yarn forward, k. 3 tog., yarn forward; rep. from * to
last 14 sts., k.2, B.1, k.3, B.1, k.2, yarn forward, sl.1,
k.1, p.s.s.o., k.3.

9th row: K.5, *yarn forward, sl.1, k.1, p.s.s.o., k.5, k. 2 tog., yarn forward, k.3; rep. from * to last 2 sts., k.2.
11th row: K.6, *yarn forward, sl.1, k.1, p.s.s.o., k.1, B.1, k.1, k. 2 tog., yarn forward, k.5; rep. from * to last st., k.1.
13th row: K.7, *yarn forward, sl.1, k.1, p.s.s.o., k.1, k. 2 tog., yarn forward, k.7; rep. from * to end.
15th row: K.3, *B.1, k.4, yarn forward, k. 3 tog., yarn forward, k.4; rep. from * to last 4 sts., B.1, k.3.
16th row: P. to end.
These 16 rows form the pattern.

No. 418   Narrow Picot Edging 8 sts.

1st row: K.3, yarn forward, k. 2 tog., (yarn round needle) twice, k. 2 tog., k.1.
2nd row: K.2, k.1 and p.1 into the 'yarn round needle twice' of previous row, k.2, yarn forward, k. 2 tog., k.1.
3rd row: K.3, yarn forward, k. 2 tog., k.1, (yarn round needle) twice, k. 2 tog., k.1.
4th row: K.2, k.1 and p.1 into the 'yarn round needle twice' of previous row, k.3, yarn forward, k. 2 tog., k.1.
5th row: K.3, yarn forward, k. 2 tog., k.2, (yarn round needle) twice, k. 2 tog., k.1.
6th row: K.2, k.1 and p.1 into the 'yarn round needle twice' of previous row, k.4, yarn forward, k. 2 tog., k.1.
7th row: K.3, yarn forward, k. 2 tog., k.6.
8th row: Cast off 3 sts., k.4, (5 sts. now on right hand needle), yarn forward, k. 2 tog., k.1.
These 8 rows form the pattern.

418 Narrow Picot Edging

No. 419   Loop Edging 6 sts.

1st row: K.2, yarn forward, k. 2 tog., (yarn round needle) twice, k. 2 tog.
2nd row: K.2, p.1, k.1, yarn forward, k. 2 tog., k.1.
3rd row: K.2, yarn forward, k. 2 tog., k.3.
4th row: Yarn forward to make a st., sl. 2 sts. knitwise, k.1, then pass 2 sl. sts. over the k.1, k.1, yarn forward, k. 2 tog., k.1.
These 4 rows form the pattern.

419 Loop Edging

420 Cloverleaf Edging

No. 420 Cloverleaf Edging 7 sts.

1st row: Sl. 1 purlwise, k.2, yarn forward, k. 2 tog., (yarn round needle) twice, k.2.

2nd row: K.3, p.1, k.2, yarn forward, k. 2 tog., k.1.

3rd row: Sl. 1 purlwise, k.2, yarn forward, k. 2 tog., (yarn round needle) twice, k. 2 tog., (yarn round needle) twice, k. 2 tog.

4th row: K.2, p.1, k.2, p.1, k.2, yarn forward, k. 2 tog., k.1.

5th row: Sl. 1 purlwise, k.2, yarn forward, k. 2 tog., k.6.

6th row: Cast off 4 sts., k.3, yarn forward, k. 2 tog., k.1.

These 6 rows form the pattern.

421 Rimini Edging

No. 421 Rimini Edging 7 sts.

1st row: Yarn forward, k. 2 tog., yarn forward, k.3, yarn forward, k. 2 tog.

2nd row: Yarn forward, k. 2 tog., k.4, yarn forward, k. 2 tog.

3rd row: Yarn forward, k. 2 tog., yarn forward, k.4, yarn forward, k. 2 tog.

4th row: Yarn forward, k. 2 tog., k.5, yarn forward, k. 2 tog.

5th row: Yarn forward, k. 2 tog., yarn forward, k.5, yarn forward, k. 2 tog.

6th row: Yarn forward, k. 2 tog., k.6, yarn forward, k. 2 tog.

7th row: Yarn forward, k. 2 tog., yarn forward, k.6, yarn forward, k. 2 tog.

8th row: Yarn forward, k. 2 tog., k.7, yarn forward, k. 2 tog.

9th row: (Yarn forward, k. 2 tog.) twice, k. 2 tog., (yarn round needle) twice, k. 2 tog., k.1, yarn forward, k. 2 tog.

10th row: Yarn forward, k. 2 tog., k.3, p.1, k.1, k. 2 tog., yarn forward, k. 2 tog.

11th row: (Yarn forward, k. 2 tog.) twice, k.4, yarn forward, k. 2 tog.

12th row: Yarn forward, k. 2 tog., k.4, k. 2 tog., yarn forward, k. 2 tog.

13th row: (Yarn forward, k. 2 tog.) twice, k.3, yarn forward, k. 2 tog.

14th row: Yarn forward, k. 2 tog., k.3, k. 2 tog., yarn forward, k. 2 tog.

15th row: (Yarn forward, k. 2 tog.) twice, k.2, yarn forward, k. 2 tog.

16th row: Yarn forward, k. 2 tog., k.2, k. 2 tog., yarn forward, k. 2 tog.

These 16 rows form the pattern.

No. 422 Nasturtium Edging 5 sts.

1st row: Sl.1, k.1, k. 2 tog., yarn forward, k.1

2nd row: K.1, (k.1, p.1, k.1, p.1, k.1) all in next st., yarn forward, k. 2 tog., k.1.

3rd row: Sl.1, k.1, yarn forward, k. 2 tog., k.5.

4th row: K.6, yarn forward, k. 2 tog., k.1.

5th row: As 3rd row.

6th row: As 4th row.

7th row: As 3rd row.

8th row: Cast off 4 sts., k.1, yarn forward, k. 2 tog., k.1.

These 8 rows form the pattern.

422 Nasturtium Edging

No. 423 Pointelle Edging 6 sts.

1st row: Yarn round needle, p. 2 tog., k.2, yarn forward, k.2.

2nd row: K.5, yarn round needle, p. 2 tog.

3rd row: Yarn round needle, p. 2 tog., k.2, yarn forward, k.1, yarn forward, k.2.

4th row: K.7, yarn round needle, p. 2 tog.

5th row: Yarn round needle, p. 2 tog., k.2, (yarn forward, k.1) 3 times, yarn forward, k.2.

6th row: Cast off 7 sts., k.3, yarn round needle, p. 2 tog.

These 6 rows form the pattern.

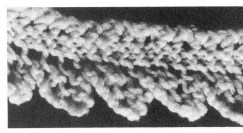

423 Pointelle Edging

No. 424 Curved Lace Edging 12 sts.

1st row: Sl. 1 purlwise, k.2, yarn forward, k. 2 tog., k.1, (yarn round needle) twice, k. 2 tog., (yarn round needle) twice, k.4.

2nd row: Sl. 1 purlwise, k.4, p.1, k.2, p.1, k.3, yarn forward, k. 2 tog., k.1.

3rd row: Sl. 1 purlwise, k.2, yarn forward, k. 2 tog., k.10.

4th row: Cast off 3 sts., k.8, yarn forward, k. 2 tog., k.1.

These 4 rows form the pattern.

424 Curved Lace Edging

No. 425 Diamond Pointelle Edging 15 sts.

1st row: K.3, yarn forward, k. 2 tog., k.3, yarn forward, k.1, yarn forward, k.6.

2nd row: K.6, yarn forward, k.3, yarn forward, k. 2 tog., k.3, yarn forward, k. 2 tog., k.1.

3rd row: K.3, yarn forward, (k. 2 tog.) twice, yarn forward, k.5, yarn forward, k.6.

4th row: Cast off 4 sts., k.1, yarn forward, k. 2 tog., k.3, k. 2 tog., yarn forward, k. 2 tog., k.1, yarn forward, k. 2 tog., k.1.

5th row: K.3, yarn forward, k. 2 tog., k.1, yarn forward, k. 2 tog., k.1, k. 2 tog., yarn forward, k.3.

6th row: K.3, yarn forward, k.1, yarn forward, sl.1, k. 2

425 Diamond Pointelle Edging

tog., p.s.s.o., yarn forward, k.4, yarn forward, k. 2 tog., k.1.

These 6 rows form the pattern.

No. 426   Aspen Leaf Edging 10 sts.

1st row: Sl.1, k.2, yarn forward, k. 2 tog., *(yarn round needle) twice, k. 2 tog.* rep. from * to * once, k.1.

2nd row: K.3, (p.1, k.2) twice, yarn forward, k. 2 tog., k.1.

3rd row: Sl.1, k.2, yarn forward, k. 2 tog., k.2, work from * to * of 1st row, twice, k.1.

4th row: K.3, p.1, k.2, p.1, k.4, yarn forward, k. 2 tog., k.1.

5th row: Sl.1, k.2, yarn forward, k. 2 tog., k.4, work from * to * of 1st row, twice, k.1.

6th row: K.3, p.1, k.2, p.1, k.6, yarn forward, k. 2 tog., k.1.

7th row: Sl.1, k.2, yarn forward, k. 2 tog., k.11.

8th row: Cast off 6 sts., k.6, yarn forward, k. 2 tog., k.1.

These 8 rows form the pattern.

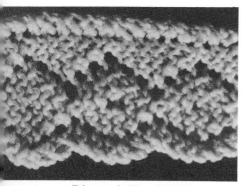

426 Aspen Leaf Edging

No. 427   Diamond Shawl Edging 11 sts.

1st row: Yarn round needle, p. 2 tog., k. to end.

2nd row: K.2, yarn forward, k.3, yarn forward, sl.1, k.1, p.s.s.o., k.2, yarn round needle, p. 2 tog.

3rd row and foll. alt. rows: As 1st row.

4th row: K.2, yarn forward, k.5, yarn forward, sl.1, k.1, p.s.s.o., k.1, yarn round needle, p. 2 tog.

6th row: K.2, yarn forward, k.3, yarn forward, sl.1, k.1, p.s.s.o., k.2, yarn forward, sl.1, k.1, p.s.s.o., yarn round needle, p. 2 tog.

8th row: K.1, k. 2 tog., yarn forward, sl.1, k.1, p.s.s.o., k.3, k. 2 tog., yarn forward, k.2, yarn round needle, p. 2 tog.

10th row: K.1, k. 2 tog., yarn forward, sl.1, k.1, p.s.s.o., k.1, k. 2 tog., yarn forward, k.3, yarn round needle, p. 2 tog.

12th row: K.1, k. 2 tog., yarn forward, sl.1, k. 2 tog., p.s.s.o., yarn forward, k.4, yarn round needle, p. 2 tog.

These 12 rows form the pattern.

427 Diamond Shawl Edging

No. 428 Pom-pon Edging 13 sts.

1st row: Sl.1, k.12.

2nd row: Sl.1, k.1, k. 2 tog., (yarn round needle) twice, k. 2 tog., k.7.

3rd row: Sl.1, k.8, p.1, k.3, working each extra loop as a made st.

4th row: Sl.1, k.12.

5th row: As 4th row.

6th row: Sl.1, k.1, k. 2 tog., (yarn round needle) twice, k. 2 tog., k.2, (yarn round needle) twice, *k.1, (yarn round needle) twice*, rep. from * to * twice more, k.2.

7th row: Working extra loops as made sts., sl.1, (k.2, p.1) 4 times, k.4, p.1, k.3.

8th and 9th rows: Sl.1, k.20.

10th row: Sl.1, k.1, k. 2 tog., (yarn round needle) twice, k. 2 tog., k.15.

11th row: Winding yarn 3 times round needle on each st., k.12, (yarn round needle) 3 times, to make 3 sts., k.5, p.1, k.3.

12th row: Sl.1, k.9, p.1, k.1, sl. 12 sts. on to right hand needle dropping extra loops, sl. these 12 long sts. back on to left hand needle and k. these 12 loops t.b.l. together counting as 1 st. on the following row.

These 12 rows form the pattern.

428 Pom-pon Edging

No. 429 Beech Leaf Edging 25 sts.

1st row: K.2, p. 2 tog., yarn round needle, p.1, k.1, yarn forward, k.5, yarn forward, sl.1, k. 2 tog., p.s.s.o., yarn forward, k.5, yarn forward, k.6.

2nd row: K.6, p.7, k.1, p.8, k.5.

3rd row: K.2, p. 2 tog., yarn round needle, p.1, k.1, yarn forward, k.1, k. 2 tog., p.1, k. 2 tog., k.1, p.1, k.1, k. 2 tog., p.1, k. 2 tog., k.1, (yarn forward and round needle making 2 loops, k. 2 tog.) twice, k.2.

4th row: K.3, dropping extra loop work k.1 and p.1 in next st., k.1, dropping extra loop work k.1 and p.1 in next st., (p.2, k.1) 3 times, p.4, k.5.

5th row: K.2, p. 2 tog., yarn round needle, p.1, (k.1, yarn forward) twice, (k. 2 tog., p.1) 3 times, k. 2 tog., (yarn forward, k.1) twice, (yarn forward, and yarn round needle making 2 loops, k. 2 tog.) twice, k.2.

6th row: K.3, (dropping extra loop k.1 and p.1 in next st., k.1) twice, p.4, (k.1, p.1) 3 times, p.4, k.5.

7th row: K.2, p. 2 tog., yarn round needle, p.1, k.1, yarn forward, k.3, yarn forward, sl.1, k. 2 tog., p.s.s.o., p.1, sl.1, k. 2 tog., p.s.s.o., yarn forward, k.3, yarn forward, k.9.

429 Beech Leaf Edging

430 Vandyke Lace Edging Broad

431 Miss Marshall's Edging

8th row: Cast off 3 sts. (1 st. now on right hand needle), k.5, p.6, k.1, p.7, k.5.
These 8 rows form the pattern.

No. 430   Vandyke Lace Edging Broad 20 sts.
1st row: Sl.1, k.1, (yarn forward, k. 2 tog.) 8 times, yarn forward, k.2.
2nd row and foll. alt. rows to 16th row: K. to end.
3rd row: Sl.1, k.4, (yarn forward, k. 2 tog.) 7 times, yarn forward, k.2.
5th row: Sl.1, k.7, (yarn forward, k. 2 tog.) 6 times, yarn forward, k.2.
7th row: Sl.1, k.10, (yarn forward, k. 2 tog.) 5 times, yarn forward, k.2.
9th row: Sl.1, k.13, (yarn forward, k. 2 tog.) 4 times, yarn forward, k.2.
11th row: Sl.1, k.16, (yarn forward, k. 2 tog.) 3 times, yarn forward, k.2.
13th row: Sl.1, k.19, (yarn forward, k. 2 tog.) twice, yarn forward, k.2.
15th row: Sl.1, k.22, yarn forward, k. 2 tog., yarn forward, k.2.
17th row: K. to end.
18th row: Cast off 8 sts., k. to end.
These 18 rows form the pattern.

No. 431   Miss Marshall's Edging 20 sts.
1st row: Sl.1, k.3, (yarn forward, k. 2 tog.) 7 times, yarn forward, k.2.
2nd, 4th, 6th and 8th rows: K. to end.
3rd row: Sl.1, k.6, (yarn forward, k. 2 tog.) 6 times, yarn forward, k.2.
5th row: Sl.1, k.9, (yarn forward, k. 2 tog.) 5 times, yarn forward, k.2.
7th row: Sl.1, k.12, (yarn forward, k. 2 tog.) 4 times, yarn forward, k.2.
9th row: Sl.1, k.23.
10th row: Cast off 4 sts., k.19.
These 10 rows form the pattern.

No. 432 Pleated Edging 16 sts.

1st row: K.1, sl.1, k.1, p.s.s.o., (yarn round needle) twice, k. 2 tog., p.8, p. twice in next st., k.2.
2nd row: K.14, p.1, k.2.
3rd row: K.1, sl.1, k.1, p.s.s.o., (yarn round needle) twice, k. 2 tog., p.9, inc. in next st., k.2.
4th row: K.12, turn, p.9, inc. in next st., k.2.
5th row: K.16, p.1, k.2.
6th row: K.1, *sl.1, k.1, p.s.s.o., (yarn round needle) twice, k. 2 tog., p.1, yarn round needle, p. 2 tog.; rep. from * once, p.3.
7th row: K.13, turn, p.9, p. 2 tog., k.2.
8th row: K.15, p.1, k.2.
9th row: K.1, sl.1, k.1, p.s.s.o., (yarn round needle) twice, k. 2 tog., p.9, p. 2 tog., k.2.
10th row: As 2nd row.
11th row: K.1, sl.1, k.1, p.s.s.o., (yarn round needle) twice, k. 2 tog., p.8, p. 2 tog., k.2.
12th row: K.13, p.1, k.2.
13th row: K.1, sl.1, k.1, p.s.s.o., (yarn round needle) twice, k. 2 tog., k.11.
14th row: K.2, p.8, turn, k.10.
15th row: As 14th row.
16th row: K.2, p.9, k.2, p.1, k.2.
These 16 rows form the pattern.

432 Pleated Edging

No. 433 Small Frill Edging 11 sts. plus 3

The pattern begins at the broadest edge, allow for each repeat of 11 sts. to reduce to 3 sts.
1st row: P.3, *k.8, p.3; rep. from * to end.
2nd row: K.3, *p.8, k.3; rep. from * to end.
3rd row: P.3, *sl.1, k.1, p.s.s.o., k.4, k. 2 tog., p.3; rep. from * to end.
4th row: K.3, *p.6, k.3; rep. from * to end.
5th row: P.3, *sl.1, k.1, sl.1, k.1., p.s.s.o., k.2, k. 2 tog., p.3; rep. from * to end.
6th row: K.3, *p.4, k.3; rep. from * to end.
7th row: P.3, *sl.1, k.1, p.s.s.o., k. 2 tog., p.3; rep. from * to end.
8th row: K.3, *p.2, k.3; rep. from * to end.
9th row: P.3, *k. 2 tog., p.3; rep. from * to end.
10th row: *K.2, k. 2 tog.; rep. from * to last 3 sts., k.3.
These 10 rows form the pattern.

433 Small Frill Edging

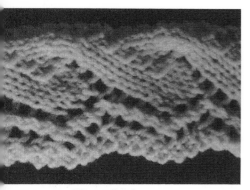

434 Wavy Edging

No. 434 Wavy Edging 13 sts.

1st row: K.2, p. to last 2 sts., k.2.

2nd row: Sl.1, k.3, yarn forward, k.5, yarn forward, k. 2 tog., yarn forward, k.2.

3rd row and foll. alt. rows: As 1st row.

4th row: Sl.1, k.4, sl.1, k. 2 tog., p.s.s.o., k.2, (yarn forward, k. 2 tog.) twice, k.1.

6th row: Sl.1, k.3, sl.1, k.1, p.s.s.o., k.2, (yarn forward, k. 2 tog.) twice, k.1.

8th row: Sl.1, k.2, sl.1, k.1, p.s.s.o., k.2, (yarn forward, k. 2 tog.) twice, k.1.

10th row: Sl.1, k.1, sl.1, k.1, p.s.s.o., k.2, (yarn forward, k. 2 tog.) twice, k.1.

12th row: K.1, sl.1, k.1, p.s.s.o., k.2, yarn forward, k.1, yarn forward, k. 2 tog., yarn forward, k.2.

14th row: Sl.1, (k.3, yarn forward) twice, k. 2 tog., yarn forward, k.2.

These 14 rows form the pattern.

435 Shamrock Insertion Lace

No. 435   Shamrock Insertion Lace 14 sts.

1st row: Sl.1, k.1, yarn round needle, p. 2 tog., k.2, (yarn round needle) twice, k.4, yarn round needle, p. 2 tog., k.2.

2nd row: Sl.1, k.1, yarn round needle, p. 2 tog., k.2, k. 2 tog., k.1, p.1, k.2, yarn round needle, p. 2 tog., k.2.

3rd row: Sl.1, k.1, yarn round needle, p. 2 tog., k.4, (yarn round needle) twice, k. 2 tog., k.1, yarn round needle, p. 2 tog., k.2.

4th row: Sl.1, k.1, yarn round needle, p. 2 tog., k.3, p.1, k. 2 tog., k.2, yarn round needle, p. 2 tog., k.2.

5th row: Sl.1, k.1, yarn round needle, p. 2 tog., k.3, (yarn round needle) twice, k.2, k. 2 tog., yarn round needle, p. 2 tog., k.2.

6th row: Sl.1, k.1, yarn round needle, p. 2 tog., k.4, p.1, k. 2 tog., k.1, yarn round needle, p. 2 tog., k.2.

7th row: Sl.1, k.1, yarn round needle, p. 2 tog., k. 2 tog., k.5, yarn round needle, p. 2 tog., k.2.

8th row: Sl.1, k.1, yarn round needle, p. 2 tog., k.6, yarn round needle, p. 2 tog., k.2.

These 8 rows form the pattern.

No. 436 Lozenge Pattern Insertion 18 sts.

1st row: Sl.1, k.2, yarn forward, sl.1, k.1, p.s.s.o., k.1, (yarn forward, k. 2 tog.) twice, k.5, yarn forward, k.2 tog., k.1.

2nd row and foll. alt. rows: Sl.1, k.2, yarn round needle, p. 2 tog., p.9, k.1, yarn forward, k. 2 tog., k.1.

3rd row: Sl.1, k.2, yarn forward, sl.1, k.1, p.s.s.o., k.2, (yarn forward, k. 2 tog.) twice, k.4, yarn forward, k. 2 tog., k.1.

5th row: Sl.1, k.2, yarn forward, sl.1, k.1, p.s.s.o., k.3, (yarn forward, k. 2 tog.) twice, k.3, yarn forward, k. 2 tog., k.1.

7th row: Sl.1, k.2, yarn forward, sl.1, k.1, p.s.s.o., k.4, (yarn forward, k.2 tog.) twice, k.2, yarn forward, k. 2 tog., k.1.

9th row: Sl.1, k.2, yarn forward, sl.1, k.1, p.s.s.o., k.10, yarn forward, k. 2 tog., k.1.

10th row: As 2nd row.

These 10 rows form the pattern.

436 Lozenge Pattern Insertion

No. 437 Rose Leaf Insertion 15 sts.

1st row: Sl.1, k.2, (yarn forward, k. 2 tog.) twice, yarn forward, k.1, yarn forward, k. 2 tog., yarn forward, k.2, yarn forward, k. 2 tog., k.1.

2nd row: Sl.1, k.2, yarn forward, k. 2 tog., p.8, k.1, yarn forward, k. 2 tog., k.1.

3rd row: Sl.1, k.2, (yarn forward, k. 2 tog.) twice, yarn forward, k.3, yarn forward, sl.1, k.1, p.s.s.o., yarn forward, k.2, yarn forward, k. 2 tog., k.1.

4th row: Sl.1, k.2, yarn forward, k. 2 tog., p.10, k.1, yarn forward, k. 2 tog., k.1.

5th row: Sl.1, k.2, (yarn forward, k. 2 tog.) twice, yarn forward, k.5, yarn forward, sl.1, k.1, p.s.s.o., yarn forward, k.2, yarn forward, k. 2 tog., k.1.

6th row: Sl.1, k.2, yarn forward, k. 2 tog., p.12, k.1, yarn forward, k. 2 tog., k.1.

7th row: Sl.1, k.2, (yarn forward, k. 2 tog.) twice, yarn forward, k.7, yarn forward, sl.1, k.1, p.s.s.o., yarn forward, k.2, yarn forward, k. 2 tog., k.1.

8th row: Sl.1, k.2, yarn forward, k. 2 tog., p.14, k.1, yarn forward, k. 2 tog., k.1.

9th row: Sl.1, k.2, yarn forward, k. 2 tog., yarn forward, sl.1, k. 2 tog., p.s.s.o., yarn forward, sl.1, k.1, p.s.s.o., k.3, (k. 2 tog., yarn forward) twice, k. 2 tog., k.1, yarn forward, k. 2 tog., k.1.

10th row: As 6th row.

11th row: Sl.1, k.2, yarn forward, k.2 tog., yarn forward,

437 Rose Leaf Insertion

sl.1, k. 2 tog., p.s.s.o., yarn forward, sl.1, k.1, p.s.s.o., k.1, (k. 2 tog., yarn forward) twice, k. 2 tog., k.1, yarn forward, k. 2 tog., k.1.

12th row: As 4th row.

13th row: Sl.1, k.2, yarn forward, k. 2 tog., (yarn forward, sl.1, k. 2 tog., p.s.s.o.) twice, (yarn forward, k. 2 tog.) twice, k.1, yarn forward, k. 2 tog., k.1.

14th row: As 2nd row.

15th row: Sl.1, k.2, yarn forward, k. 2 tog., (yarn forward, sl.1, k. 2 tog., p.s.s.o.) twice, (yarn forward, k. 2 tog., k.1) twice.

16th row: Sl.1, k.2, yarn forward, k. 2 tog., p.6, k.1, yarn forward, k. 2 tog., k.1.

These 16 rows form the pattern.

No. 438 Crown of Glory Insertion 22 sts.

1st row: Sl.1, k.10, (yarn round needle) twice, k.11.

2nd row: Sl.1, k.3, p.7, (k.1, p.1, k.1, p.1, k.1) all in next st., p.7, k.4.

3rd row: Sl.1, k.2, sl.1, k.1, p.s.s.o., k.17, k. 2 tog., k.3.

4th row: Sl.1, k.3, p.17, k.4.

5th row: Sl.1, k.2, sl.1, k.1, p.s.s.o., k.5, (yarn forward, k.1) 5 times, yarn forward, k.5, k. 2 tog., k.3.

6th row: Sl.1, k.3, p.21, k.4.

7th row: Sl.1, k.2, sl.1, k.1, p.s.s.o., k.19, k. 2 tog., k.3.

8th row: Sl.1, k.3, p.19, k.4.

9th row: Sl.1, k.2, sl.1, k.1, p.s.s.o., k.3, (yarn forward, k. 2 tog.) 6 times, k.2, k. 2 tog., k.3.

10th row: As 4th row.

11th row: Sl.1, k.2, sl.1, k.1, p.s.s.o., k.15, k. 2 tog., k.3.

12th row: Sl.1, k.3, p.15, k.4.

13th row: Sl.1, k.2, sl.1, k.1, p.s.s.o., (yarn forward, k. 2 tog.) 7 times, k.4.

14th row: Sl.1, k.21.

15th and 16th rows: As 14th row.

These 16 rows form the pattern.

438 Crown of Glory Insertion

439–443 Petit Choux Pattern worked in a variety of widely differing yarns

439

440

441

442

443

GLOSSARY

Knitwise: a term generally used in slipping stitches from the left hand needle to the right by inserting the point of the right hand needle into the loop, as if to knit it.

Pass the slipped stitch over: the slipped stitch(es) is the first to be passed on to the right hand needle; insert the point of the left hand needle into this loop and lift it over the last stitch(es) on right hand needle and off the needle. Note that some patterns require two stitches to be passed over the worked stitch.

Purlwise: slipping a stitch from the left hand needle to the right by inserting the point of the right hand needle into the loop, as if to purl it.

Tension, gauge: the number of stitches and/or rows measured to a given number of centimetres or inches.

Through back loop: knit or purl through the back of the stitch instead of the front; to knit, this means inserting the point of the right hand needle into the centre of the loop from the right hand side through to the back; to purl, this means inserting the point of the right hand needle from the back from the left hand side. The same technique is used for working two stitches together through back of loops.

*: this asterisk indicates the beginning of a pattern repeat; a semi-colon indicates the conclusion.

( ): brackets (parentheses) are used within pattern repeats where the method contained within the brackets is to be worked for the number of times indicated immediately following the bracket signs, e.g. (k. 2 tog.) twice.

Yarn forward: a method of making a stitch by bringing the yarn forward between two knit stitches and over the top of the needle to work the following knit stitch.

Yarn round needle: this is the method of making a stitch when the yarn is already in the forward position and a purl stitch follows.

CONVERSION CHART

Knitting Needles

U.K. Old sizes	Metric (mm)	U.S.A.	EUROPEAN (mm)
000	10	15	9
00	9	13	$8\frac{1}{2}$
0	8	12	8
1	$7\frac{1}{2}$	11	$7\frac{1}{2}$
2	7	$10\frac{1}{2}$	7
3	$6\frac{1}{2}$	10	$6\frac{1}{2}$
4	6	9	6
5	$5\frac{1}{2}$	8	$5\frac{1}{2}$
6	5	7	5
7	$4\frac{1}{2}$	6	$4\frac{1}{2}$
8	4	5	4
9	$3\frac{3}{4}$	4	$3\frac{1}{2}$
10	$3\frac{1}{4}$	3	—
11	3	2	3
12	$2\frac{3}{4}$	1	$2\frac{1}{2}$
13	$2\frac{1}{4}$	0	—
14	2	00	2

Crochet Hooks

U.K. (mm)	U.S.A.	EUROPEAN (mm)
7	K/$10\frac{1}{2}$	7
6.5	J/10	6.5
6	I/9	6
5.5	H/8	5.5
5	—	5
4.5	G/6	4.5
4	F/5	4
3.5	E/4	3.5
3	C/2	3
2.5	B/1	2.5

BIBLIOGRAPHY

Abbey, Barbara, *Knitting Lace*, The Viking Press Inc., 1974

Thomas, Mary, *Book of Knitting Patterns*, Hodder and Stoughton, 1935

Thompson, Gladys, *Patterns for Guernseys, Jerseys and Arans*, Dover Publications, 1975

Walker, Barbara, *A Treasury of Knitting Patterns*, Charles Scribner's Sons, New York, 1968

SUPPLIERS

U.K.
To obtain information about stockists of the yarn used for the samples in this book write to the following address:
Wendy Press Office,
Carter and Parker Ltd,
Guiseley,
W. Yorks,
LS20 9PD

U.S.A.
For distributors of Wendy yarns write to:
Wendy Yarns U.S.A.,
PO Box 11672,
Milwaukee,
Wisconsin,
53211

CANADA
For distributors of Wendy yarns write to:
White Buffalo Mills Ltd,
545 Assiniboine Avenue,
Brandon,
Manitoba,
R7A 0G3

To obtain information about the beads and sequins used in this book write to:
Wycraft,
The Craft Shop,
78 High Street,
Ramsgate,
Kent.